Dungeo

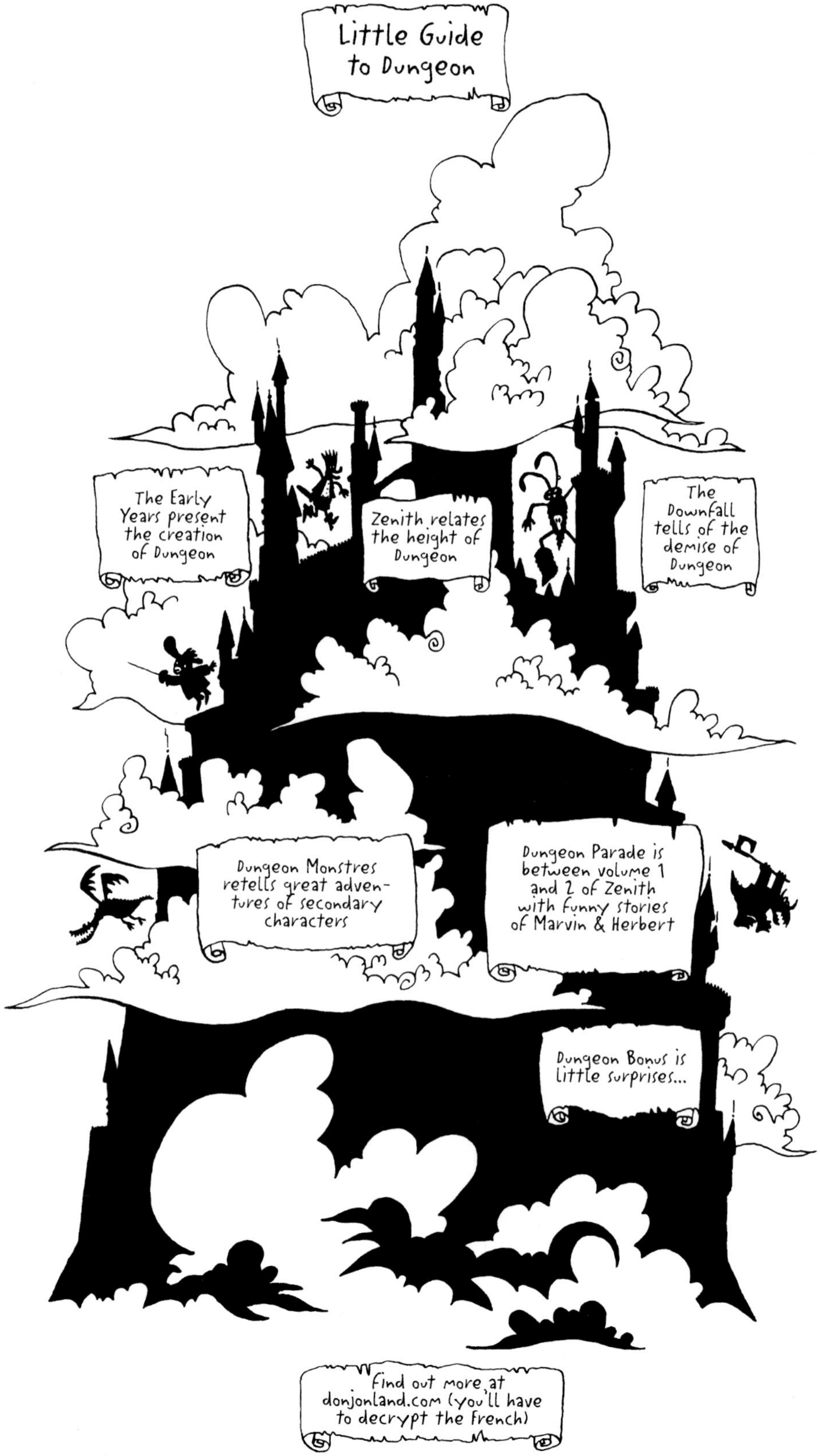
Little Guide to Dungeon
The Early Years present the creation of Dungeon
Zenith relates the height of Dungeon
The Downfall tells of the demise of Dungeon
Dungeon Monstres retells great adventures of secondary characters
Dungeon Parade is between volume 1 and 2 of Zenith with funny stories of Marvin & Herbert
Dungeon Bonus is little surprises...
Find out more at donjonland.com (you'll have to decrypt the French)

Dungeon

The Early Years

Volume 1:

The Night Shirt

Christophe BLAIN, art
Joann SFAR, Lewis TRONDHEIM, story

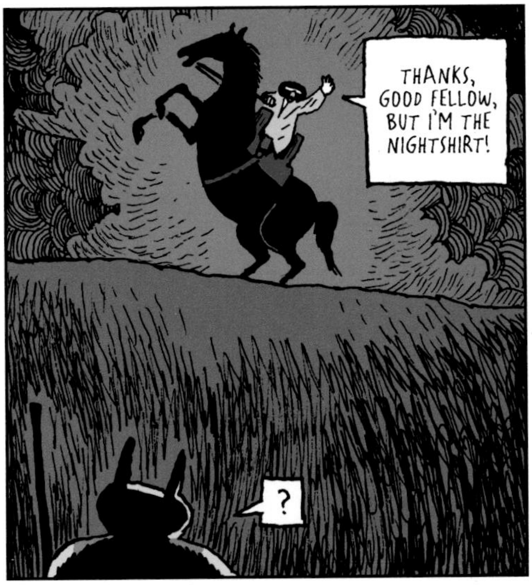
THANKS, GOOD FELLOW, BUT I'M THE NIGHTSHIRT!
?

NANTIER • BEALL • MINOUSTCHINE
Publishing inc.
new york

Also available from Trondheim:
Dungeon Zenith, vols. 1, 2: $14.95 each
Mr. O, $13.95
with Thierry Robin:
Li'l Santa, $14.95
Happy Halloween, Li'l Santa, $14.95
With Manu Larcenet:
Astronauts of the Future, vol. 1, $14.95

Add $3 P&H first item $1 each additional.

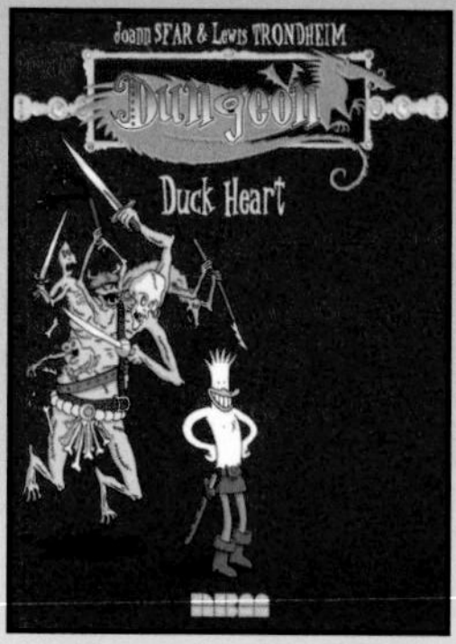
Joann SFAR & Lewis TRONDHEIM
Dungeon
Duck Heart

Write for our complete catalog
of over 200 graphic novels:

NBM
555 8th Ave., Suite 1202
New York, NY 10018
www.nbmpublishing.com

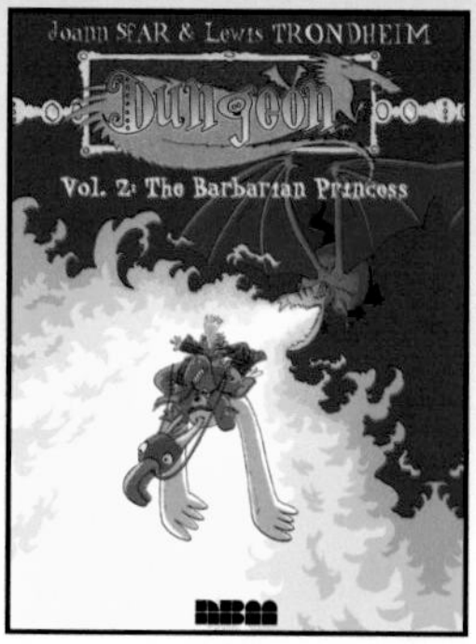
Joann SFAR & Lewis TRONDHEIM
Dungeon
Vol. 2: The Barbarian Princess

Originally published in French in 2 books:
Donjon Potron-Minet:
La Chemise de la Nuit and
Un Justicier dans L'Ennui
ISBN-10: 1-56163-439-5
ISBN-13: 978-1-56163-439-2

Translation by Joe Johnson
Lettering by Ortho
Printed in China

3 2 1

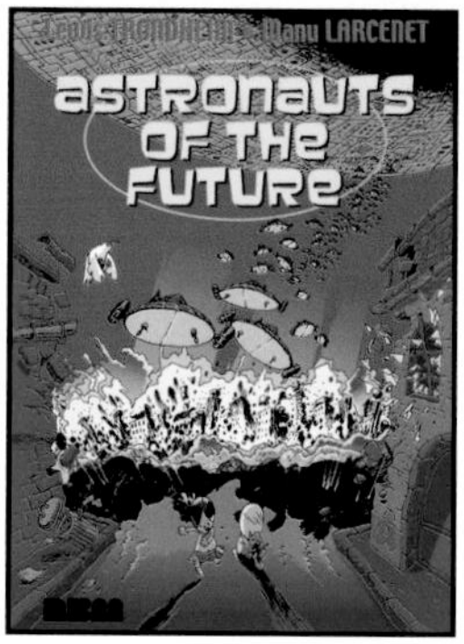
Manu LARCENET
ASTRONAUTS OF THE FUTURE

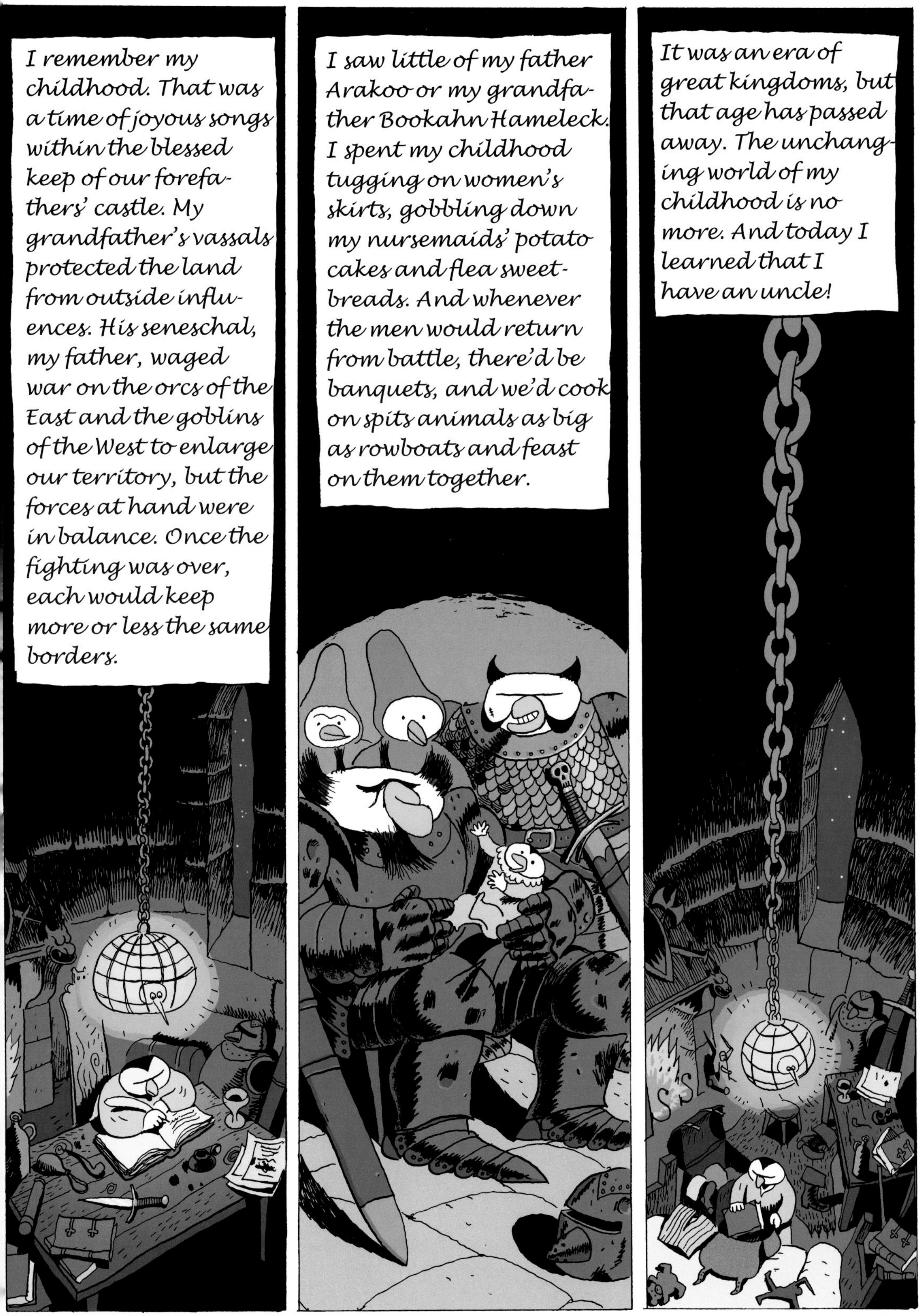
I remember my childhood. That was a time of joyous songs within the blessed keep of our forefathers' castle. My grandfather's vassals protected the land from outside influences. His seneschal, my father, waged war on the orcs of the East and the goblins of the West to enlarge our territory, but the forces at hand were in balance. Once the fighting was over, each would keep more or less the same borders.
I saw little of my father Arakoo or my grandfather Bookahn Hameleck. I spent my childhood tugging on women's skirts, gobbling down my nursemaids' potato cakes and flea sweetbreads. And whenever the men would return from battle, there'd be banquets, and we'd cook on spits animals as big as rowboats and feast on them together.
It was an era of great kingdoms, but that age has passed away. The unchanging world of my childhood is no more. And today I learned that I have an uncle!

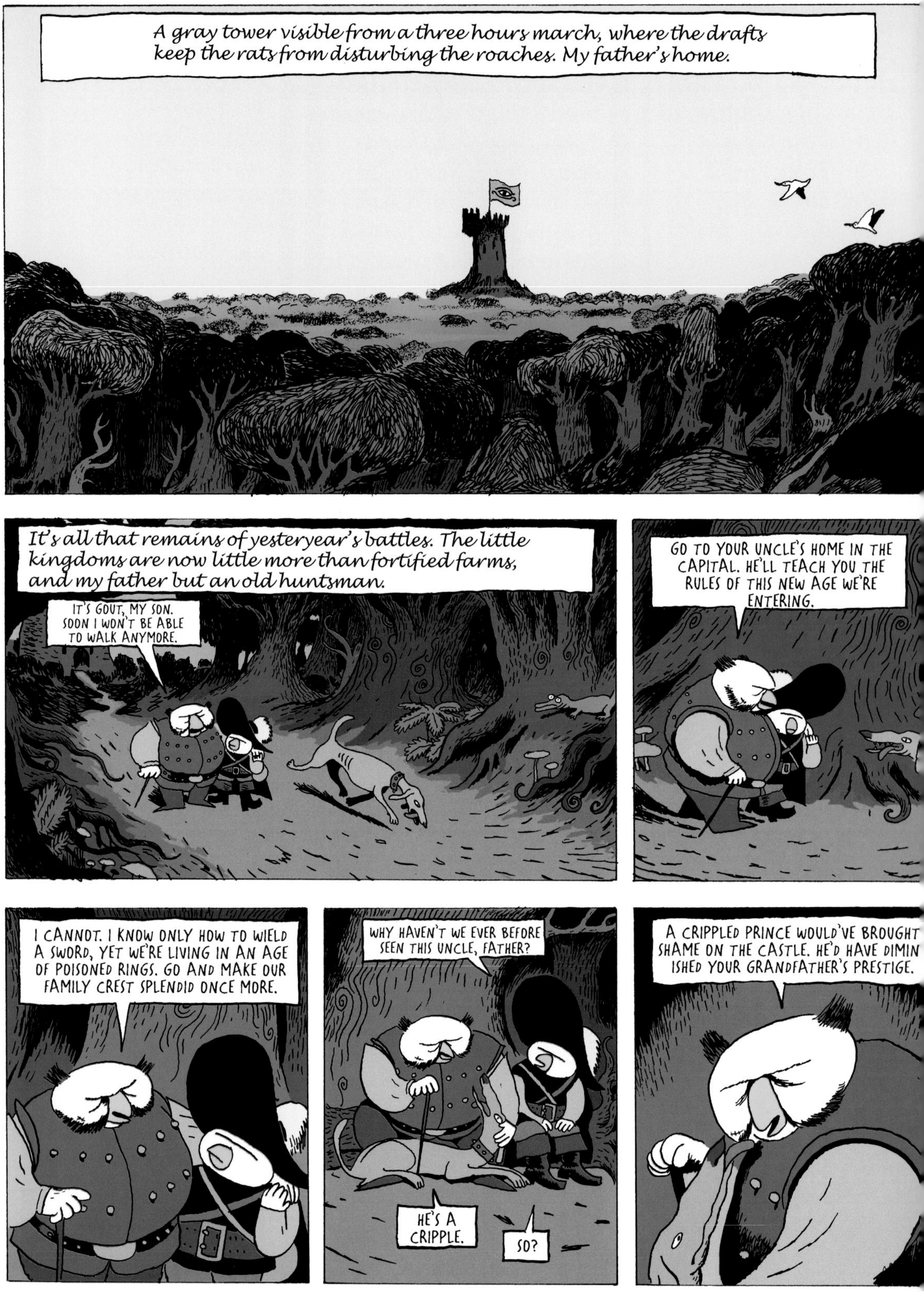
A gray tower visible from a three hours march, where the drafts keep the rats from disturbing the roaches. My father's home.
It's all that remains of yesteryear's battles. The little kingdoms are now little more than fortified farms, and my father but an old huntsman.
IT'S GOUT, MY SON. SOON I WON'T BE ABLE TO WALK ANYMORE.
GO TO YOUR UNCLE'S HOME IN THE CAPITAL. HE'LL TEACH YOU THE RULES OF THIS NEW AGE WE'RE ENTERING.
I CANNOT. I KNOW ONLY HOW TO WIELD A SWORD, YET WE'RE LIVING IN AN AGE OF POISONED RINGS. GO AND MAKE OUR FAMILY CREST SPLENDID ONCE MORE.
WHY HAVEN'T WE EVER BEFORE SEEN THIS UNCLE, FATHER?
HE'S A CRIPPLE.
SO?
A CRIPPLED PRINCE WOULD'VE BROUGHT SHAME ON THE CASTLE. HE'D HAVE DIMIN ISHED YOUR GRANDFATHER'S PRESTIGE.

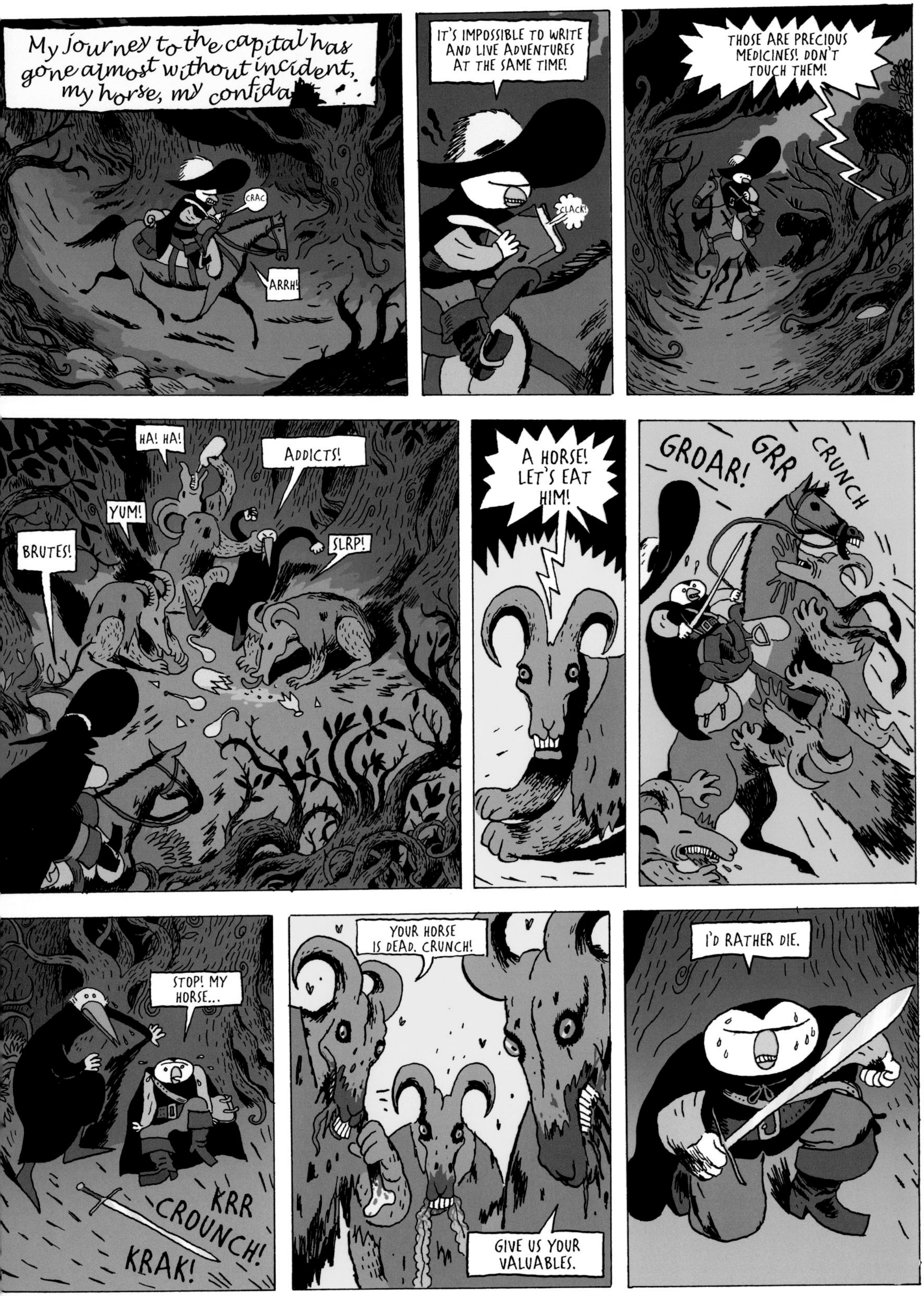
My journey to the capital has gone almost without incident, my horse, my confida
CRAC
ARRH!
IT'S IMPOSSIBLE TO WRITE AND LIVE ADVENTURES AT THE SAME TIME!
CLACK!
THOSE ARE PRECIOUS MEDICINES! DON'T TOUCH THEM!
HA! HA!
ADDICTS!
YUM!
BRUTES!
SLRP!
A HORSE! LET'S EAT HIM!
GROAR!
GRR
CRUNCH
STOP! MY HORSE...
KRR
CROUNCH!
KRAK!
YOUR HORSE IS DEAD. CRUNCH!
GIVE US YOUR VALUABLES.
I'D RATHER DIE.

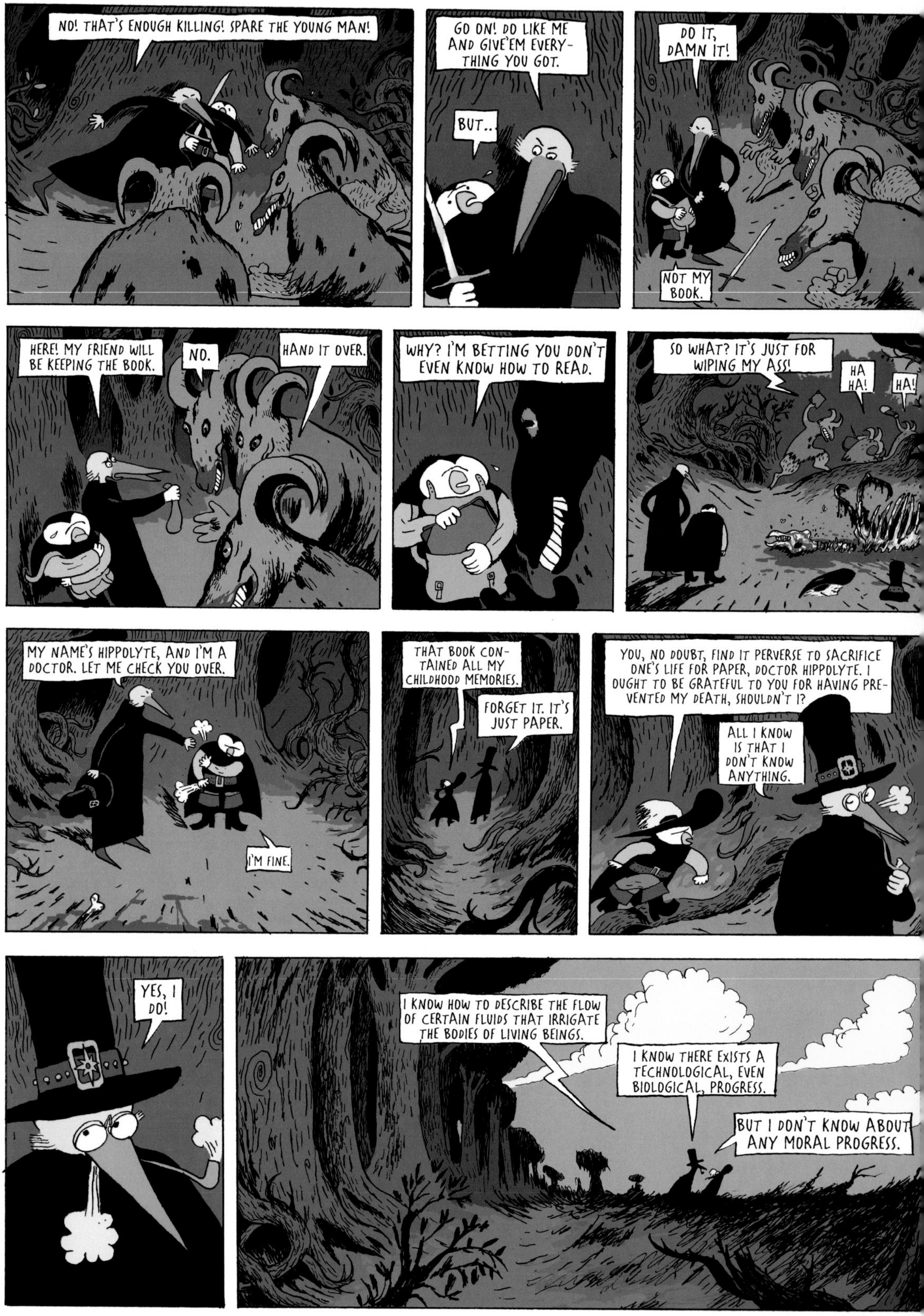
NO! THAT'S ENOUGH KILLING! SPARE THE YOUNG MAN!
GO ON! DO LIKE ME AND GIVE'EM EVERY-THING YOU GOT.
BUT...
DO IT, DAMN IT!
NOT MY BOOK.
HERE! MY FRIEND WILL BE KEEPING THE BOOK.
NO.
HAND IT OVER.
WHY? I'M BETTING YOU DON'T EVEN KNOW HOW TO READ.
SO WHAT? IT'S JUST FOR WIPING MY ASS!
HA HA!
HA!
MY NAME'S HIPPOLYTE, AND I'M A DOCTOR. LET ME CHECK YOU OVER.
I'M FINE.
THAT BOOK CONTAINED ALL MY CHILDHOOD MEMORIES.
FORGET IT. IT'S JUST PAPER.
YOU, NO DOUBT, FIND IT PERVERSE TO SACRIFICE ONE'S LIFE FOR PAPER, DOCTOR HIPPOLYTE. I OUGHT TO BE GRATEFUL TO YOU FOR HAVING PREVENTED MY DEATH, SHOULDN'T I?
ALL I KNOW IS THAT I DON'T KNOW ANYTHING.
YES, I DO!
I KNOW HOW TO DESCRIBE THE FLOW OF CERTAIN FLUIDS THAT IRRIGATE THE BODIES OF LIVING BEINGS.
I KNOW THERE EXISTS A TECHNOLOGICAL, EVEN BIOLOGICAL, PROGRESS.
BUT I DON'T KNOW ABOUT ANY MORAL PROGRESS.

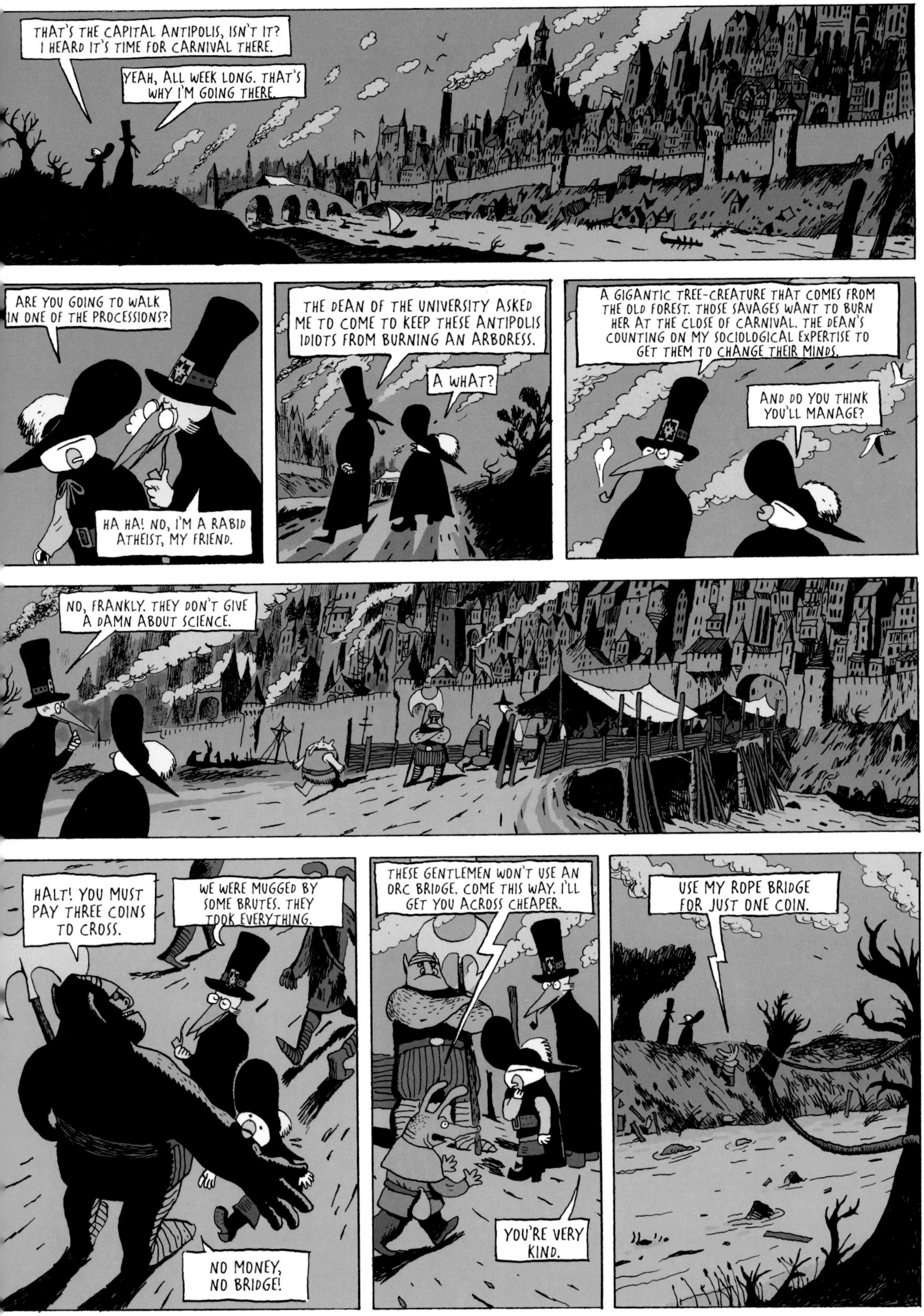
THAT'S THE CAPITAL ANTIPOLIS, ISN'T IT? I HEARD IT'S TIME FOR CARNIVAL THERE.
YEAH, ALL WEEK LONG. THAT'S WHY I'M GOING THERE.
ARE YOU GOING TO WALK IN ONE OF THE PROCESSIONS?
HA HA! NO, I'M A RABID ATHEIST, MY FRIEND.
THE DEAN OF THE UNIVERSITY ASKED ME TO COME TO KEEP THESE ANTIPOLIS IDIOTS FROM BURNING AN ARBORESS.
A WHAT?
A GIGANTIC TREE-CREATURE THAT COMES FROM THE OLD FOREST. THOSE SAVAGES WANT TO BURN HER AT THE CLOSE OF CARNIVAL. THE DEAN'S COUNTING ON MY SOCIOLOGICAL EXPERTISE TO GET THEM TO CHANGE THEIR MINDS.
AND DO YOU THINK YOU'LL MANAGE?
NO, FRANKLY. THEY DON'T GIVE A DAMN ABOUT SCIENCE.
HALT! YOU MUST PAY THREE COINS TO CROSS.
WE WERE MUGGED BY SOME BRUTES. THEY TOOK EVERYTHING.
NO MONEY, NO BRIDGE!
THESE GENTLEMEN WON'T USE AN ORC BRIDGE. COME THIS WAY. I'LL GET YOU ACROSS CHEAPER.
YOU'RE VERY KIND.
USE MY ROPE BRIDGE FOR JUST ONE COIN.

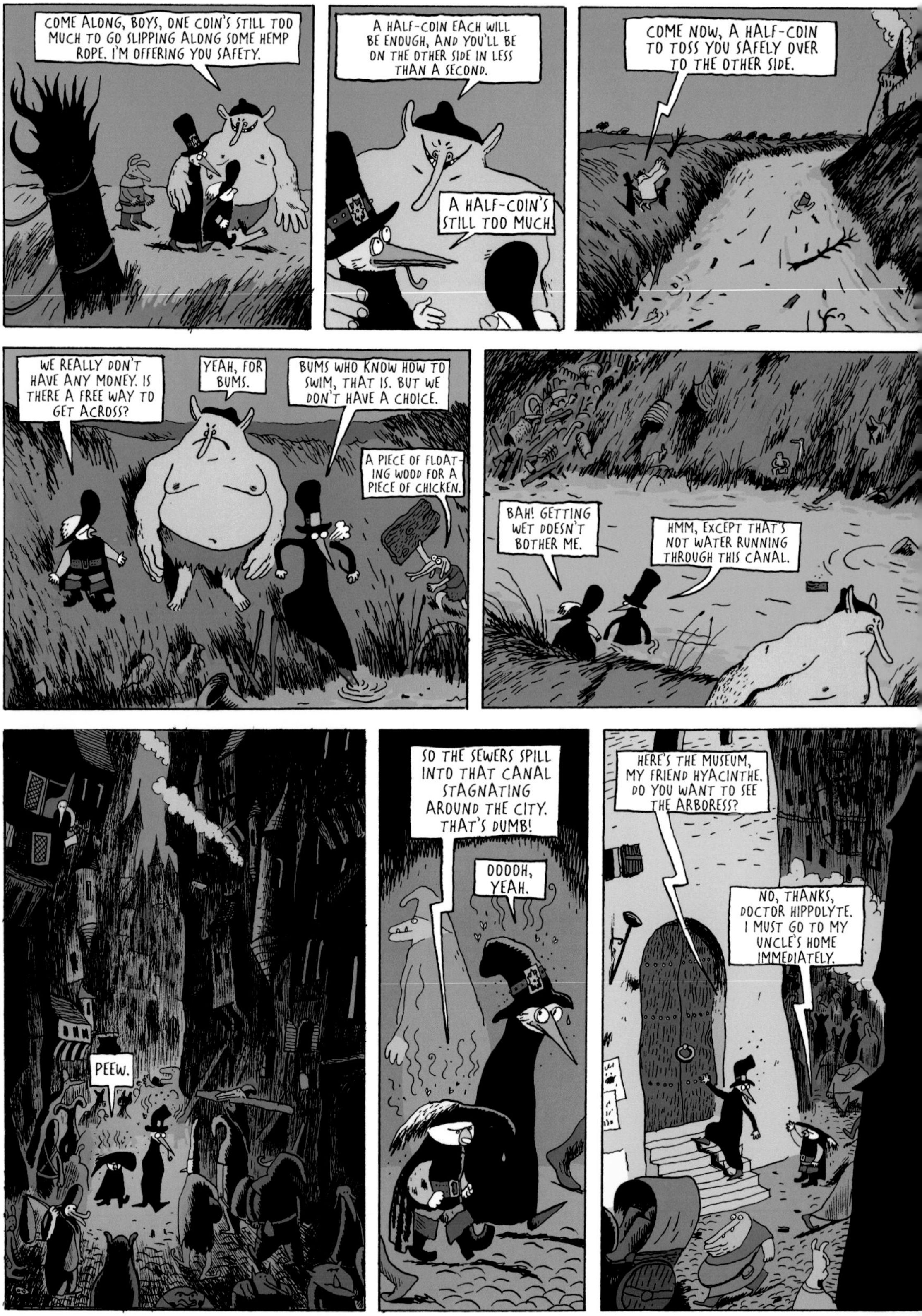
COME ALONG, BOYS, ONE COIN'S STILL TOO MUCH TO GO SLIPPING ALONG SOME HEMP ROPE. I'M OFFERING YOU SAFETY.
A HALF-COIN EACH WILL BE ENOUGH, AND YOU'LL BE ON THE OTHER SIDE IN LESS THAN A SECOND.
A HALF-COIN'S STILL TOO MUCH.
COME NOW, A HALF-COIN TO TOSS YOU SAFELY OVER TO THE OTHER SIDE.
WE REALLY DON'T HAVE ANY MONEY. IS THERE A FREE WAY TO GET ACROSS?
YEAH, FOR BUMS.
BUMS WHO KNOW HOW TO SWIM, THAT IS. BUT WE DON'T HAVE A CHOICE.
A PIECE OF FLOATING WOOD FOR A PIECE OF CHICKEN.
BAH! GETTING WET DOESN'T BOTHER ME.
HMM, EXCEPT THAT'S NOT WATER RUNNING THROUGH THIS CANAL.
PEEW.
SO THE SEWERS SPILL INTO THAT CANAL STAGNATING AROUND THE CITY. THAT'S DUMB!
OOOOH, YEAH.
HERE'S THE MUSEUM, MY FRIEND HYACINTHE. DO YOU WANT TO SEE THE ARBORESS?
NO, THANKS, DOCTOR HIPPOLYTE. I MUST GO TO MY UNCLE'S HOME IMMEDIATELY.

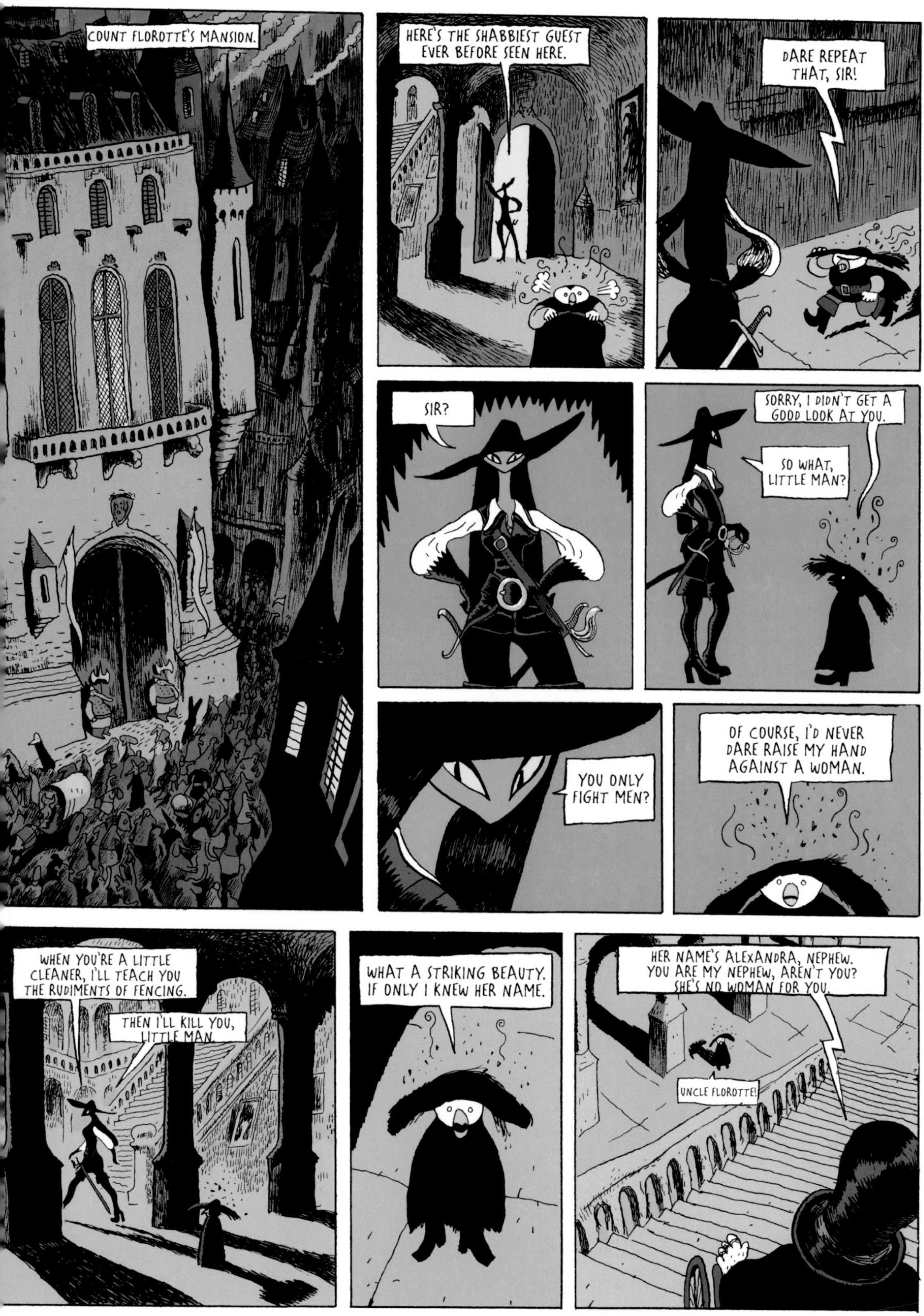
COUNT FLOROTTE'S MANSION.
HERE'S THE SHABBIEST GUEST EVER BEFORE SEEN HERE.
DARE REPEAT THAT, SIR!
SIR?
SORRY, I DIDN'T GET A GOOD LOOK AT YOU.
SO WHAT, LITTLE MAN?
YOU ONLY FIGHT MEN?
OF COURSE, I'D NEVER DARE RAISE MY HAND AGAINST A WOMAN.
WHEN YOU'RE A LITTLE CLEANER, I'LL TEACH YOU THE RUDIMENTS OF FENCING.
THEN I'LL KILL YOU, LITTLE MAN.
WHAT A STRIKING BEAUTY. IF ONLY I KNEW HER NAME.
HER NAME'S ALEXANDRA, NEPHEW. YOU ARE MY NEPHEW, AREN'T YOU? SHE'S NO WOMAN FOR YOU.
UNCLE FLOROTTE!

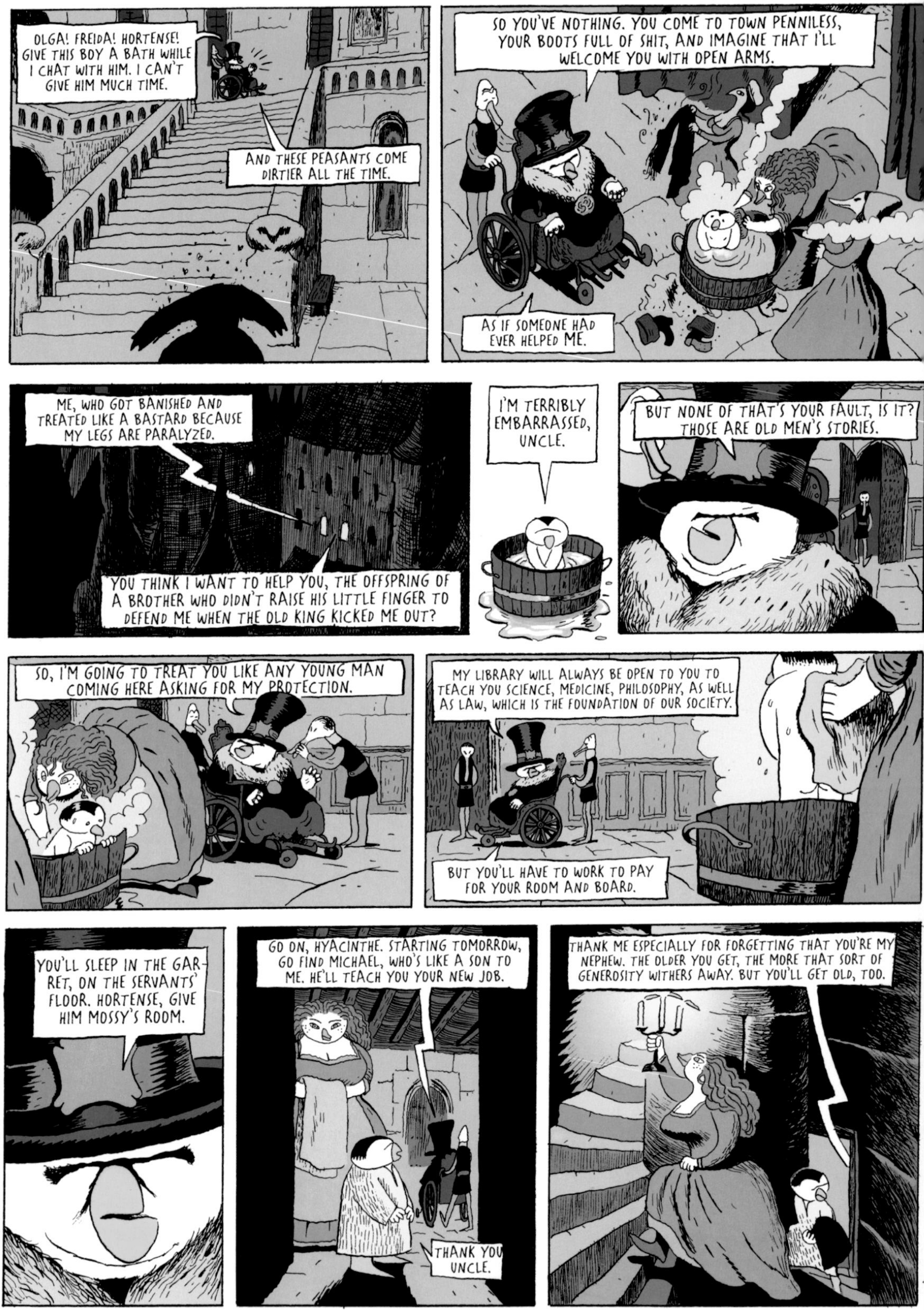
OLGA! FREIDA! HORTENSE! GIVE THIS BODY A BATH WHILE I CHAT WITH HIM. I CAN'T GIVE HIM MUCH TIME.
AND THESE PEASANTS COME DIRTIER ALL THE TIME.
SO YOU'VE NOTHING. YOU COME TO TOWN PENNILESS, YOUR BOOTS FULL OF SHIT, AND IMAGINE THAT I'LL WELCOME YOU WITH OPEN ARMS.
AS IF SOMEONE HAD EVER HELPED ME.
ME, WHO GOT BANISHED AND TREATED LIKE A BASTARD BECAUSE MY LEGS ARE PARALYZED.
YOU THINK I WANT TO HELP YOU, THE OFFSPRING OF A BROTHER WHO DIDN'T RAISE HIS LITTLE FINGER TO DEFEND ME WHEN THE OLD KING KICKED ME OUT?
I'M TERRIBLY EMBARRASSED, UNCLE.
BUT NONE OF THAT'S YOUR FAULT, IS IT? THOSE ARE OLD MEN'S STORIES.
SO, I'M GOING TO TREAT YOU LIKE ANY YOUNG MAN COMING HERE ASKING FOR MY PROTECTION.
MY LIBRARY WILL ALWAYS BE OPEN TO YOU TO TEACH YOU SCIENCE, MEDICINE, PHILOSOPHY, AS WELL AS LAW, WHICH IS THE FOUNDATION OF OUR SOCIETY.
BUT YOU'LL HAVE TO WORK TO PAY FOR YOUR ROOM AND BOARD.
YOU'LL SLEEP IN THE GARRET, ON THE SERVANTS' FLOOR. HORTENSE, GIVE HIM MOSSY'S ROOM.
GO ON, HYACINTHE. STARTING TOMORROW, GO FIND MICHAEL, WHO'S LIKE A SON TO ME. HE'LL TEACH YOU YOUR NEW JOB.
THANK YOU UNCLE.
THANK ME ESPECIALLY FOR FORGETTING THAT YOU'RE MY NEPHEW. THE OLDER YOU GET, THE MORE THAT SORT OF GENEROSITY WITHERS AWAY. BUT YOU'LL GET OLD, TOO.

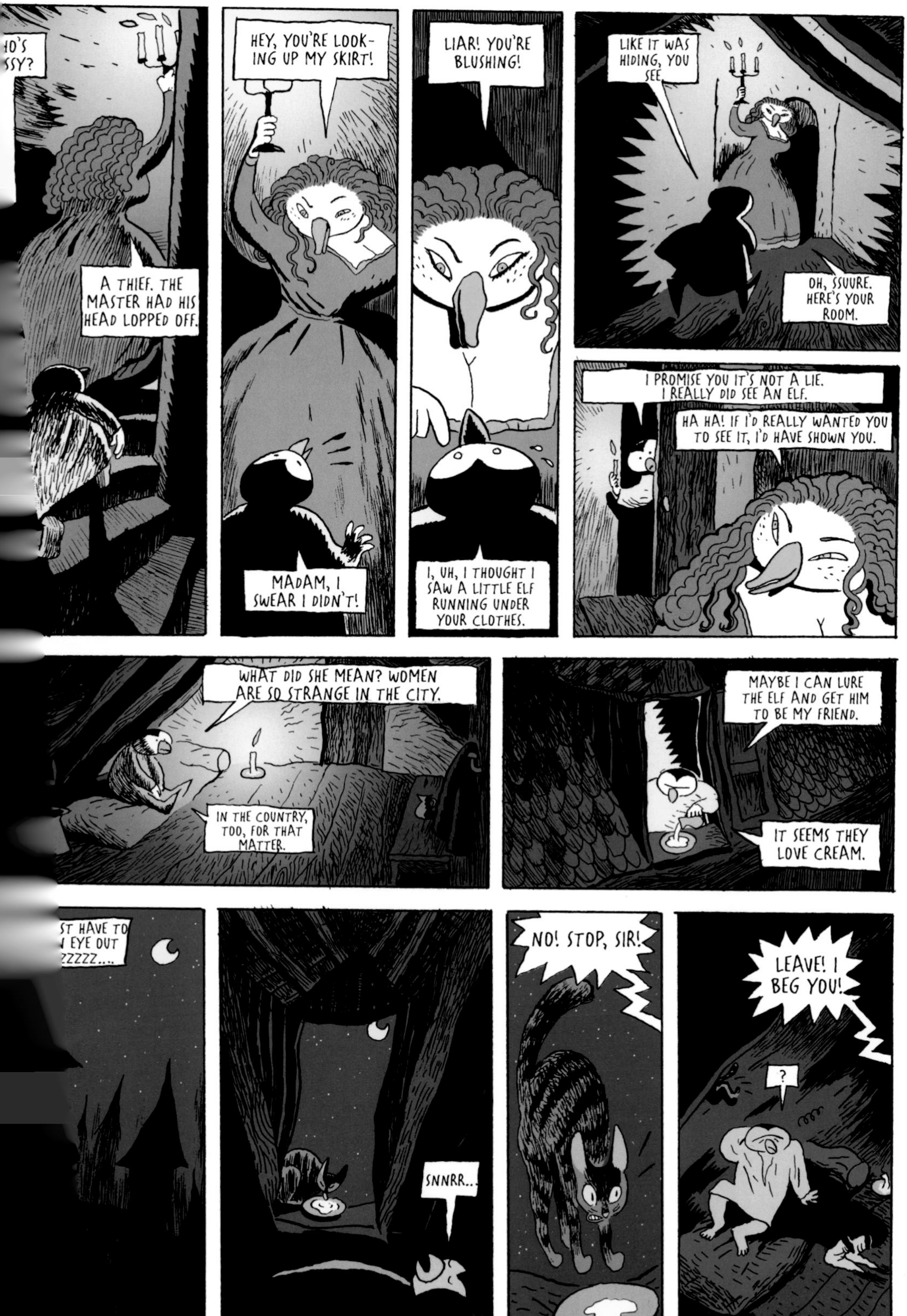
HO'S
SSY?
A THIEF. THE MASTER HAD HIS HEAD LOPPED OFF.
HEY, YOU'RE LOOKING UP MY SKIRT!
MADAM, I SWEAR I DIDN'T!
LIAR! YOU'RE BLUSHING!
I, UH, I THOUGHT I SAW A LITTLE ELF RUNNING UNDER YOUR CLOTHES.
LIKE IT WAS HIDING, YOU SEE.
OH, SSUURE. HERE'S YOUR ROOM.
I PROMISE YOU IT'S NOT A LIE. I REALLY DID SEE AN ELF.
HA HA! IF I'D REALLY WANTED YOU TO SEE IT, I'D HAVE SHOWN YOU.
WHAT DID SHE MEAN? WOMEN ARE SO STRANGE IN THE CITY.
IN THE COUNTRY, TOO, FOR THAT MATTER.
MAYBE I CAN LURE THE ELF AND GET HIM TO BE MY FRIEND.
IT SEEMS THEY LOVE CREAM.
ST HAVE TO
EYE OUT
ZZZZZ....
SNNRR...
NO! STOP, SIR!
LEAVE! I BEG YOU!
?

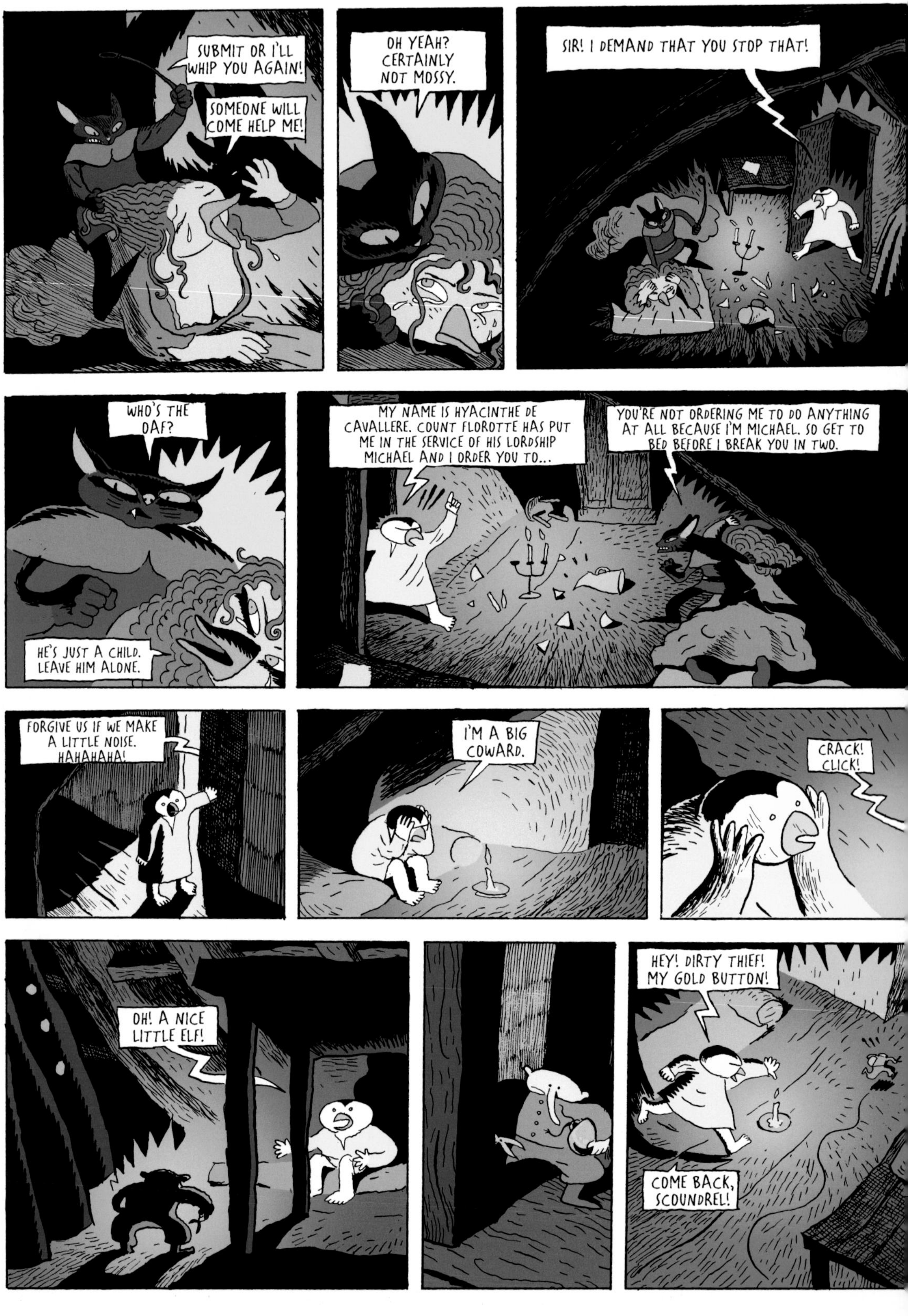
SUBMIT OR I'LL WHIP YOU AGAIN!
SOMEONE WILL COME HELP ME!
OH YEAH? CERTAINLY NOT MOSSY.
SIR! I DEMAND THAT YOU STOP THAT!
WHO'S THE OAF?
HE'S JUST A CHILD. LEAVE HIM ALONE.
MY NAME IS HYACINTHE DE CAVALLERE. COUNT FLOROTTE HAS PUT ME IN THE SERVICE OF HIS LORDSHIP MICHAEL AND I ORDER YOU TO...
YOU'RE NOT ORDERING ME TO DO ANYTHING AT ALL BECAUSE I'M MICHAEL. SO GET TO BED BEFORE I BREAK YOU IN TWO.
FORGIVE US IF WE MAKE A LITTLE NOISE. HAHAHAHA!
I'M A BIG COWARD.
CRACK! CLICK!
OH! A NICE LITTLE ELF!
HEY! DIRTY THIEF! MY GOLD BUTTON!
COME BACK, SCOUNDREL!

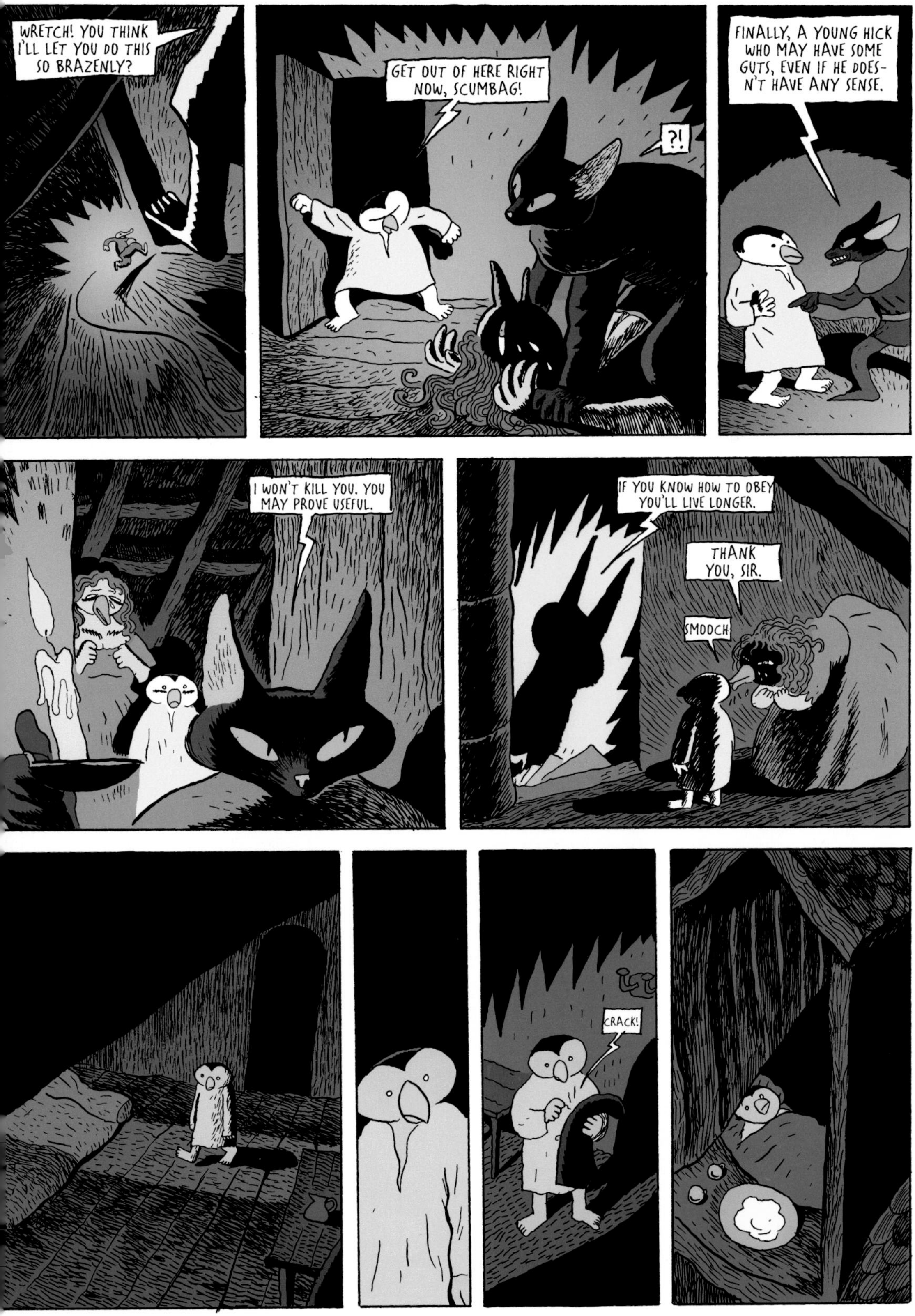
WRETCH! YOU THINK I'LL LET YOU DO THIS SO BRAZENLY?
GET OUT OF HERE RIGHT NOW, SCUMBAG!
?!
FINALLY, A YOUNG HICK WHO MAY HAVE SOME GUTS, EVEN IF HE DOESN'T HAVE ANY SENSE.
I WON'T KILL YOU. YOU MAY PROVE USEFUL.
IF YOU KNOW HOW TO OBEY YOU'LL LIVE LONGER.
THANK YOU, SIR.
SMOOCH
CRACK!

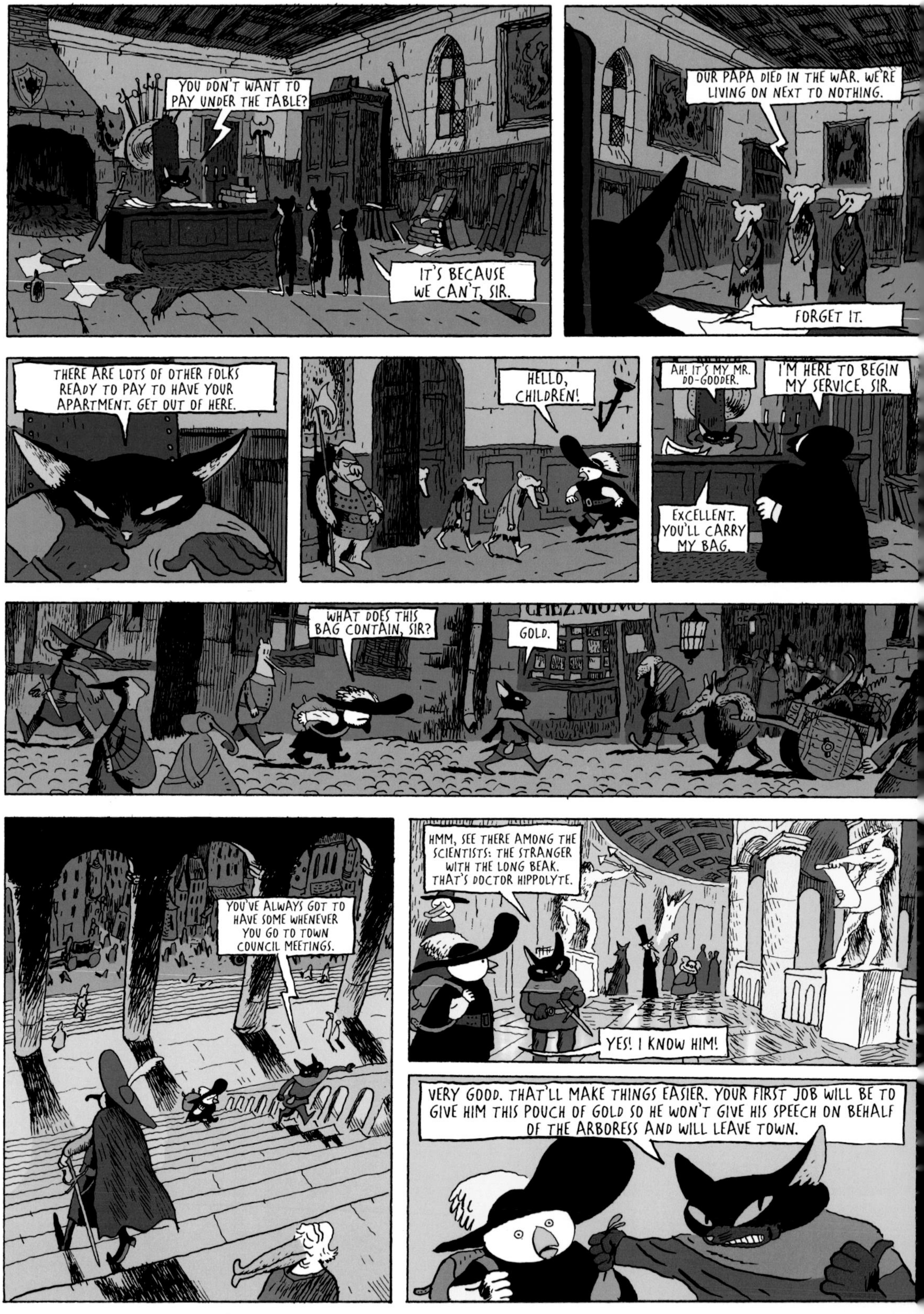

YOU DON'T WANT TO PAY UNDER THE TABLE?
IT'S BECAUSE WE CAN'T, SIR.
OUR PAPA DIED IN THE WAR. WE'RE LIVING ON NEXT TO NOTHING.
FORGET IT.
THERE ARE LOTS OF OTHER FOLKS READY TO PAY TO HAVE YOUR APARTMENT. GET OUT OF HERE.
HELLO, CHILDREN!
AH! IT'S MY MR. DO-GOODER.
I'M HERE TO BEGIN MY SERVICE, SIR.
EXCELLENT. YOU'LL CARRY MY BAG.
WHAT DOES THIS BAG CONTAIN, SIR?
GOLD.
YOU'VE ALWAYS GOT TO HAVE SOME WHENEVER YOU GO TO TOWN COUNCIL MEETINGS.
HMM, SEE THERE AMONG THE SCIENTISTS: THE STRANGER WITH THE LONG BEAK. THAT'S DOCTOR HIPPOLYTE.
YES! I KNOW HIM!
VERY GOOD. THAT'LL MAKE THINGS EASIER. YOUR FIRST JOB WILL BE TO GIVE HIM THIS POUCH OF GOLD SO HE WON'T GIVE HIS SPEECH ON BEHALF OF THE ARBORESS AND WILL LEAVE TOWN.

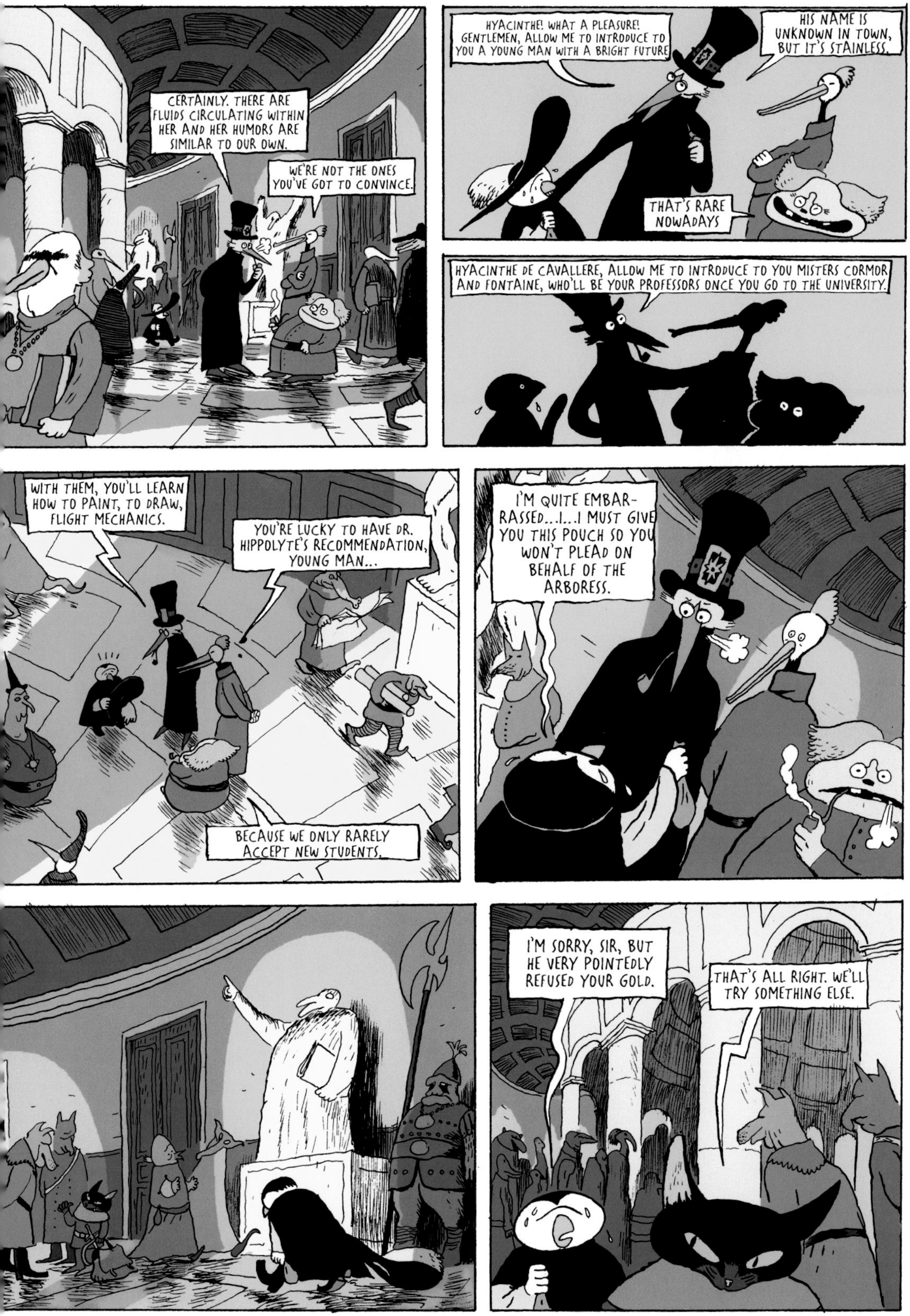

CERTAINLY. THERE ARE FLUIDS CIRCULATING WITHIN HER AND HER HUMORS ARE SIMILAR TO OUR OWN.
WE'RE NOT THE ONES YOU'VE GOT TO CONVINCE.
HYACINTHE! WHAT A PLEASURE! GENTLEMEN, ALLOW ME TO INTRODUCE TO YOU A YOUNG MAN WITH A BRIGHT FUTURE
HIS NAME IS UNKNOWN IN TOWN, BUT IT'S STAINLESS.
THAT'S RARE NOWADAYS
HYACINTHE DE CAVALLERE, ALLOW ME TO INTRODUCE TO YOU MISTERS CORMOR AND FONTAINE, WHO'LL BE YOUR PROFESSORS ONCE YOU GO TO THE UNIVERSITY.
WITH THEM, YOU'LL LEARN HOW TO PAINT, TO DRAW, FLIGHT MECHANICS.
YOU'RE LUCKY TO HAVE DR. HIPPOLYTE'S RECOMMENDATION, YOUNG MAN...
BECAUSE WE ONLY RARELY ACCEPT NEW STUDENTS.
I'M QUITE EMBARRASSED...I...I MUST GIVE YOU THIS POUCH SO YOU WON'T PLEAD ON BEHALF OF THE ARBORESS.
I'M SORRY, SIR, BUT HE VERY POINTEDLY REFUSED YOUR GOLD.
THAT'S ALL RIGHT. WE'LL TRY SOMETHING ELSE.

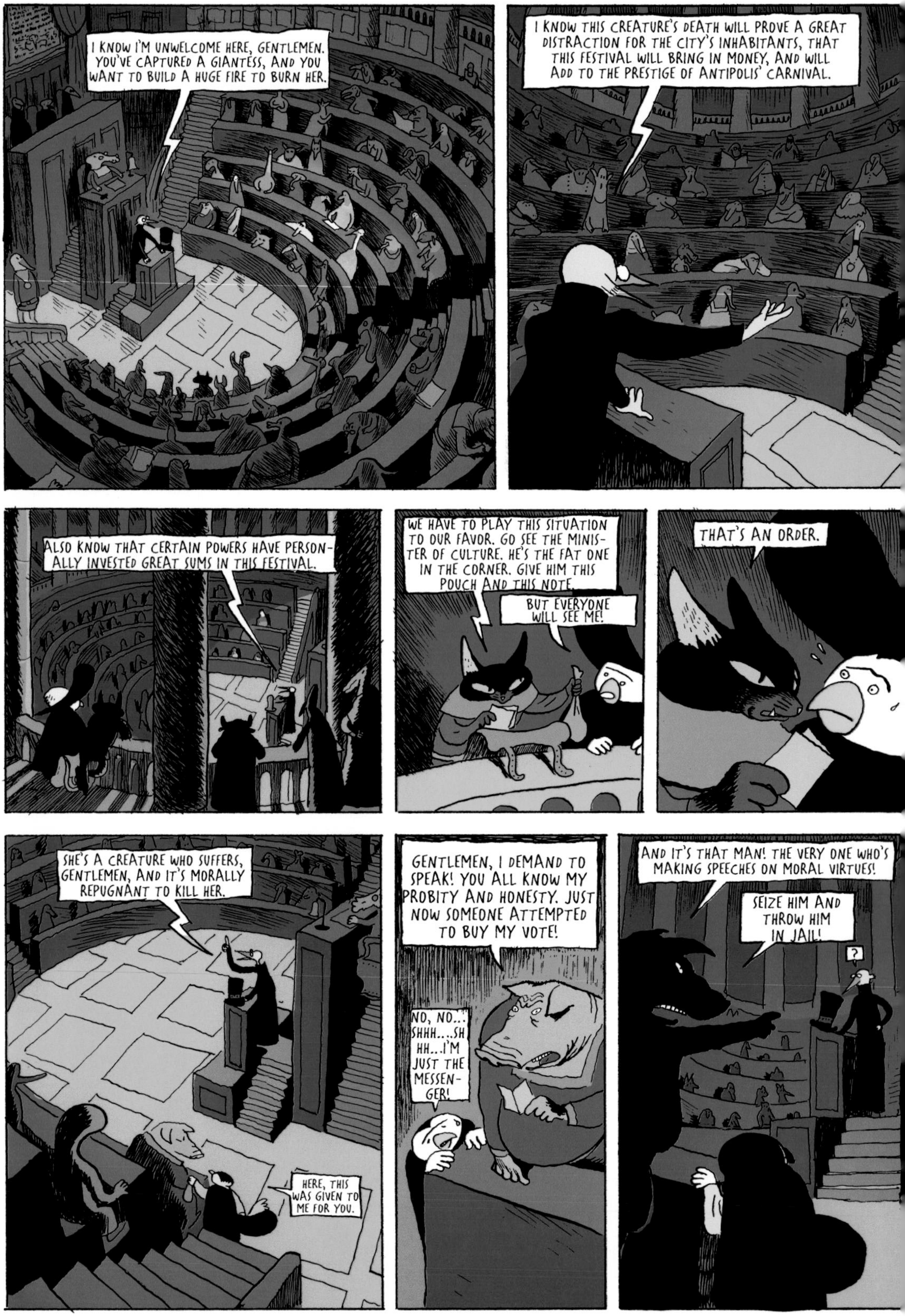
I KNOW I'M UNWELCOME HERE, GENTLEMEN. YOU'VE CAPTURED A GIANTESS, AND YOU WANT TO BUILD A HUGE FIRE TO BURN HER.
I KNOW THIS CREATURE'S DEATH WILL PROVE A GREAT DISTRACTION FOR THE CITY'S INHABITANTS, THAT THIS FESTIVAL WILL BRING IN MONEY, AND WILL ADD TO THE PRESTIGE OF ANTIPOLIS' CARNIVAL.
ALSO KNOW THAT CERTAIN POWERS HAVE PERSONALLY INVESTED GREAT SUMS IN THIS FESTIVAL.
WE HAVE TO PLAY THIS SITUATION TO OUR FAVOR. GO SEE THE MINISTER OF CULTURE. HE'S THE FAT ONE IN THE CORNER. GIVE HIM THIS POUCH AND THIS NOTE.
BUT EVERYONE WILL SEE ME!
THAT'S AN ORDER.
SHE'S A CREATURE WHO SUFFERS, GENTLEMEN, AND IT'S MORALLY REPUGNANT TO KILL HER.
HERE, THIS WAS GIVEN TO ME FOR YOU.
GENTLEMEN, I DEMAND TO SPEAK! YOU ALL KNOW MY PROBITY AND HONESTY. JUST NOW SOMEONE ATTEMPTED TO BUY MY VOTE!
NO, NO... SHHH...SHHH...I'M JUST THE MESSENGER!
AND IT'S THAT MAN! THE VERY ONE WHO'S MAKING SPEECHES ON MORAL VIRTUES!
SEIZE HIM AND THROW HIM IN JAIL!
?

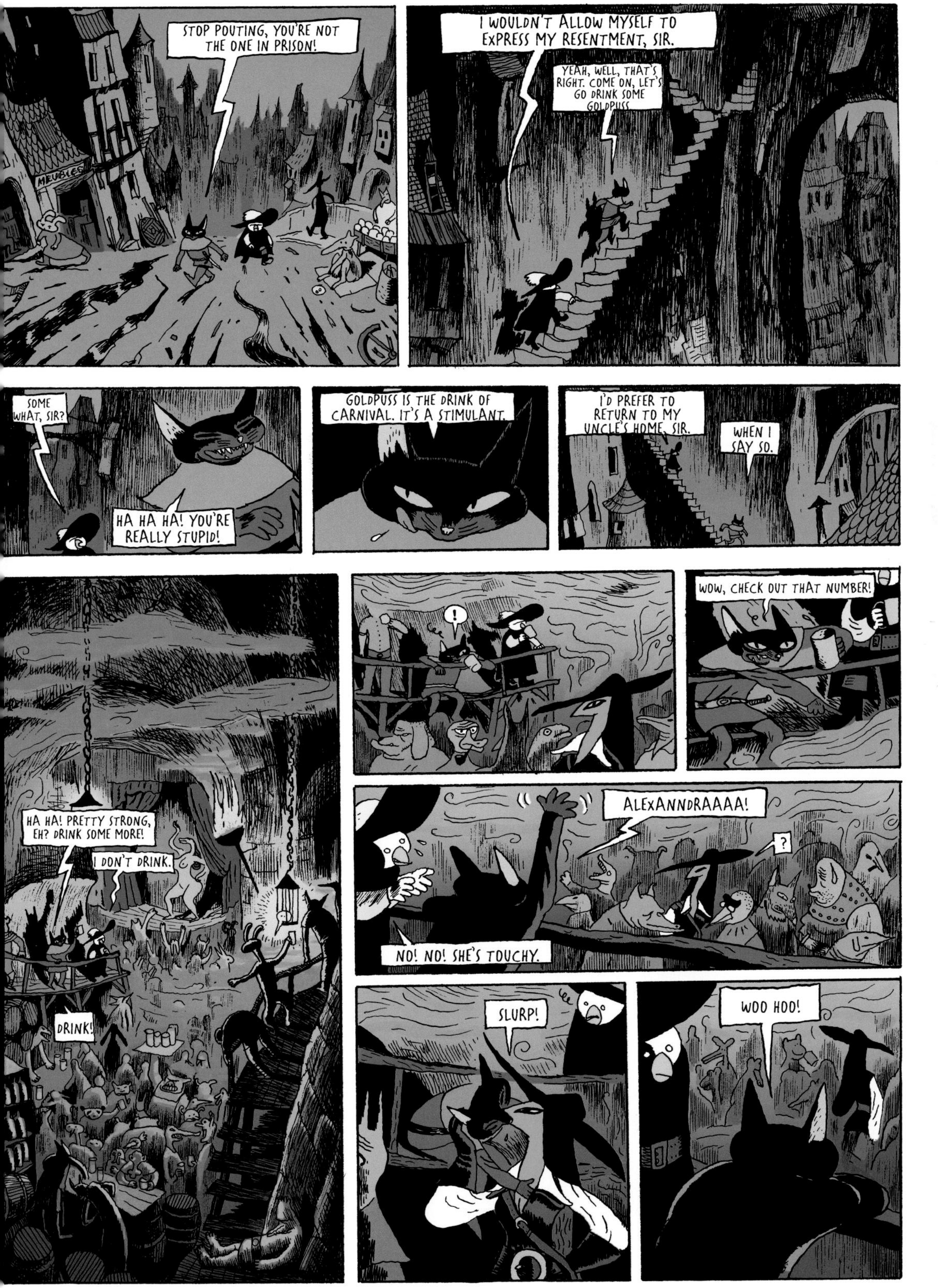
STOP POUTING, YOU'RE NOT THE ONE IN PRISON!
MEUBLES
I WOULDN'T ALLOW MYSELF TO EXPRESS MY RESENTMENT, SIR.
YEAH, WELL, THAT'S RIGHT. COME ON, LET'S GO DRINK SOME GOLDPUSS
SOME WHAT, SIR?
HA HA HA! YOU'RE REALLY STUPID!
GOLDPUSS IS THE DRINK OF CARNIVAL. IT'S A STIMULANT.
I'D PREFER TO RETURN TO MY UNCLE'S HOME, SIR.
WHEN I SAY SO.
HA HA! PRETTY STRONG, EH? DRINK SOME MORE!
I DON'T DRINK.
DRINK!
!
WOW, CHECK OUT THAT NUMBER!
ALEXANNDRAAAA!
?
NO! NO! SHE'S TOUCHY.
SLURP!
WOO HOO!

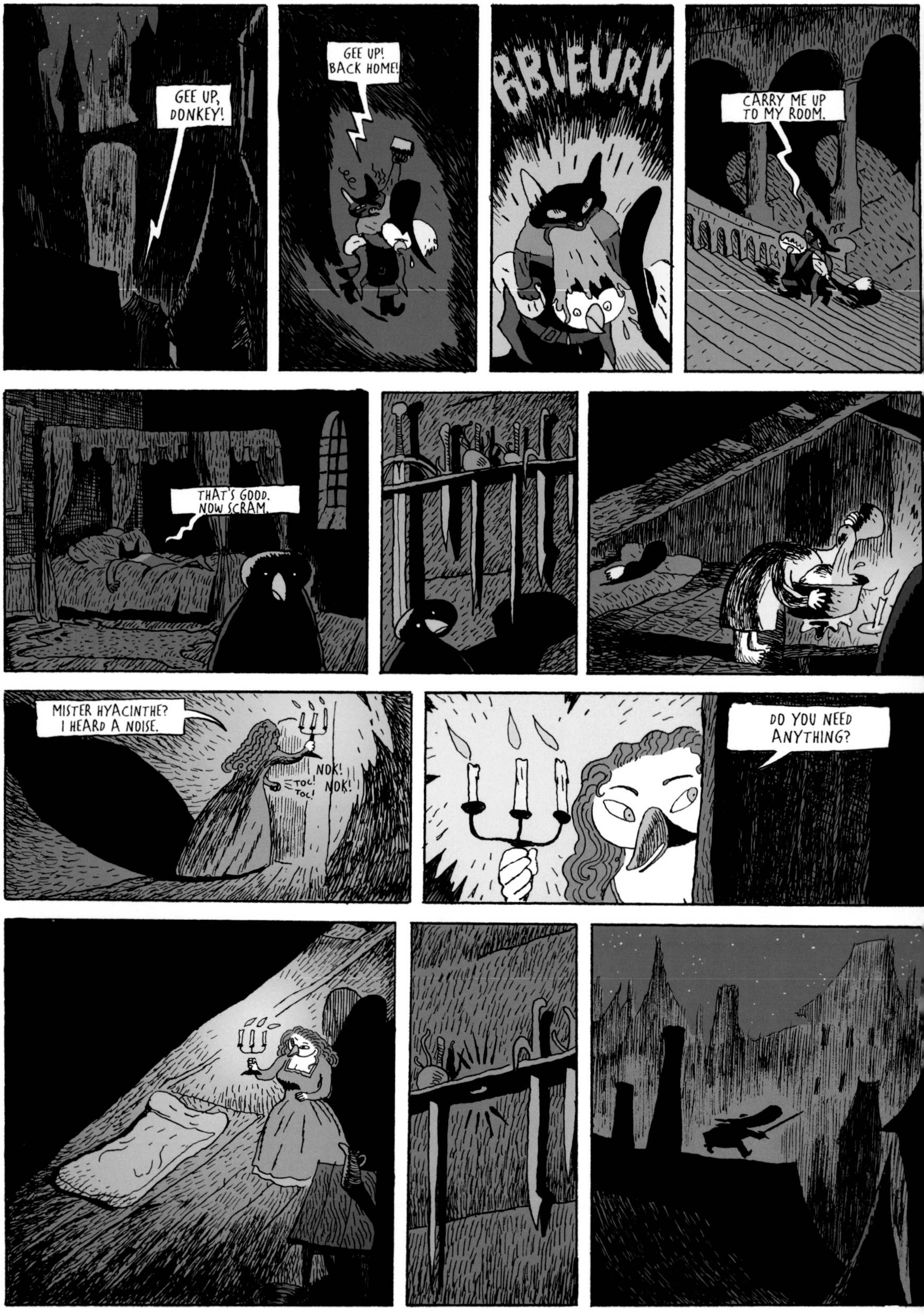
GEE UP, DONKEY!
GEE UP! BACK HOME!
BBLEURK
CARRY ME UP TO MY ROOM.
THAT'S GOOD. NOW SCRAM.
MISTER HYACINTHE? I HEARD A NOISE.
TOC! TOC!
NOK! NOK!
DO YOU NEED ANYTHING?

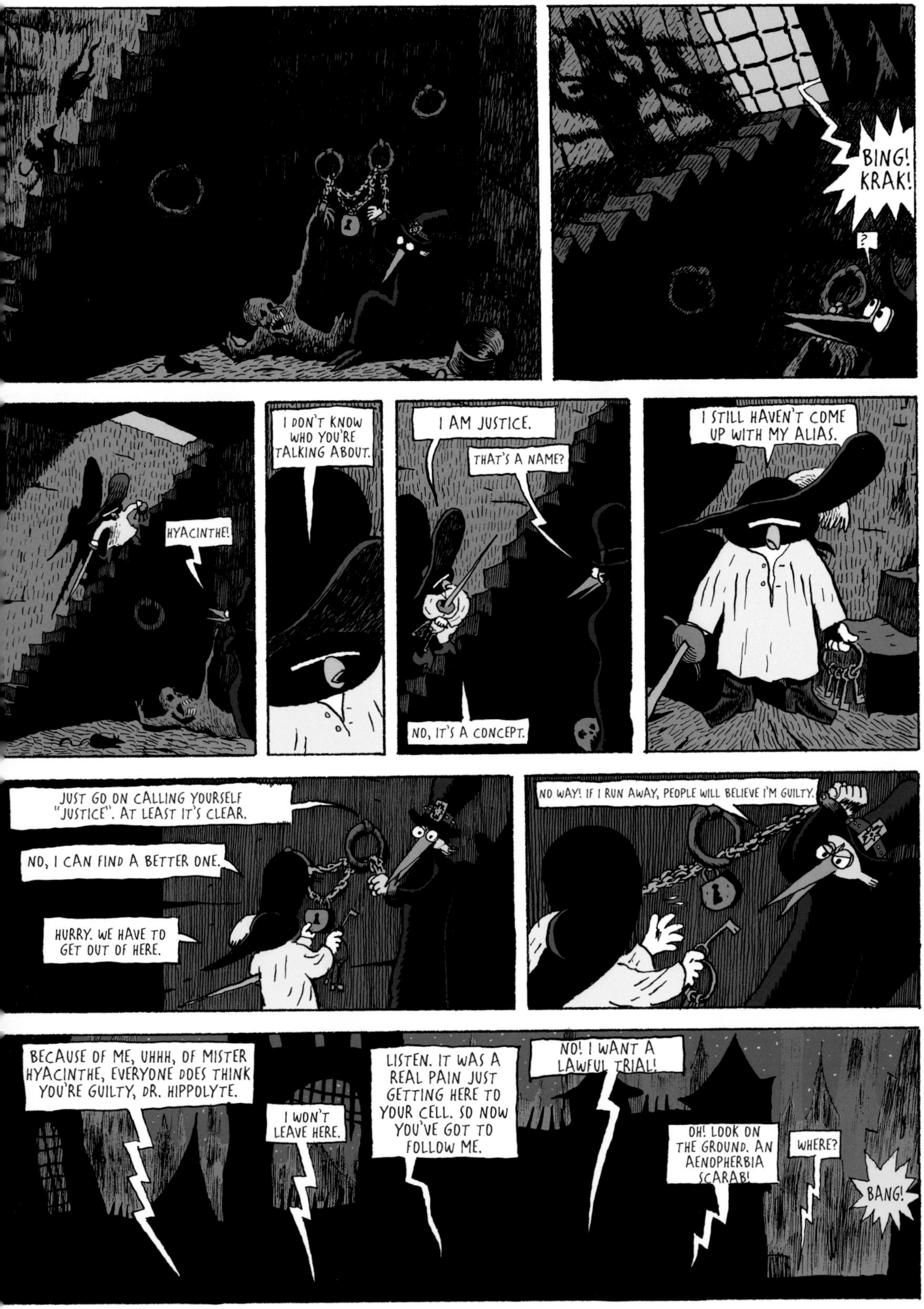
BING! KRAK!
?
HYACINTHE!
I DON'T KNOW WHO YOU'RE TALKING ABOUT.
I AM JUSTICE.
THAT'S A NAME?
NO, IT'S A CONCEPT.
I STILL HAVEN'T COME UP WITH MY ALIAS.
JUST GO ON CALLING YOURSELF "JUSTICE". AT LEAST IT'S CLEAR.
NO, I CAN FIND A BETTER ONE.
HURRY. WE HAVE TO GET OUT OF HERE.
NO WAY! IF I RUN AWAY, PEOPLE WILL BELIEVE I'M GUILTY.
BECAUSE OF ME, UHHH, OF MISTER HYACINTHE, EVERYONE DOES THINK YOU'RE GUILTY, DR. HIPPOLYTE.
I WON'T LEAVE HERE.
LISTEN. IT WAS A REAL PAIN JUST GETTING HERE TO YOUR CELL. SO NOW YOU'VE GOT TO FOLLOW ME.
NO! I WANT A LAWFUL TRIAL!
OH! LOOK ON THE GROUND. AN AENOPHERBIA SCARAB!
WHERE?
BANG!

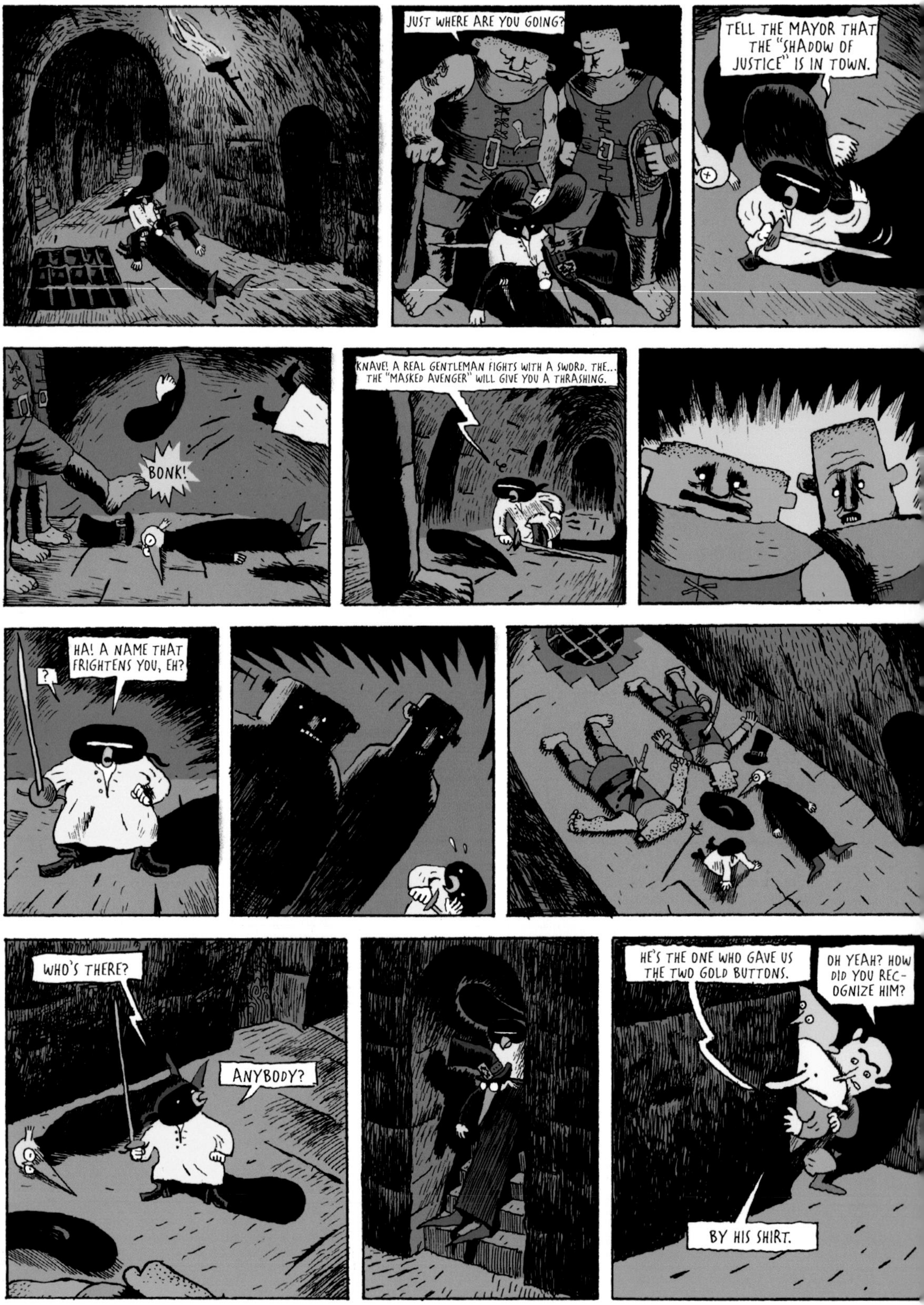
JUST WHERE ARE YOU GOING?
TELL THE MAYOR THAT THE "SHADOW OF JUSTICE" IS IN TOWN.
BONK!
KNAVE! A REAL GENTLEMAN FIGHTS WITH A SWORD. THE... THE "MASKED AVENGER" WILL GIVE YOU A THRASHING.
?
HA! A NAME THAT FRIGHTENS YOU, EH?
WHO'S THERE?
ANYBODY?
HE'S THE ONE WHO GAVE US THE TWO GOLD BUTTONS.
OH YEAH? HOW DID YOU REC-OGNIZE HIM?
BY HIS SHIRT.

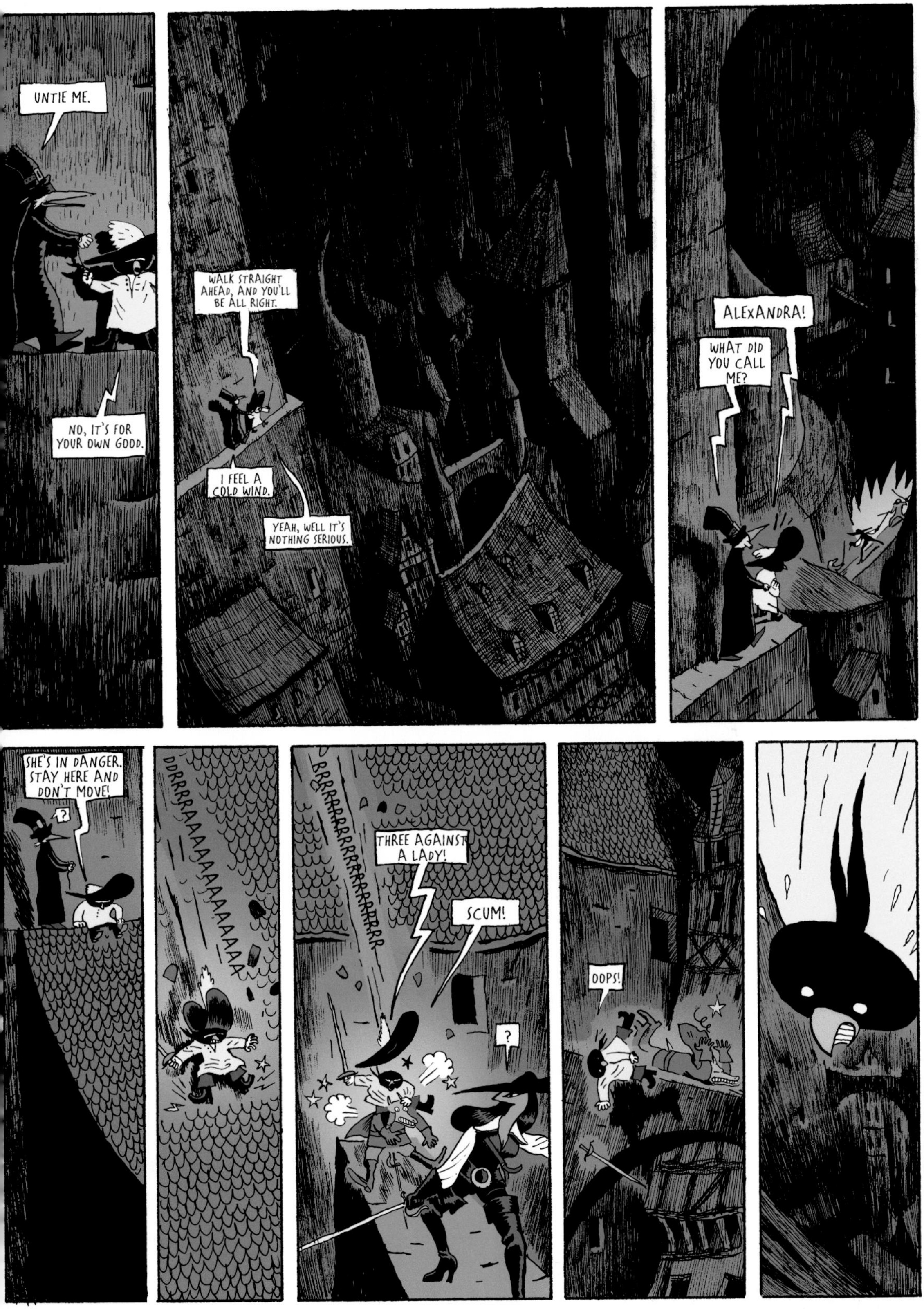
UNTIE ME.
NO, IT'S FOR YOUR OWN GOOD.
WALK STRAIGHT AHEAD, AND YOU'LL BE ALL RIGHT.
I FEEL A COLD WIND.
YEAH, WELL IT'S NOTHING SERIOUS.
ALEXANDRA!
WHAT DID YOU CALL ME?
SHE'S IN DANGER. STAY HERE AND DON'T MOVE!
?
DDRRRRAAAAAAAAAAAAAA
RRRRRRRRRRRRRRRRRR
THREE AGAINST A LADY!
SCUM!
?
OOPS!

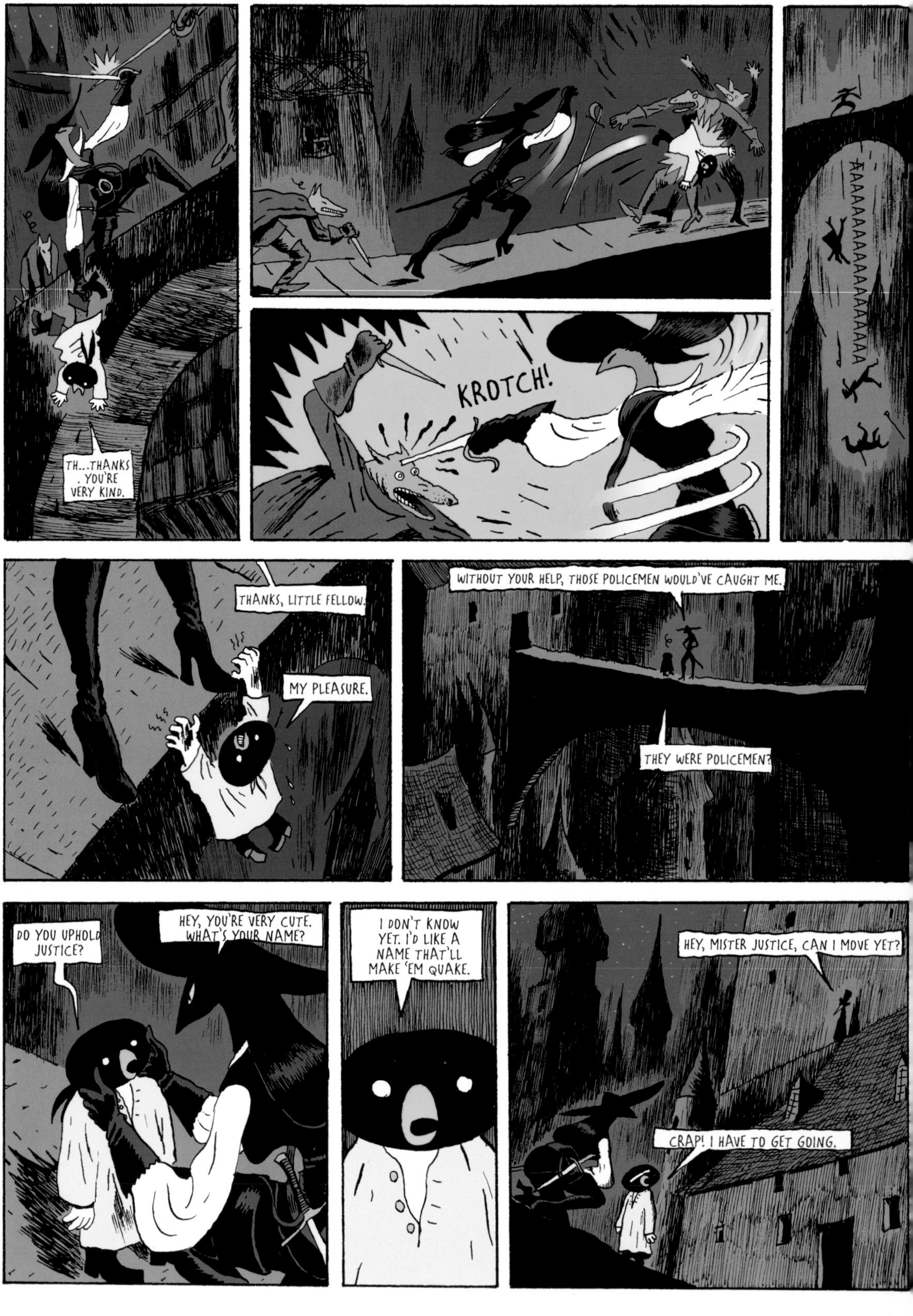
TH...THANKS. YOU'RE VERY KIND.
KROTCH!
AAAAAAAAAAAAAAAAAAA
THANKS, LITTLE FELLOW.
MY PLEASURE.
WITHOUT YOUR HELP, THOSE POLICEMEN WOULD'VE CAUGHT ME.
THEY WERE POLICEMEN?
DO YOU UPHOLD JUSTICE?
HEY, YOU'RE VERY CUTE. WHAT'S YOUR NAME?
I DON'T KNOW YET. I'D LIKE A NAME THAT'LL MAKE 'EM QUAKE.
HEY, MISTER JUSTICE, CAN I MOVE YET?
CRAP! I HAVE TO GET GOING.

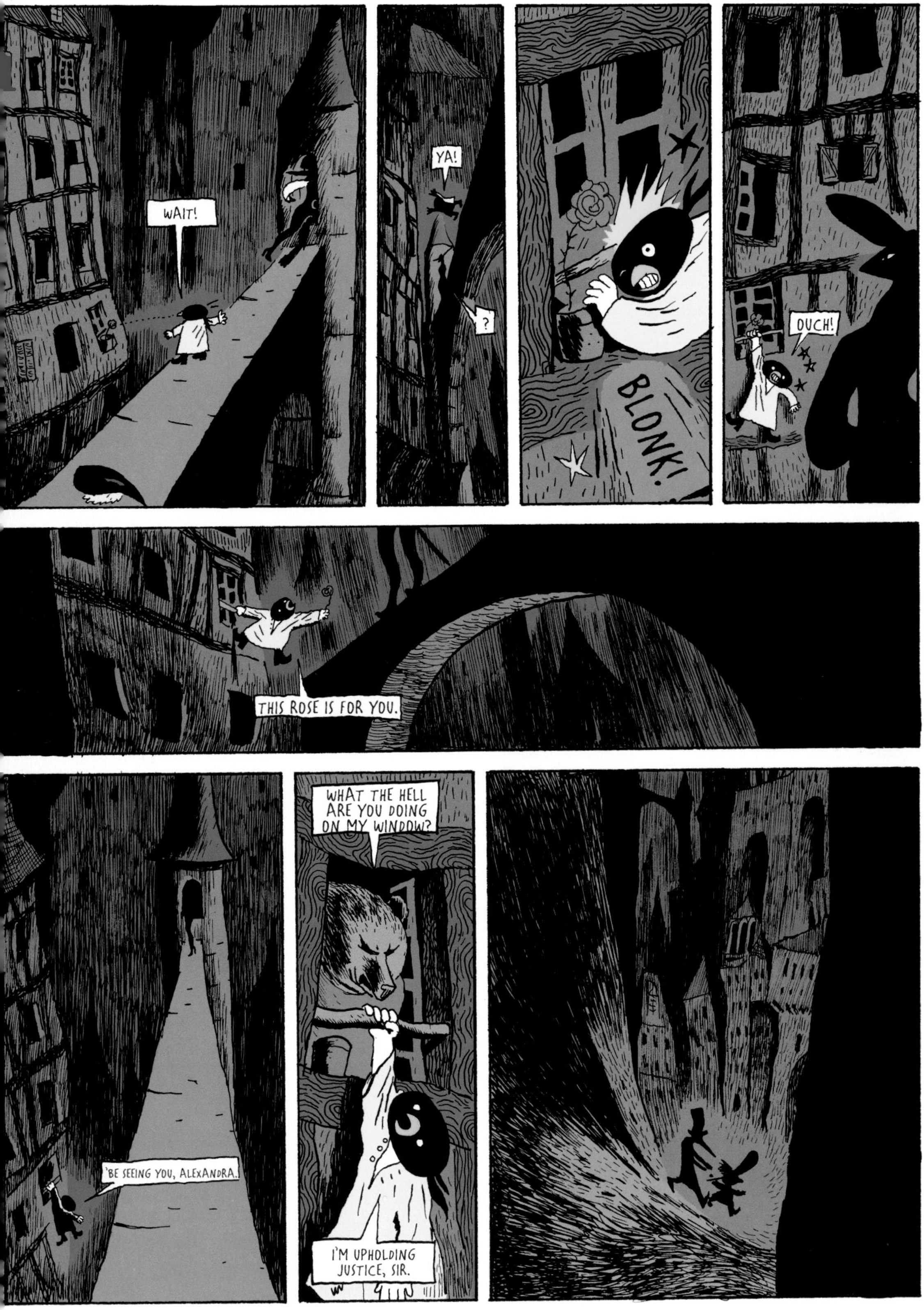
WAIT!
YA!
?
BLONK!
OUCH!
THIS ROSE IS FOR YOU.
'BE SEEING YOU, ALEXANDRA.
WHAT THE HELL ARE YOU DOING ON MY WINDOW?
I'M UPHOLDING JUSTICE, SIR.

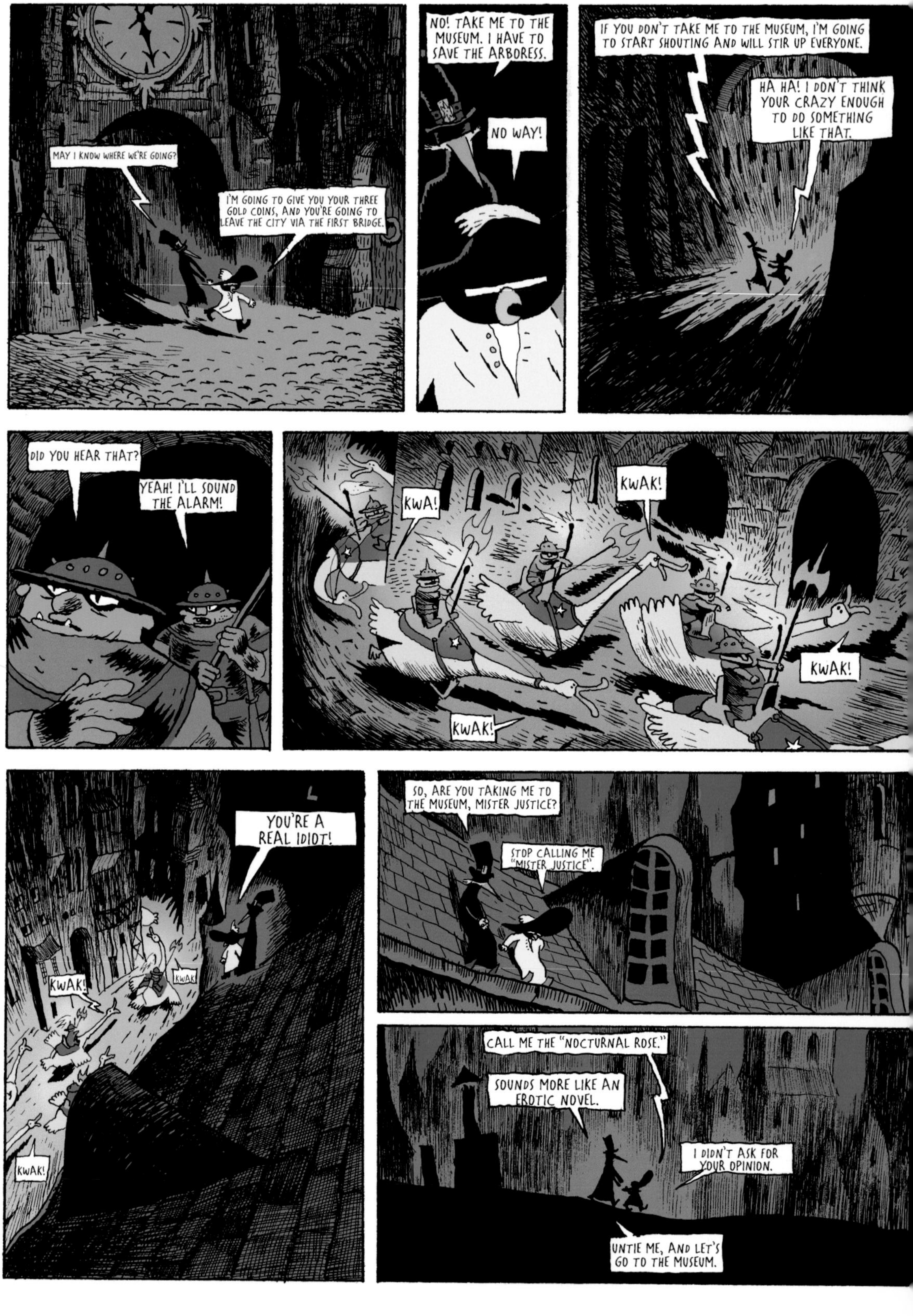

MAY I KNOW WHERE WE'RE GOING?
I'M GOING TO GIVE YOU YOUR THREE GOLD COINS, AND YOU'RE GOING TO LEAVE THE CITY VIA THE FIRST BRIDGE.
NO! TAKE ME TO THE MUSEUM. I HAVE TO SAVE THE ARBORESS.
NO WAY!
IF YOU DON'T TAKE ME TO THE MUSEUM, I'M GOING TO START SHOUTING AND WILL STIR UP EVERYONE.
HA HA! I DON'T THINK YOUR CRAZY ENOUGH TO DO SOMETHING LIKE THAT.
DID YOU HEAR THAT?
YEAH! I'LL SOUND THE ALARM!
KWA!
KWAK!
KWAK!
KWAK!
YOU'RE A REAL IDIOT!
KWAK!
KWAK!
KWAK!
SO, ARE YOU TAKING ME TO THE MUSEUM, MISTER JUSTICE?
STOP CALLING ME "MISTER JUSTICE".
CALL ME THE "NOCTURNAL ROSE."
SOUNDS MORE LIKE AN EROTIC NOVEL.
I DIDN'T ASK FOR YOUR OPINION.
UNTIE ME, AND LET'S GO TO THE MUSEUM.

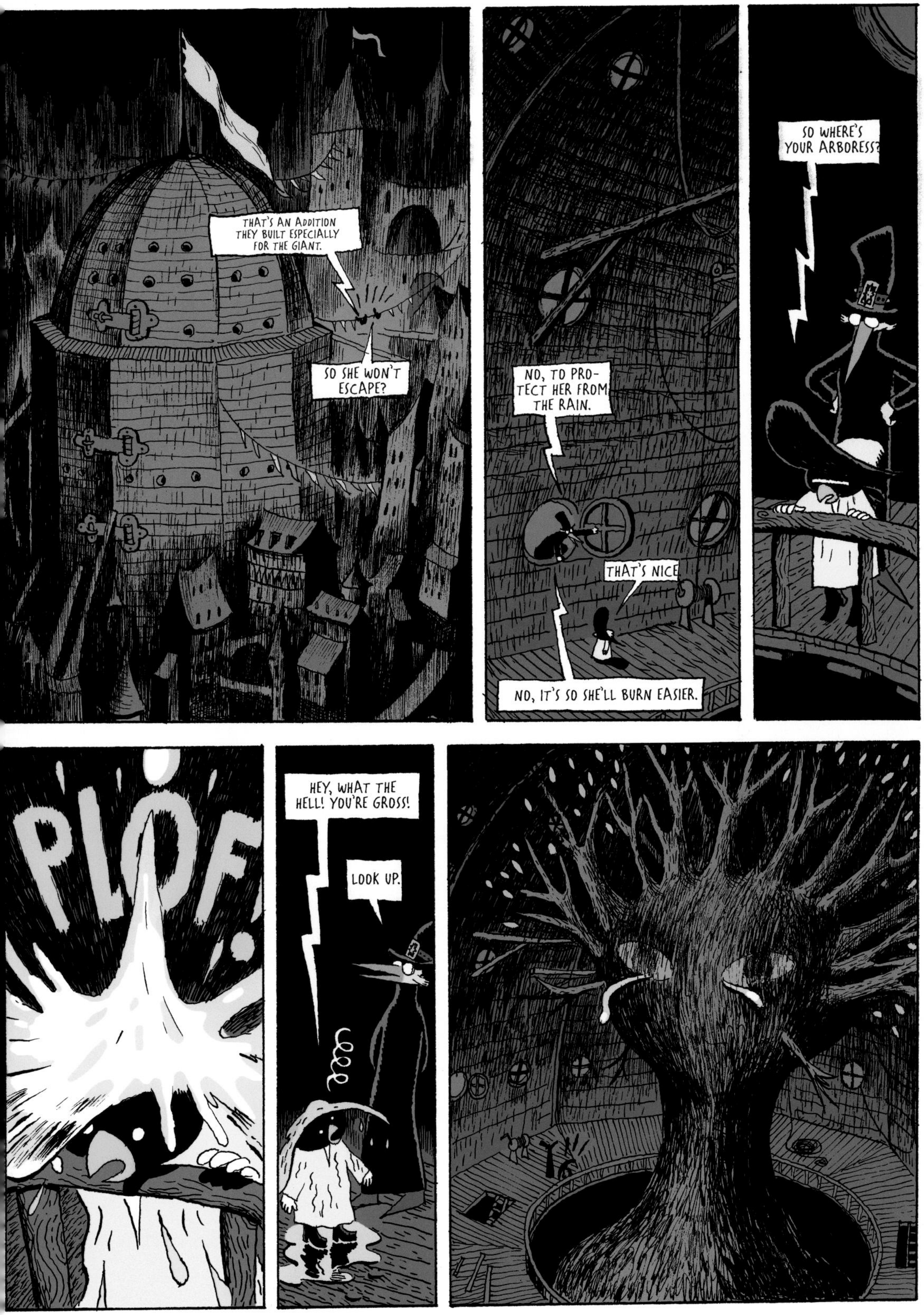
THAT'S AN ADDITION THEY BUILT ESPECIALLY FOR THE GIANT.
SO SHE WON'T ESCAPE?
NO, TO PROTECT HER FROM THE RAIN.
THAT'S NICE
NO, IT'S SO SHE'LL BURN EASIER.
SO WHERE'S YOUR ARBORESS?
PLOF!
HEY, WHAT THE HELL! YOU'RE GROSS!
LOOK UP.

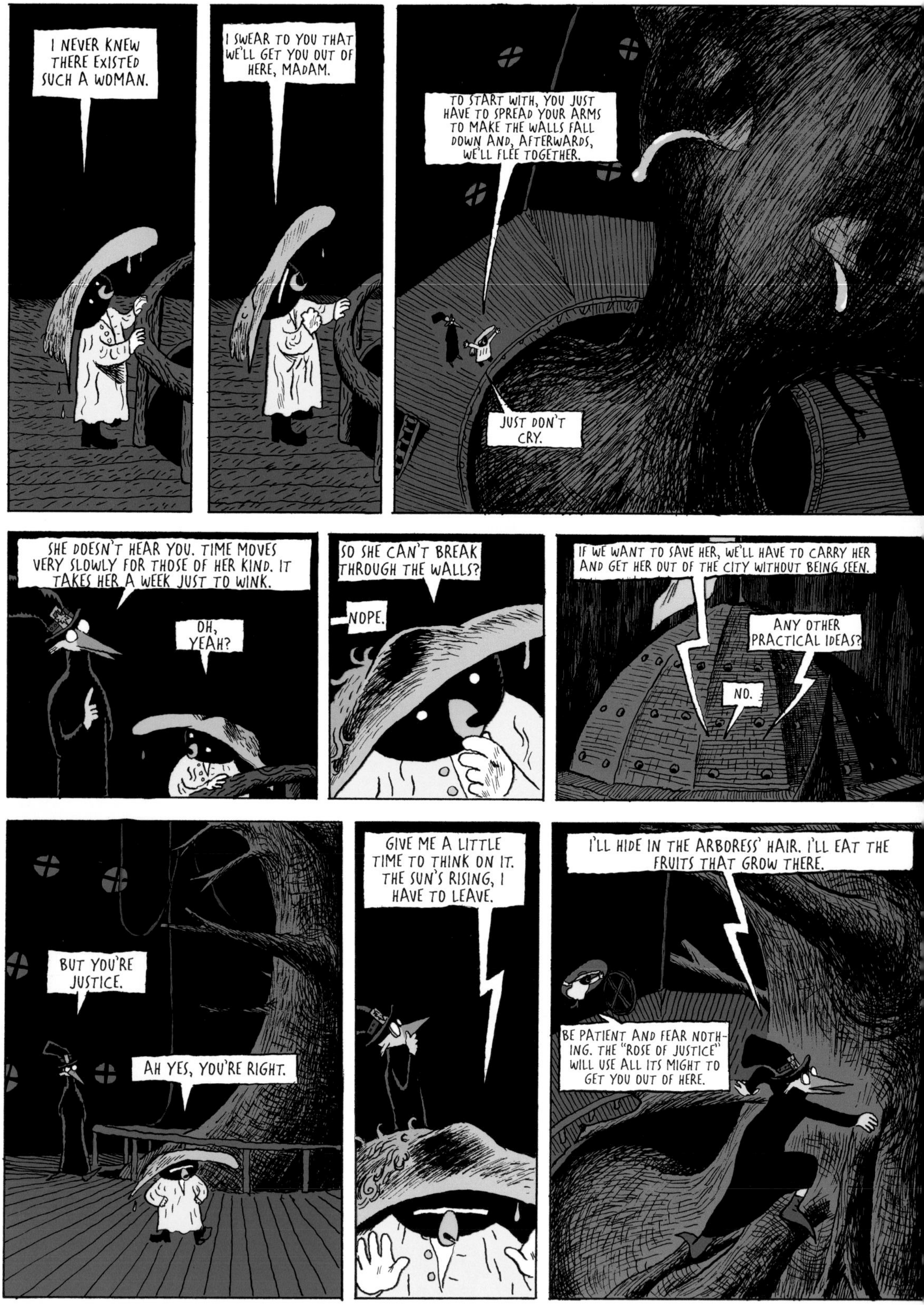
I NEVER KNEW THERE EXISTED SUCH A WOMAN.
I SWEAR TO YOU THAT WE'LL GET YOU OUT OF HERE, MADAM.
TO START WITH, YOU JUST HAVE TO SPREAD YOUR ARMS TO MAKE THE WALLS FALL DOWN AND, AFTERWARDS, WE'LL FLEE TOGETHER.
JUST DON'T CRY.
SHE DOESN'T HEAR YOU. TIME MOVES VERY SLOWLY FOR THOSE OF HER KIND. IT TAKES HER A WEEK JUST TO WINK.
OH, YEAH?
SO SHE CAN'T BREAK THROUGH THE WALLS?
NOPE.
IF WE WANT TO SAVE HER, WE'LL HAVE TO CARRY HER AND GET HER OUT OF THE CITY WITHOUT BEING SEEN.
ANY OTHER PRACTICAL IDEAS?
NO.
BUT YOU'RE JUSTICE.
AH YES, YOU'RE RIGHT.
GIVE ME A LITTLE TIME TO THINK ON IT. THE SUN'S RISING, I HAVE TO LEAVE.
I'LL HIDE IN THE ARBORESS' HAIR. I'LL EAT THE FRUITS THAT GROW THERE.
BE PATIENT AND FEAR NOTHING. THE "ROSE OF JUSTICE" WILL USE ALL ITS MIGHT TO GET YOU OUT OF HERE.

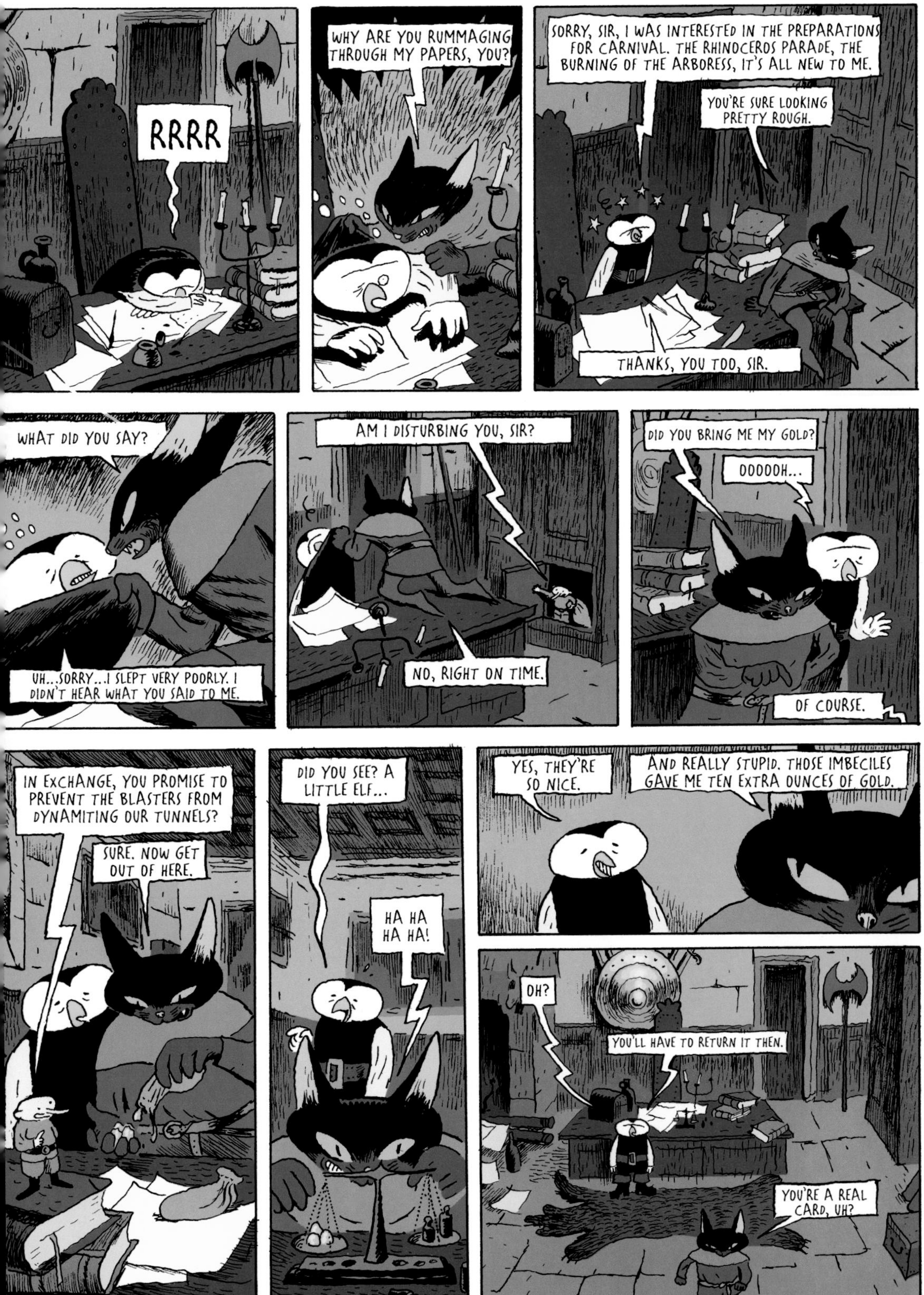
RRRR
WHY ARE YOU RUMMAGING THROUGH MY PAPERS, YOU?
SORRY, SIR, I WAS INTERESTED IN THE PREPARATIONS FOR CARNIVAL. THE RHINOCEROS PARADE, THE BURNING OF THE ARBORESS, IT'S ALL NEW TO ME.
YOU'RE SURE LOOKING PRETTY ROUGH.
THANKS, YOU TOO, SIR.
WHAT DID YOU SAY?
UH...SORRY...I SLEPT VERY POORLY. I DIDN'T HEAR WHAT YOU SAID TO ME.
AM I DISTURBING YOU, SIR?
NO, RIGHT ON TIME.
DID YOU BRING ME MY GOLD?
OOOOOH...
OF COURSE.
IN EXCHANGE, YOU PROMISE TO PREVENT THE BLASTERS FROM DYNAMITING OUR TUNNELS?
SURE. NOW GET OUT OF HERE.
DID YOU SEE? A LITTLE ELF...
HA HA HA HA!
YES, THEY'RE SO NICE.
AND REALLY STUPID. THOSE IMBECILES GAVE ME TEN EXTRA OUNCES OF GOLD.
OH?
YOU'LL HAVE TO RETURN IT THEN.
YOU'RE A REAL CARD, UH?

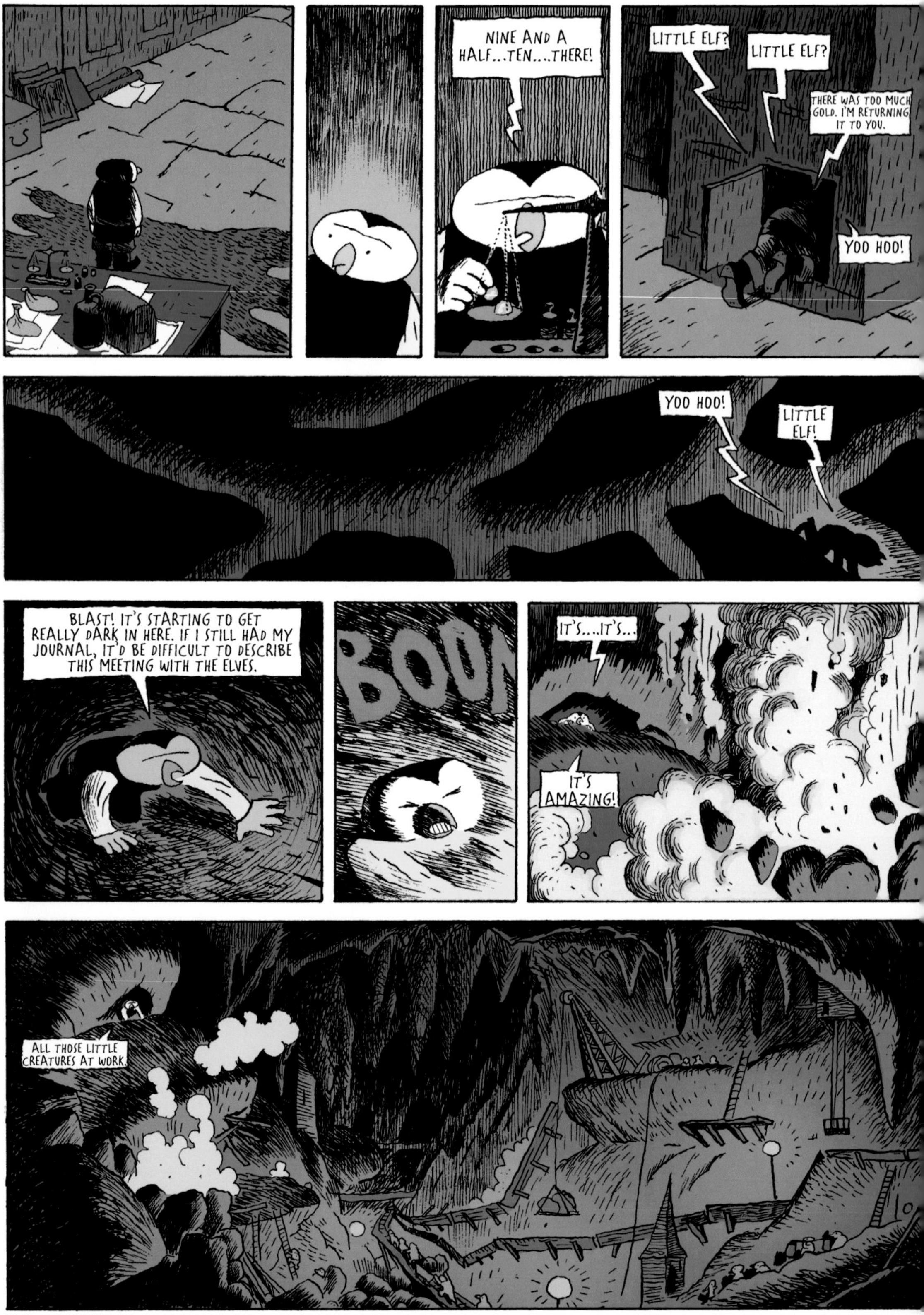
NINE AND A HALF...TEN....THERE!
LITTLE ELF?
LITTLE ELF?
THERE WAS TOO MUCH GOLD. I'M RETURNING IT TO YOU.
YOO HOO!
YOO HOO!
LITTLE ELF!
BLAST! IT'S STARTING TO GET REALLY DARK IN HERE. IF I STILL HAD MY JOURNAL, IT'D BE DIFFICULT TO DESCRIBE THIS MEETING WITH THE ELVES.
BOOM
IT'S....IT'S...
IT'S AMAZING!
ALL THOSE LITTLE CREATURES AT WORK.

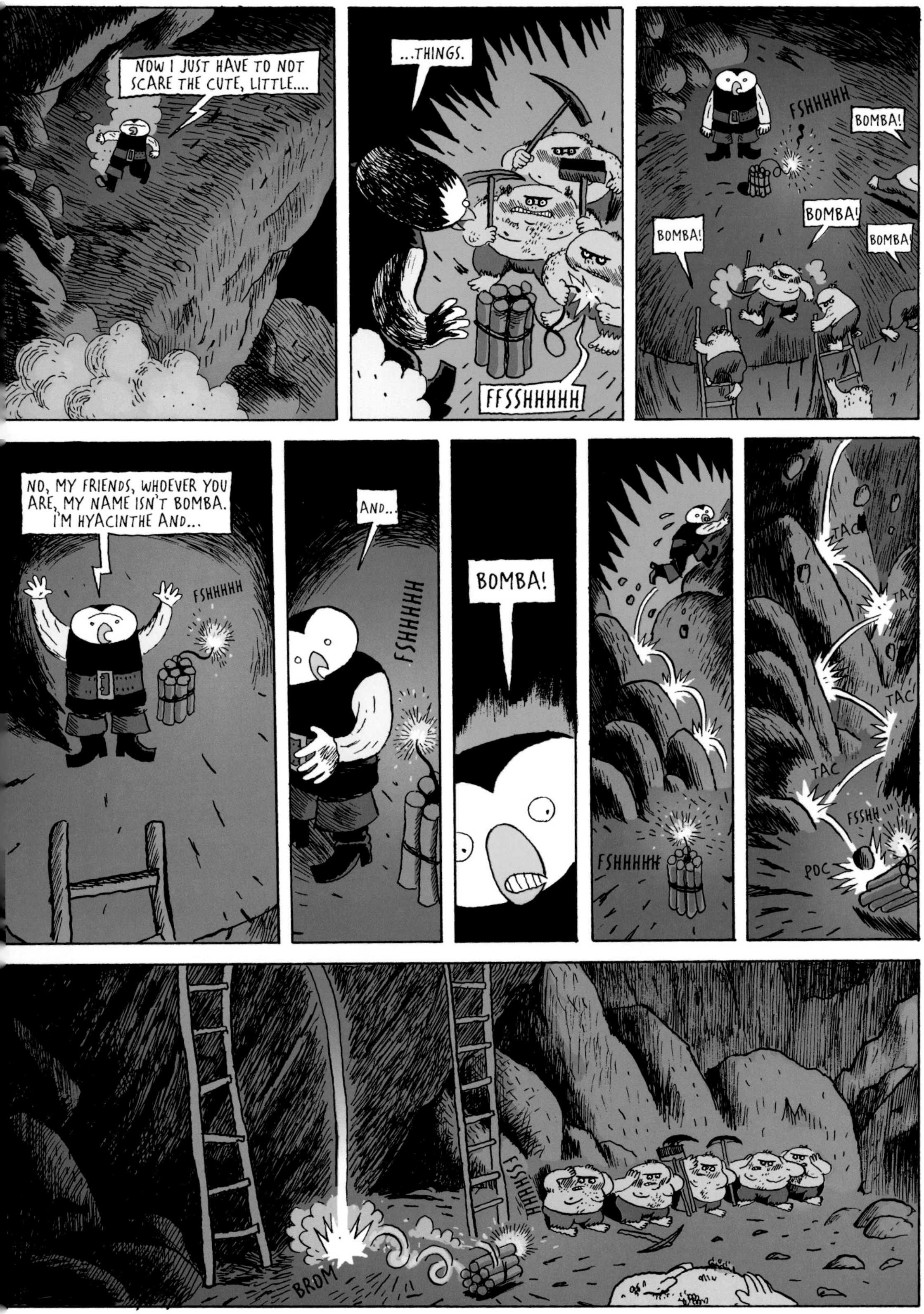

NOW I JUST HAVE TO NOT SCARE THE CUTE, LITTLE....
...THINGS.
FFSSHHHHH
FSHHHHH
BOMBA!
BOMBA!
BOMBA!
BOMBA!
NO, MY FRIENDS, WHOEVER YOU ARE, MY NAME ISN'T BOMBA. I'M HYACINTHE AND...
FSHHHHH
AND...
FSHHHHH
BOMBA!
FSHHHHH
TAC
TAC
TAC
TAC
FSSHH
POC
FSSHHH
BROM

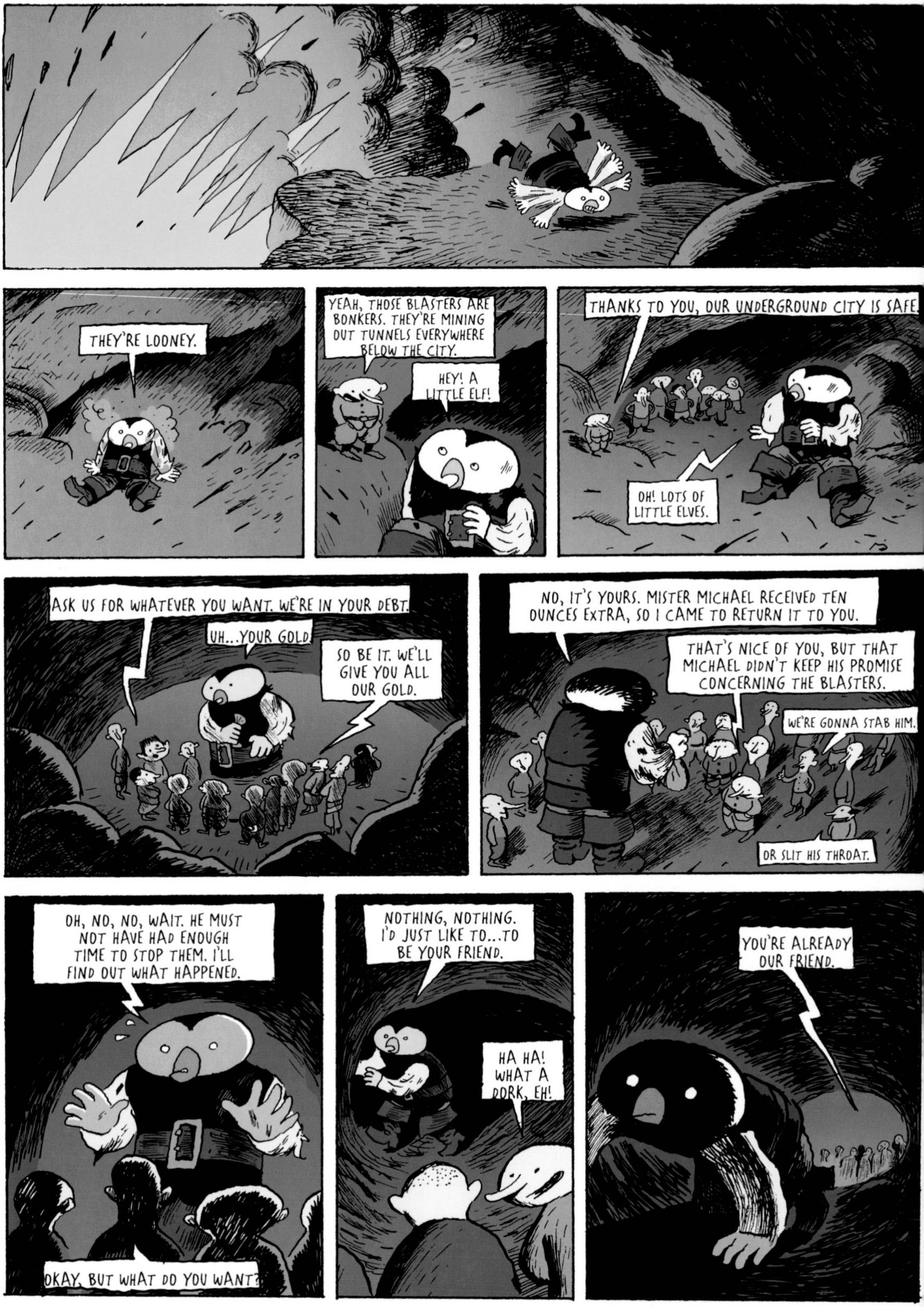
THEY'RE LOONEY.
YEAH, THOSE BLASTERS ARE BONKERS. THEY'RE MINING OUT TUNNELS EVERYWHERE BELOW THE CITY.
HEY! A LITTLE ELF!
THANKS TO YOU, OUR UNDERGROUND CITY IS SAFE.
OH! LOTS OF LITTLE ELVES.
ASK US FOR WHATEVER YOU WANT. WE'RE IN YOUR DEBT.
UH...YOUR GOLD.
SO BE IT. WE'LL GIVE YOU ALL OUR GOLD.
NO, IT'S YOURS. MISTER MICHAEL RECEIVED TEN OUNCES EXTRA, SO I CAME TO RETURN IT TO YOU.
THAT'S NICE OF YOU, BUT THAT MICHAEL DIDN'T KEEP HIS PROMISE CONCERNING THE BLASTERS.
WE'RE GONNA STAB HIM.
OR SLIT HIS THROAT.
OH, NO, NO, WAIT. HE MUST NOT HAVE HAD ENOUGH TIME TO STOP THEM. I'LL FIND OUT WHAT HAPPENED.
OKAY, BUT WHAT DO YOU WANT?
NOTHING, NOTHING. I'D JUST LIKE TO...TO BE YOUR FRIEND.
HA HA! WHAT A DORK, EH!
YOU'RE ALREADY OUR FRIEND.

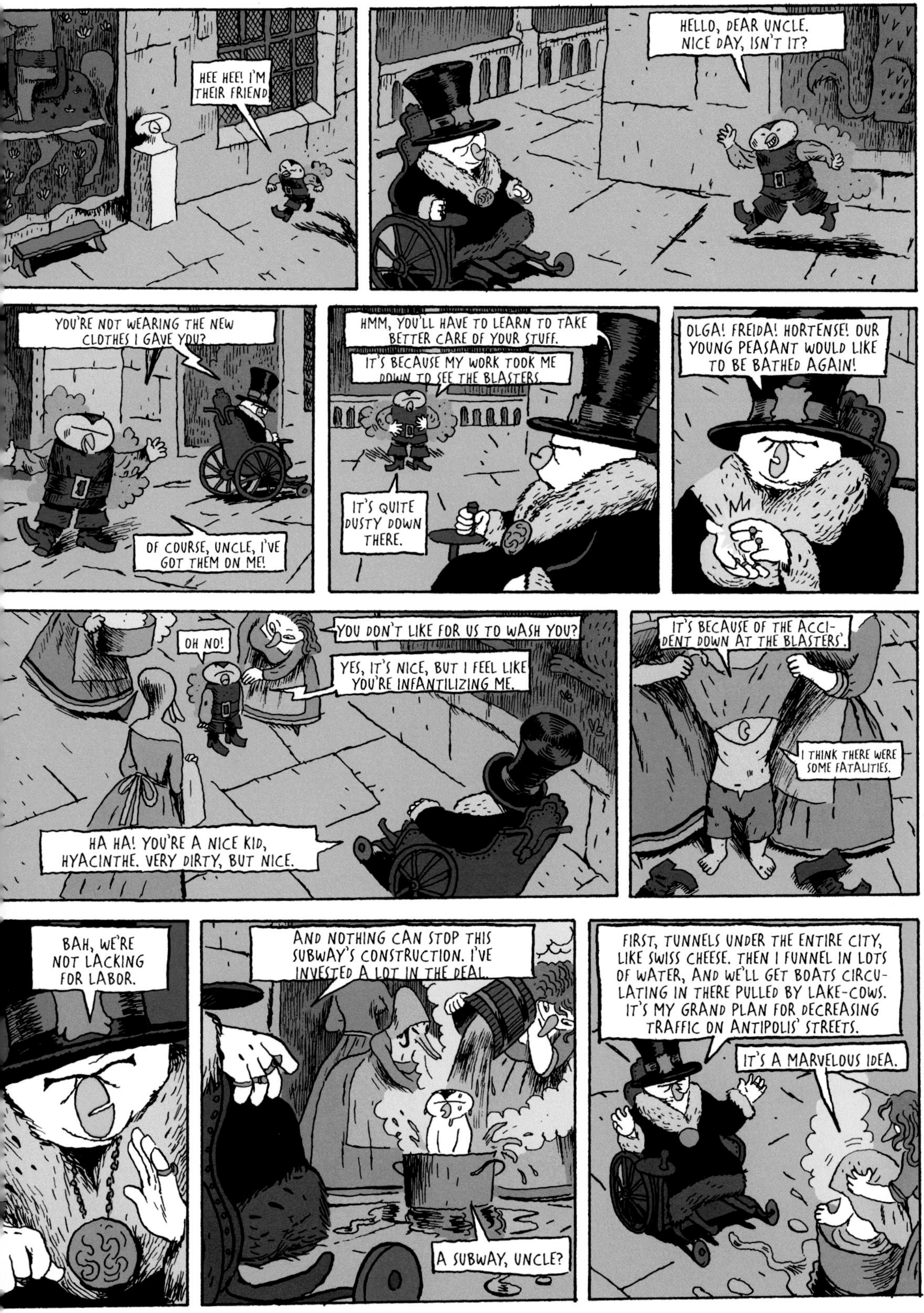
HEE HEE! I'M THEIR FRIEND.
HELLO, DEAR UNCLE. NICE DAY, ISN'T IT?
YOU'RE NOT WEARING THE NEW CLOTHES I GAVE YOU?
OF COURSE, UNCLE, I'VE GOT THEM ON ME!
HMM, YOU'LL HAVE TO LEARN TO TAKE BETTER CARE OF YOUR STUFF.
IT'S BECAUSE MY WORK TOOK ME DOWN TO SEE THE BLASTERS.
IT'S QUITE DUSTY DOWN THERE.
OLGA! FREIDA! HORTENSE! OUR YOUNG PEASANT WOULD LIKE TO BE BATHED AGAIN!
OH NO!
YOU DON'T LIKE FOR US TO WASH YOU?
YES, IT'S NICE, BUT I FEEL LIKE YOU'RE INFANTILIZING ME.
HA HA! YOU'RE A NICE KID, HYACINTHE. VERY DIRTY, BUT NICE.
IT'S BECAUSE OF THE ACCI-DENT DOWN AT THE BLASTERS'.
I THINK THERE WERE SOME FATALITIES.
BAH, WE'RE NOT LACKING FOR LABOR.
AND NOTHING CAN STOP THIS SUBWAY'S CONSTRUCTION. I'VE INVESTED A LOT IN THE DEAL.
A SUBWAY, UNCLE?
FIRST, TUNNELS UNDER THE ENTIRE CITY, LIKE SWISS CHEESE. THEN I FUNNEL IN LOTS OF WATER, AND WE'LL GET BOATS CIRCU-LATING IN THERE PULLED BY LAKE-COWS. IT'S MY GRAND PLAN FOR DECREASING TRAFFIC ON ANTIPOLIS' STREETS.
IT'S A MARVELOUS IDEA.

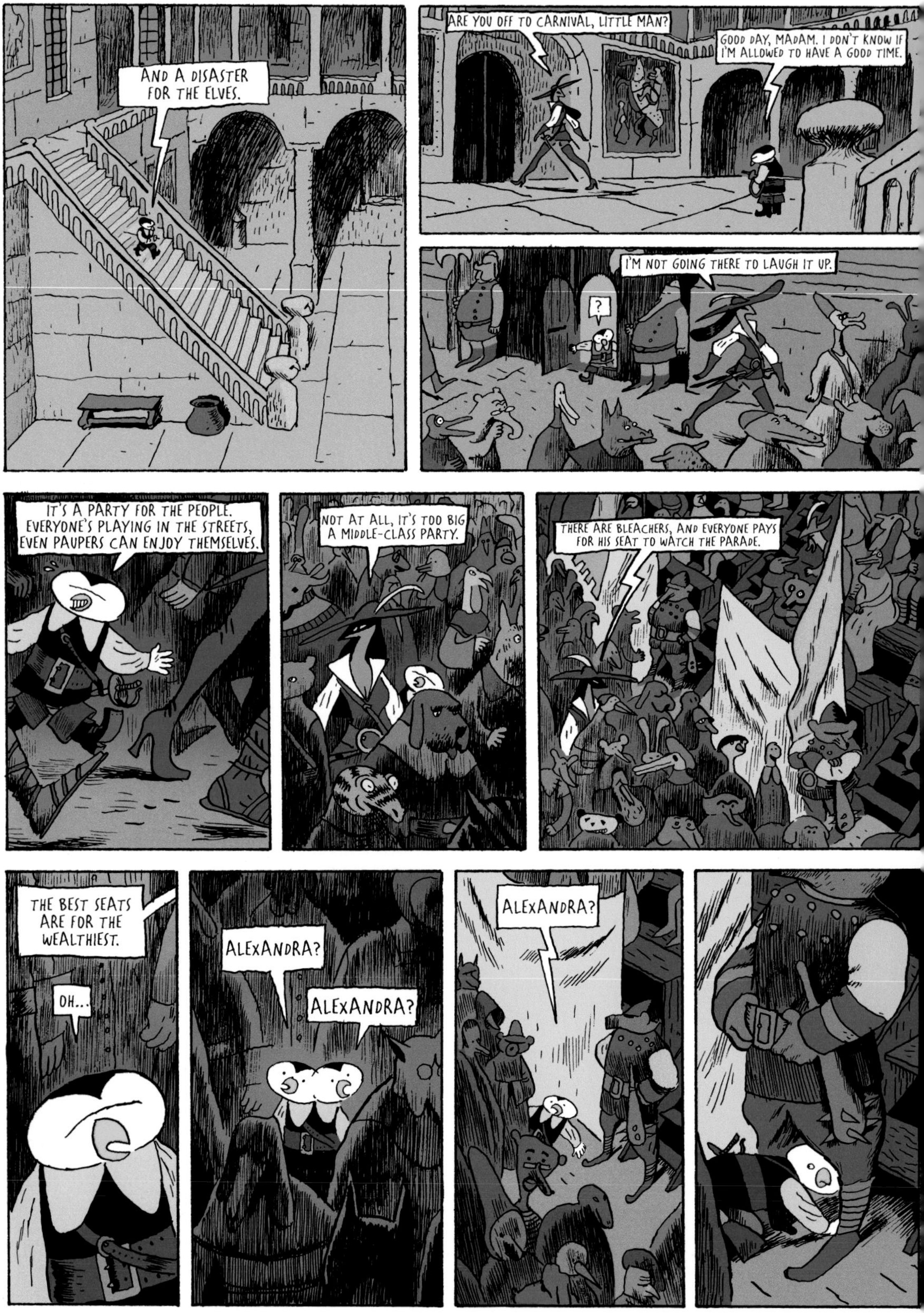
AND A DISASTER FOR THE ELVES.
ARE YOU OFF TO CARNIVAL, LITTLE MAN?
GOOD DAY, MADAM. I DON'T KNOW IF I'M ALLOWED TO HAVE A GOOD TIME.
I'M NOT GOING THERE TO LAUGH IT UP.
?
IT'S A PARTY FOR THE PEOPLE. EVERYONE'S PLAYING IN THE STREETS, EVEN PAUPERS CAN ENJOY THEMSELVES.
NOT AT ALL, IT'S TOO BIG A MIDDLE-CLASS PARTY.
THERE ARE BLEACHERS, AND EVERYONE PAYS FOR HIS SEAT TO WATCH THE PARADE.
THE BEST SEATS ARE FOR THE WEALTHIEST.
OH...
ALEXANDRA?
ALEXANDRA?
ALEXANDRA?

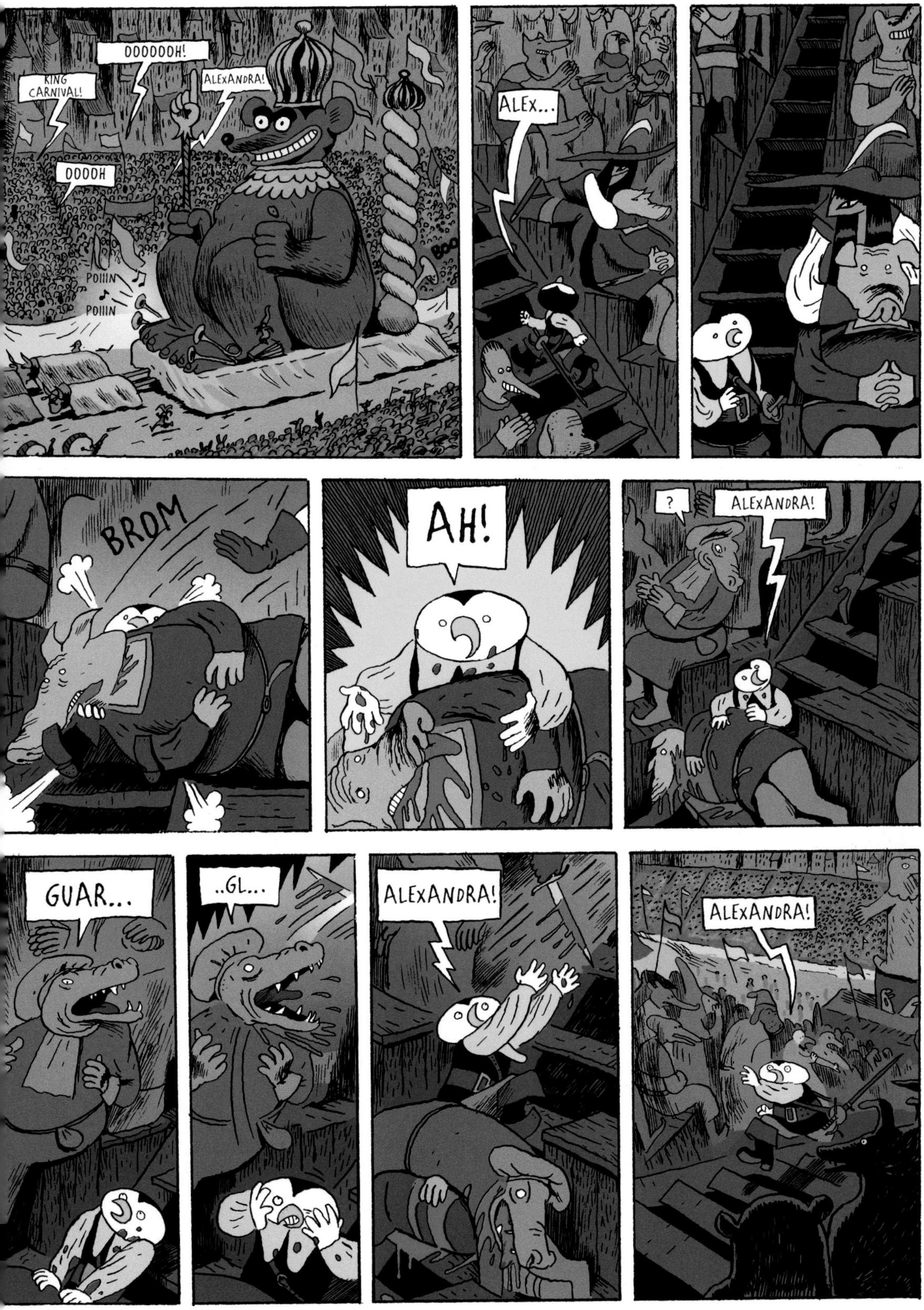
KING CARNIVAL!
OOOOOOH!
ALEXANDRA!
OOOOH
POIIIN
POIIIN
ALEX...
BROM
AH!
?
ALEXANDRA!
GUAR...
..GL...
ALEXANDRA!
ALEXANDRA!

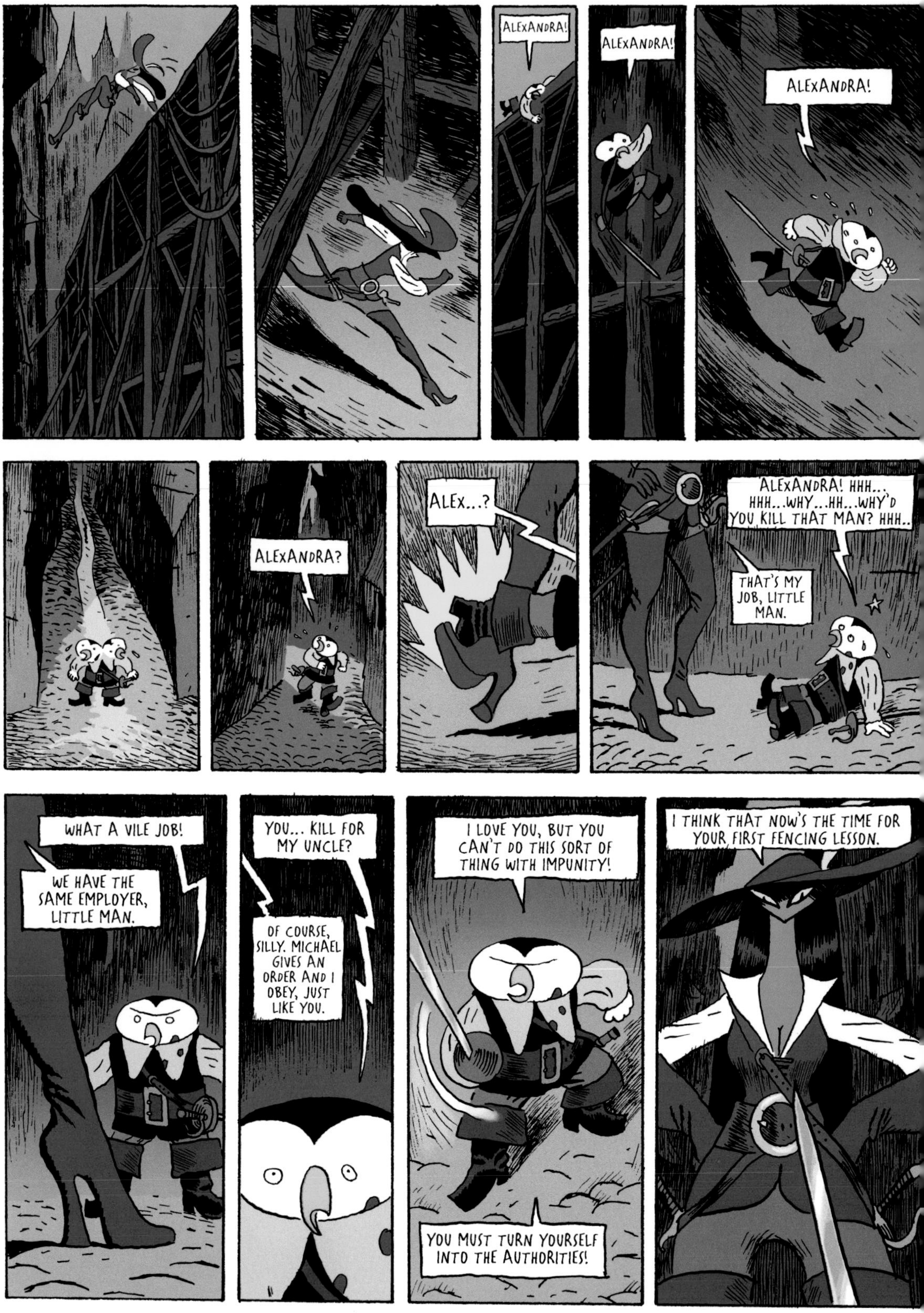
ALEXANDRA!
ALEXANDRA!
ALEXANDRA!
ALEXANDRA?
ALEX...?
ALEXANDRA! HHH... HHH...WHY...HH...WHY'D YOU KILL THAT MAN? HHH..
THAT'S MY JOB, LITTLE MAN.
WHAT A VILE JOB!
WE HAVE THE SAME EMPLOYER, LITTLE MAN.
YOU... KILL FOR MY UNCLE?
OF COURSE, SILLY. MICHAEL GIVES AN ORDER AND I OBEY, JUST LIKE YOU.
I LOVE YOU, BUT YOU CAN'T DO THIS SORT OF THING WITH IMPUNITY!
YOU MUST TURN YOURSELF INTO THE AUTHORITIES!
I THINK THAT NOW'S THE TIME FOR YOUR FIRST FENCING LESSON.

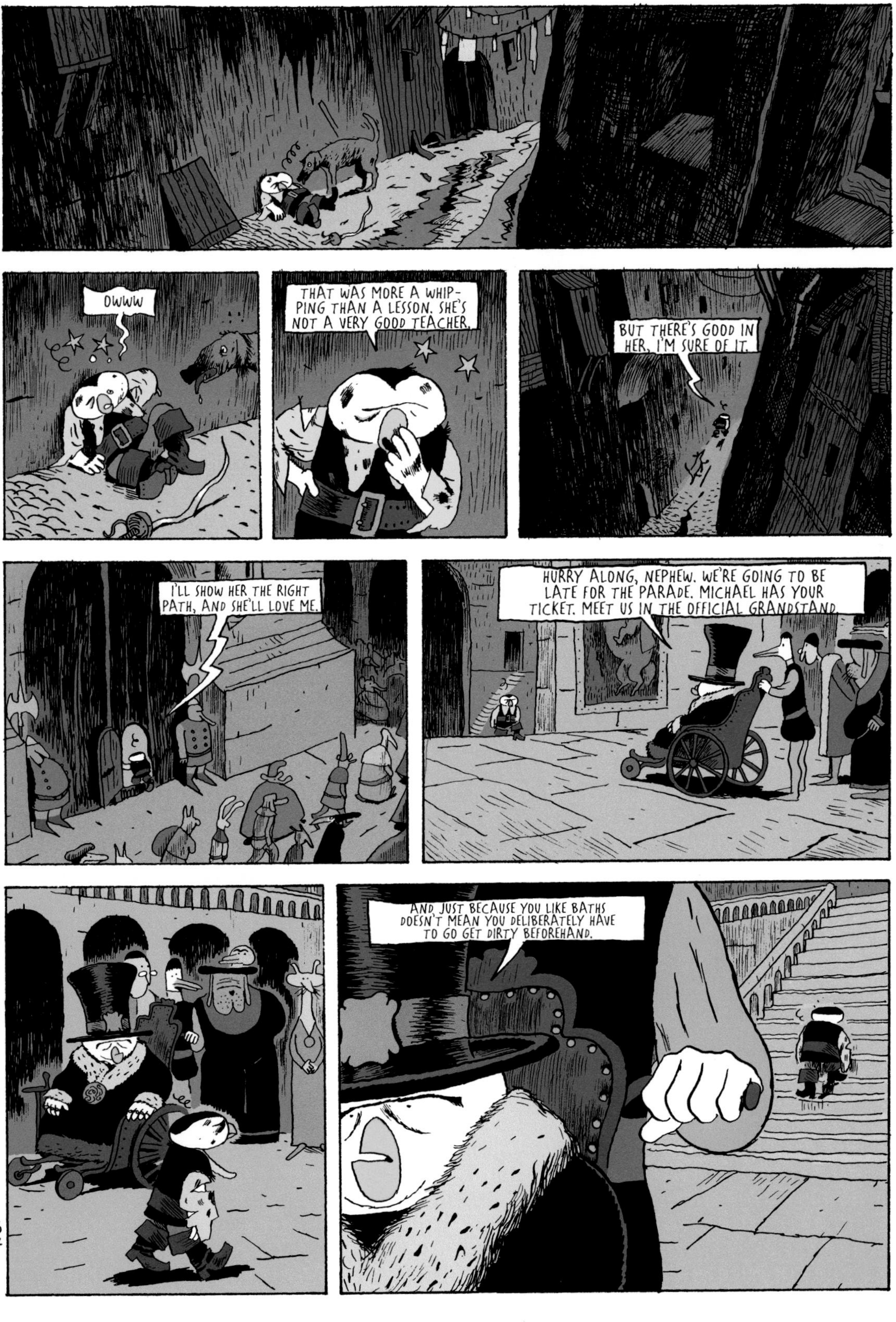
OWWW
THAT WAS MORE A WHIP-PING THAN A LESSON. SHE'S NOT A VERY GOOD TEACHER.
BUT THERE'S GOOD IN HER, I'M SURE OF IT.
I'LL SHOW HER THE RIGHT PATH, AND SHE'LL LOVE ME.
HURRY ALONG, NEPHEW. WE'RE GOING TO BE LATE FOR THE PARADE. MICHAEL HAS YOUR TICKET. MEET US IN THE OFFICIAL GRANDSTAND.
AND JUST BECAUSE YOU LIKE BATHS DOESN'T MEAN YOU DELIBERATELY HAVE TO GO GET DIRTY BEFOREHAND.

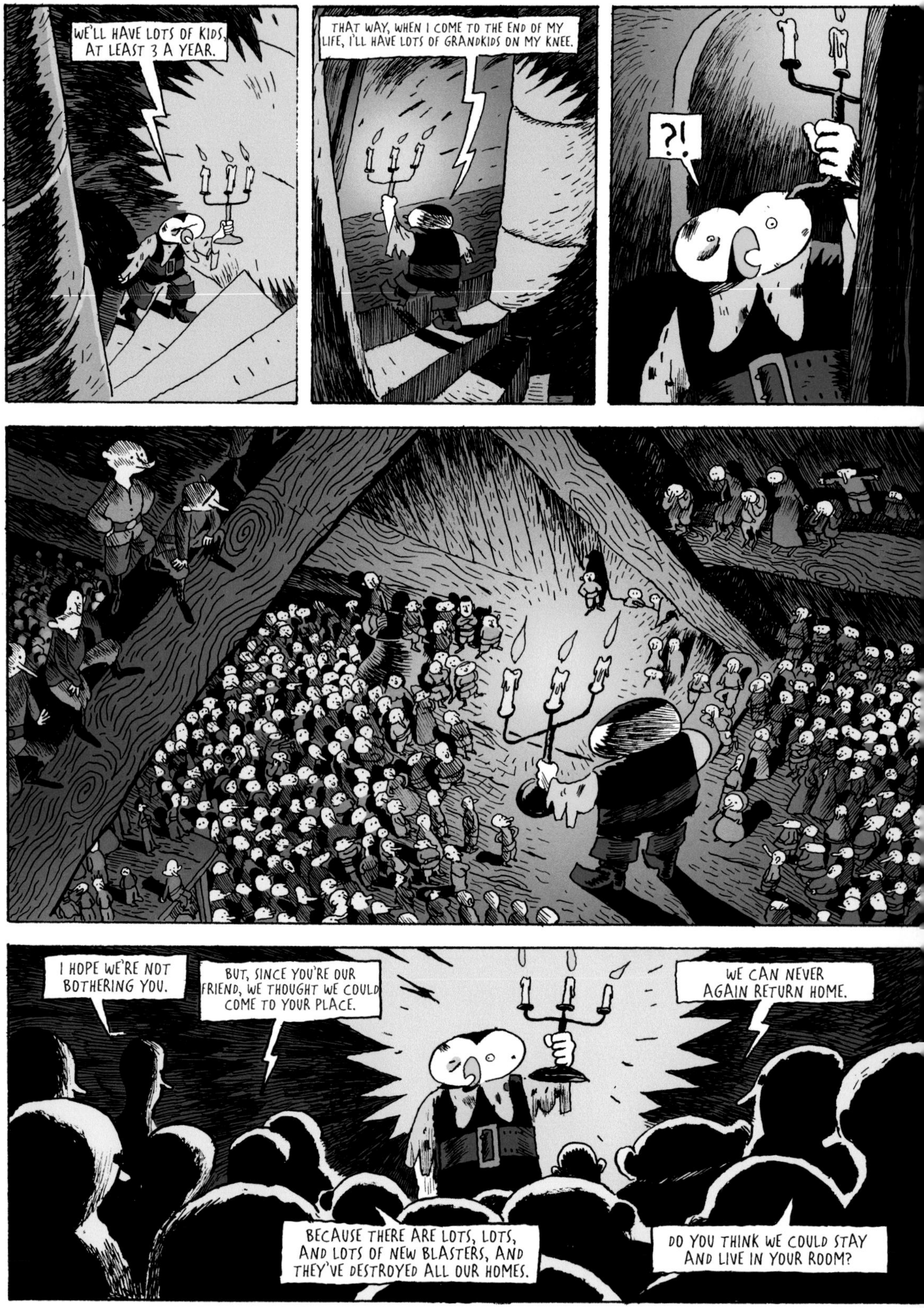
WE'LL HAVE LOTS OF KIDS, AT LEAST 3 A YEAR.
THAT WAY, WHEN I COME TO THE END OF MY LIFE, I'LL HAVE LOTS OF GRANDKIDS ON MY KNEE.
?!
I HOPE WE'RE NOT BOTHERING YOU.
BUT, SINCE YOU'RE OUR FRIEND, WE THOUGHT WE COULD COME TO YOUR PLACE.
WE CAN NEVER AGAIN RETURN HOME.
BECAUSE THERE ARE LOTS, LOTS, AND LOTS OF NEW BLASTERS, AND THEY'VE DESTROYED ALL OUR HOMES.
DO YOU THINK WE COULD STAY AND LIVE IN YOUR ROOM?

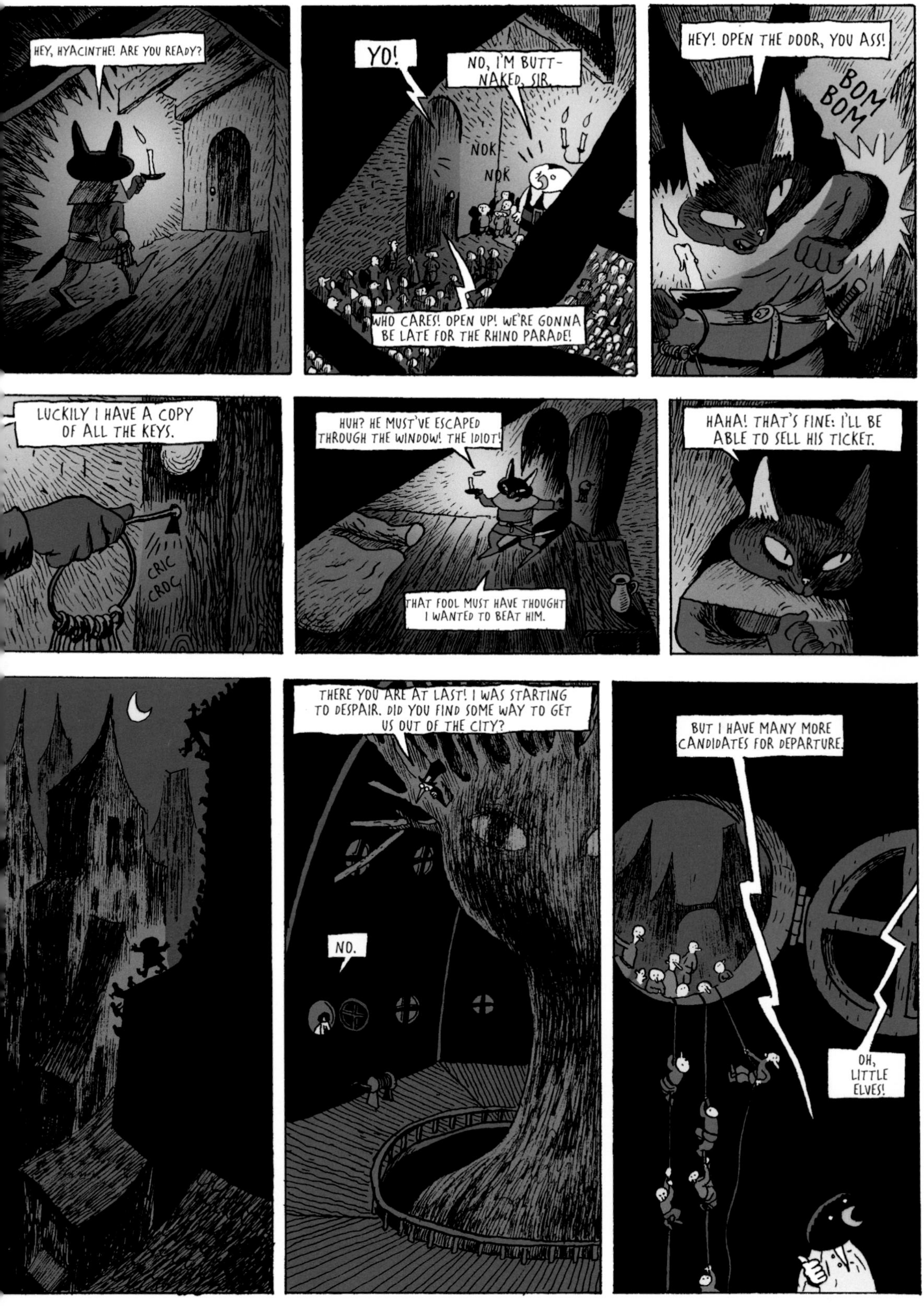
HEY, HYACINTHE! ARE YOU READY?
YO!
NO, I'M BUTT-NAKED, SIR.
NOK NOK
WHO CARES! OPEN UP! WE'RE GONNA BE LATE FOR THE RHINO PARADE!
HEY! OPEN THE DOOR, YOU ASS!
BOM BOM
LUCKILY I HAVE A COPY OF ALL THE KEYS.
CRIC CROC
HUH? HE MUST'VE ESCAPED THROUGH THE WINDOW! THE IDIOT!
THAT FOOL MUST HAVE THOUGHT I WANTED TO BEAT HIM.
HAHA! THAT'S FINE: I'LL BE ABLE TO SELL HIS TICKET.
THERE YOU ARE AT LAST! I WAS STARTING TO DESPAIR. DID YOU FIND SOME WAY TO GET US OUT OF THE CITY?
NO.
BUT I HAVE MANY MORE CANDIDATES FOR DEPARTURE.
OH, LITTLE ELVES!

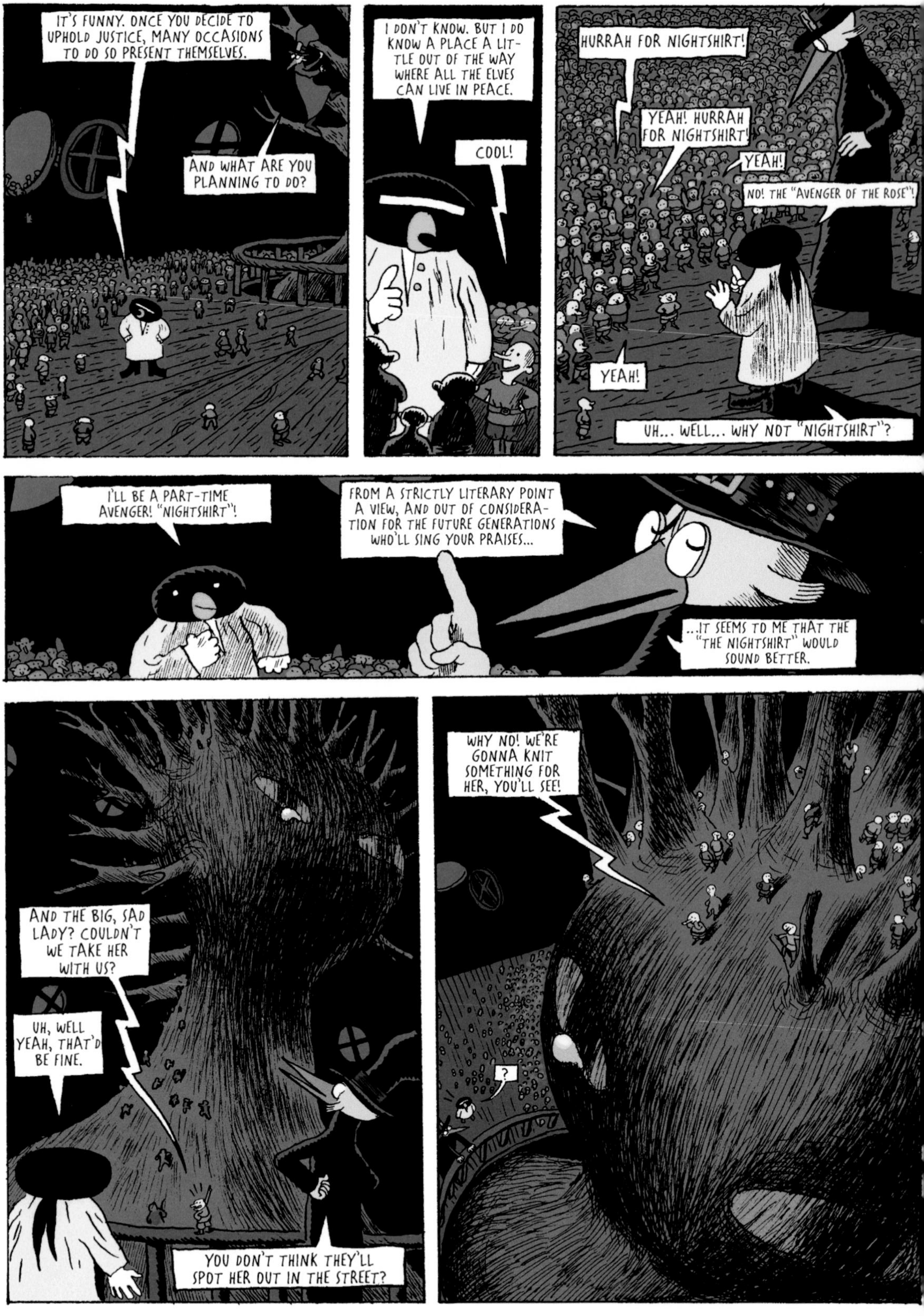
IT'S FUNNY. ONCE YOU DECIDE TO UPHOLD JUSTICE, MANY OCCASIONS TO DO SO PRESENT THEMSELVES.
AND WHAT ARE YOU PLANNING TO DO?
I DON'T KNOW. BUT I DO KNOW A PLACE A LITTLE OUT OF THE WAY WHERE ALL THE ELVES CAN LIVE IN PEACE.
COOL!
HURRAH FOR NIGHTSHIRT!
YEAH! HURRAH FOR NIGHTSHIRT!
YEAH!
NO! THE "AVENGER OF THE ROSE"!
YEAH!
UH... WELL... WHY NOT "NIGHTSHIRT"?
I'LL BE A PART-TIME AVENGER! "NIGHTSHIRT"!
FROM A STRICTLY LITERARY POINT A VIEW, AND OUT OF CONSIDERATION FOR THE FUTURE GENERATIONS WHO'LL SING YOUR PRAISES...
...IT SEEMS TO ME THAT THE "THE NIGHTSHIRT" WOULD SOUND BETTER.
AND THE BIG, SAD LADY? COULDN'T WE TAKE HER WITH US?
UH, WELL YEAH, THAT'D BE FINE.
YOU DON'T THINK THEY'LL SPOT HER OUT IN THE STREET?
WHY NO! WE'RE GONNA KNIT SOMETHING FOR HER, YOU'LL SEE!
?

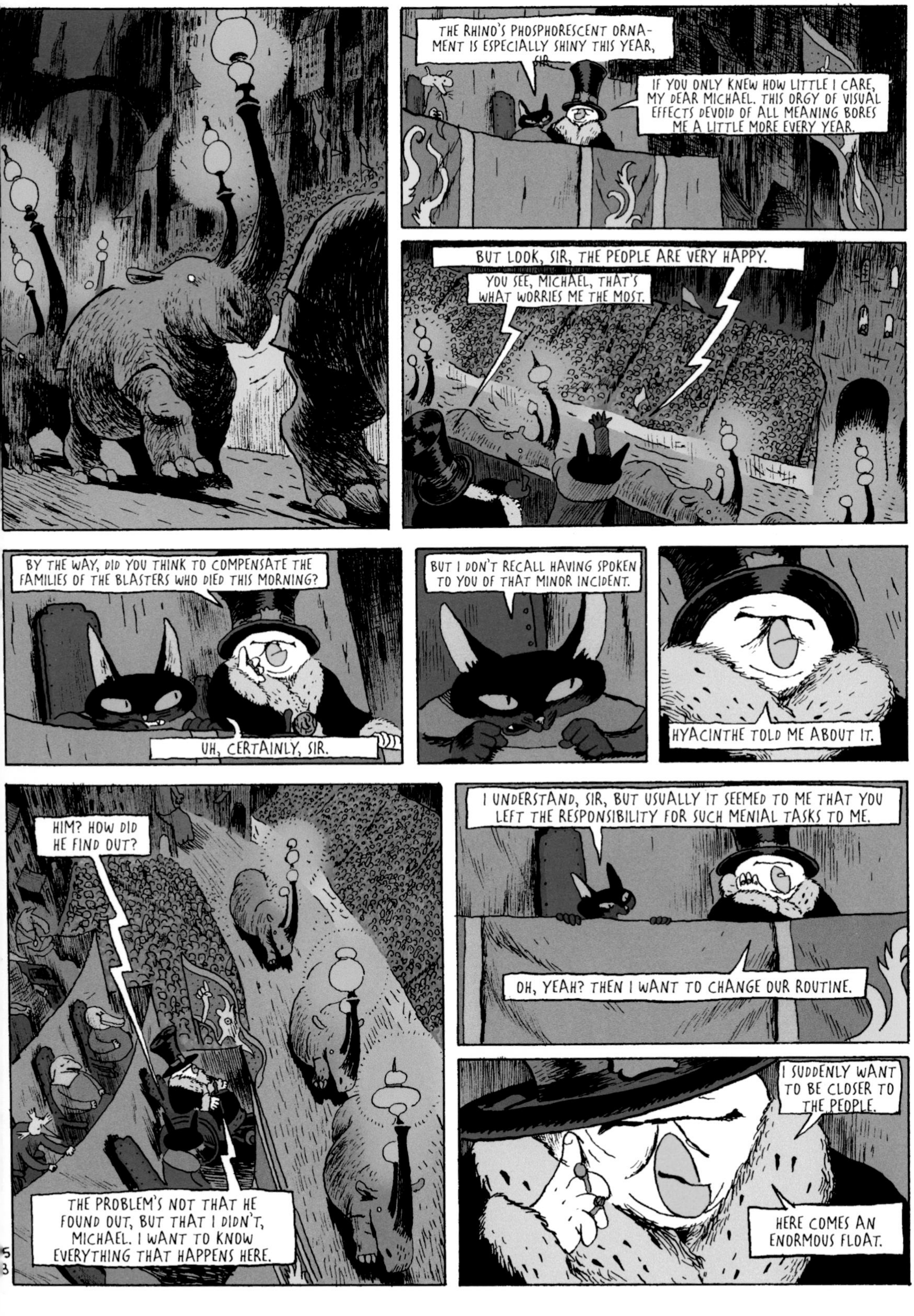
THE RHINO'S PHOSPHORESCENT ORNAMENT IS ESPECIALLY SHINY THIS YEAR, SIR.
IF YOU ONLY KNEW HOW LITTLE I CARE, MY DEAR MICHAEL. THIS ORGY OF VISUAL EFFECTS DEVOID OF ALL MEANING BORES ME A LITTLE MORE EVERY YEAR.
BUT LOOK, SIR, THE PEOPLE ARE VERY HAPPY.
YOU SEE, MICHAEL, THAT'S WHAT WORRIES ME THE MOST.
BY THE WAY, DID YOU THINK TO COMPENSATE THE FAMILIES OF THE BLASTERS WHO DIED THIS MORNING?
UH, CERTAINLY, SIR.
BUT I DON'T RECALL HAVING SPOKEN TO YOU OF THAT MINOR INCIDENT.
HYACINTHE TOLD ME ABOUT IT.
HIM? HOW DID HE FIND OUT?
THE PROBLEM'S NOT THAT HE FOUND OUT, BUT THAT I DIDN'T, MICHAEL. I WANT TO KNOW EVERYTHING THAT HAPPENS HERE.
I UNDERSTAND, SIR, BUT USUALLY IT SEEMED TO ME THAT YOU LEFT THE RESPONSIBILITY FOR SUCH MENIAL TASKS TO ME.
OH, YEAH? THEN I WANT TO CHANGE OUR ROUTINE.
I SUDDENLY WANT TO BE CLOSER TO THE PEOPLE.
HERE COMES AN ENORMOUS FLOAT.

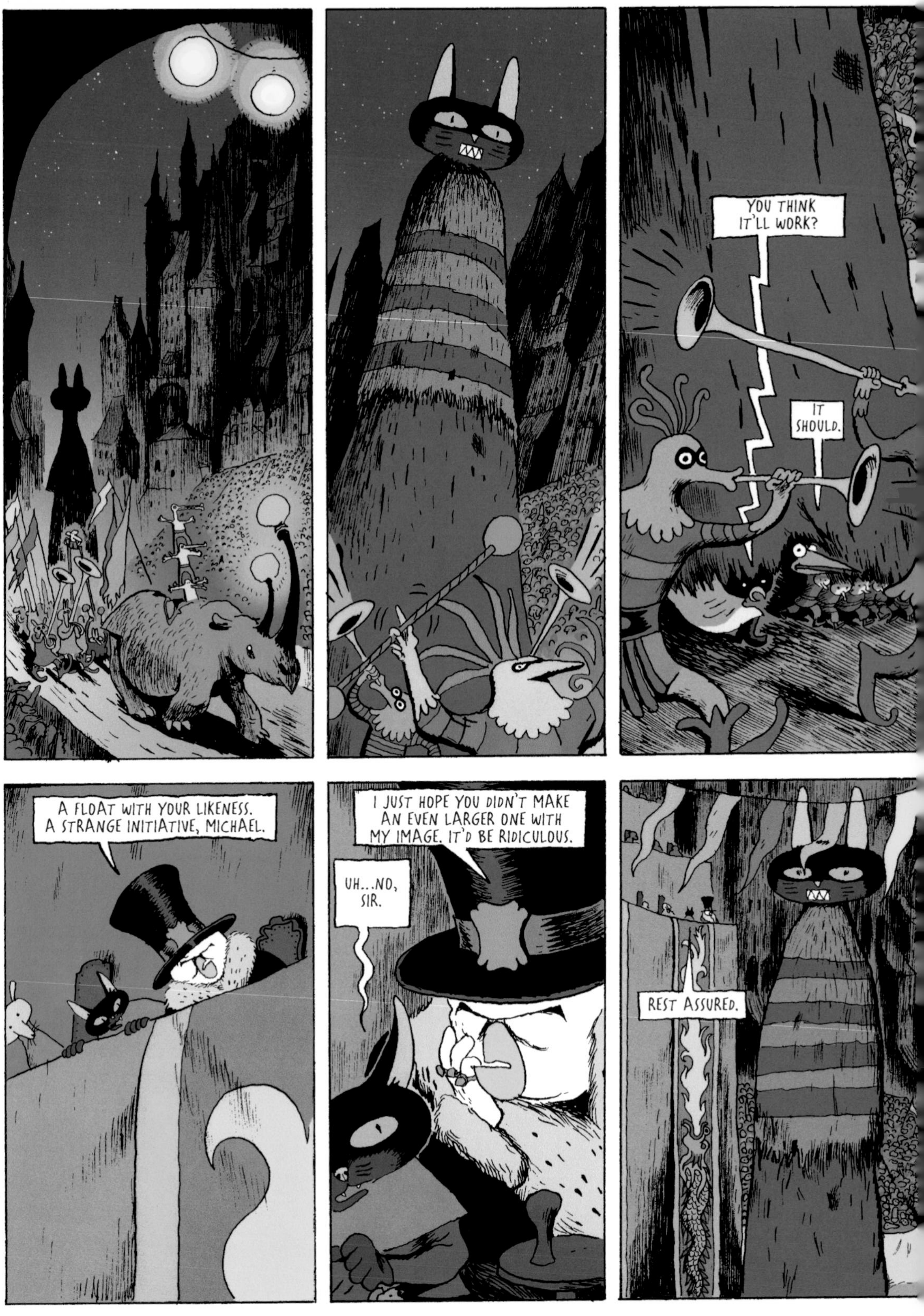
YOU THINK IT'LL WORK?
IT SHOULD.
A FLOAT WITH YOUR LIKENESS. A STRANGE INITIATIVE, MICHAEL.
I JUST HOPE YOU DIDN'T MAKE AN EVEN LARGER ONE WITH MY IMAGE. IT'D BE RIDICULOUS.
UH...NO, SIR.
REST ASSURED.

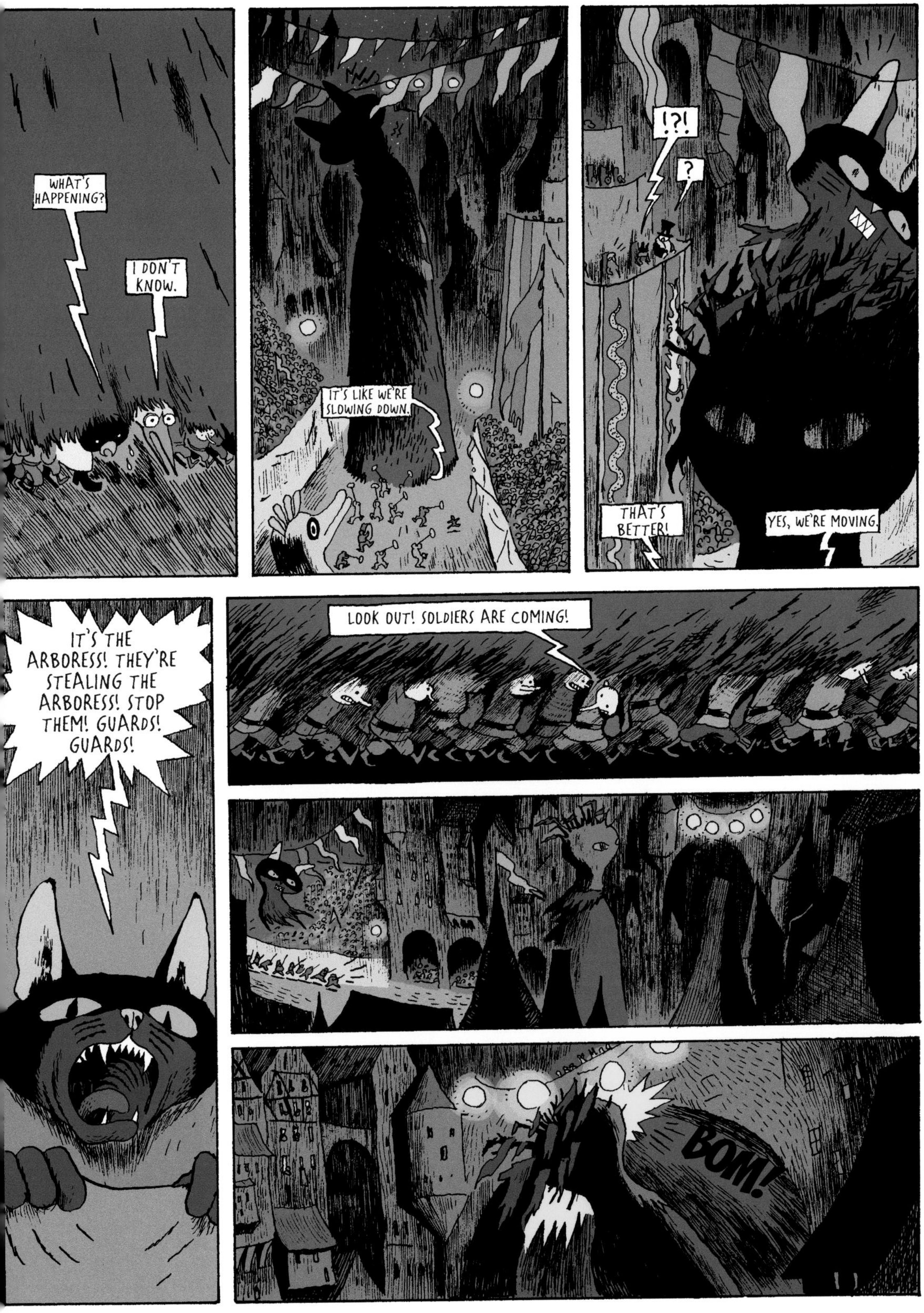
WHAT'S HAPPENING?
I DON'T KNOW.
IT'S LIKE WE'RE SLOWING DOWN.
!?!
?
THAT'S BETTER!
YES, WE'RE MOVING.
IT'S THE ARBORESS! THEY'RE STEALING THE ARBORESS! STOP THEM! GUARDS! GUARDS!
LOOK OUT! SOLDIERS ARE COMING!
BOM!

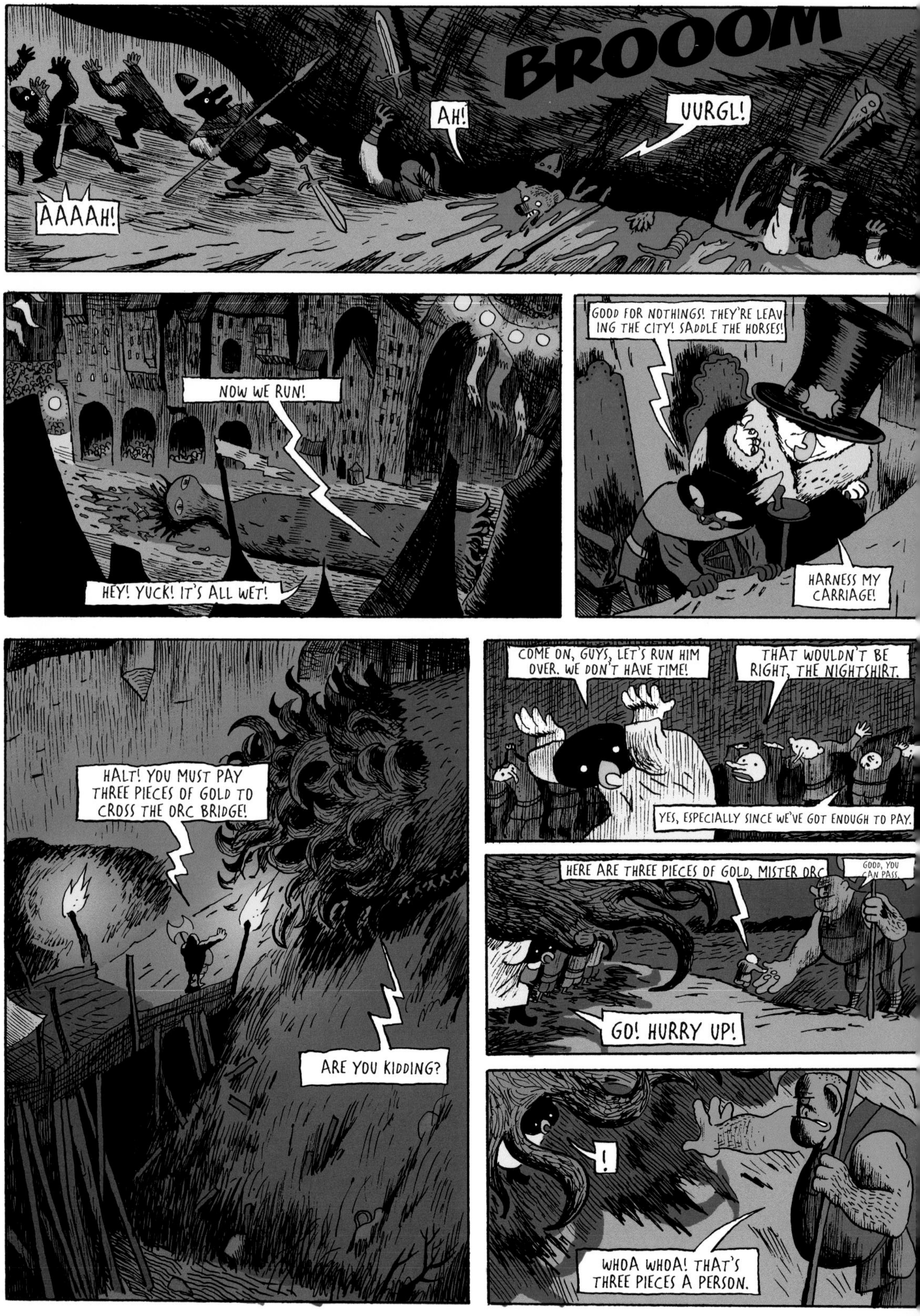
BROOOM
AAAAH!
AH!
UURGL!
NOW WE RUN!
HEY! YUCK! IT'S ALL WET!
GOOD FOR NOTHINGS! THEY'RE LEAVING THE CITY! SADDLE THE HORSES!
HARNESS MY CARRIAGE!
HALT! YOU MUST PAY THREE PIECES OF GOLD TO CROSS THE ORC BRIDGE!
ARE YOU KIDDING?
COME ON, GUYS, LET'S RUN HIM OVER. WE DON'T HAVE TIME!
THAT WOULDN'T BE RIGHT, THE NIGHTSHIRT.
YES, ESPECIALLY SINCE WE'VE GOT ENOUGH TO PAY.
HERE ARE THREE PIECES OF GOLD, MISTER ORC
GOOD, YOU CAN PASS.
GO! HURRY UP!
!
WHOA WHOA! THAT'S THREE PIECES A PERSON.

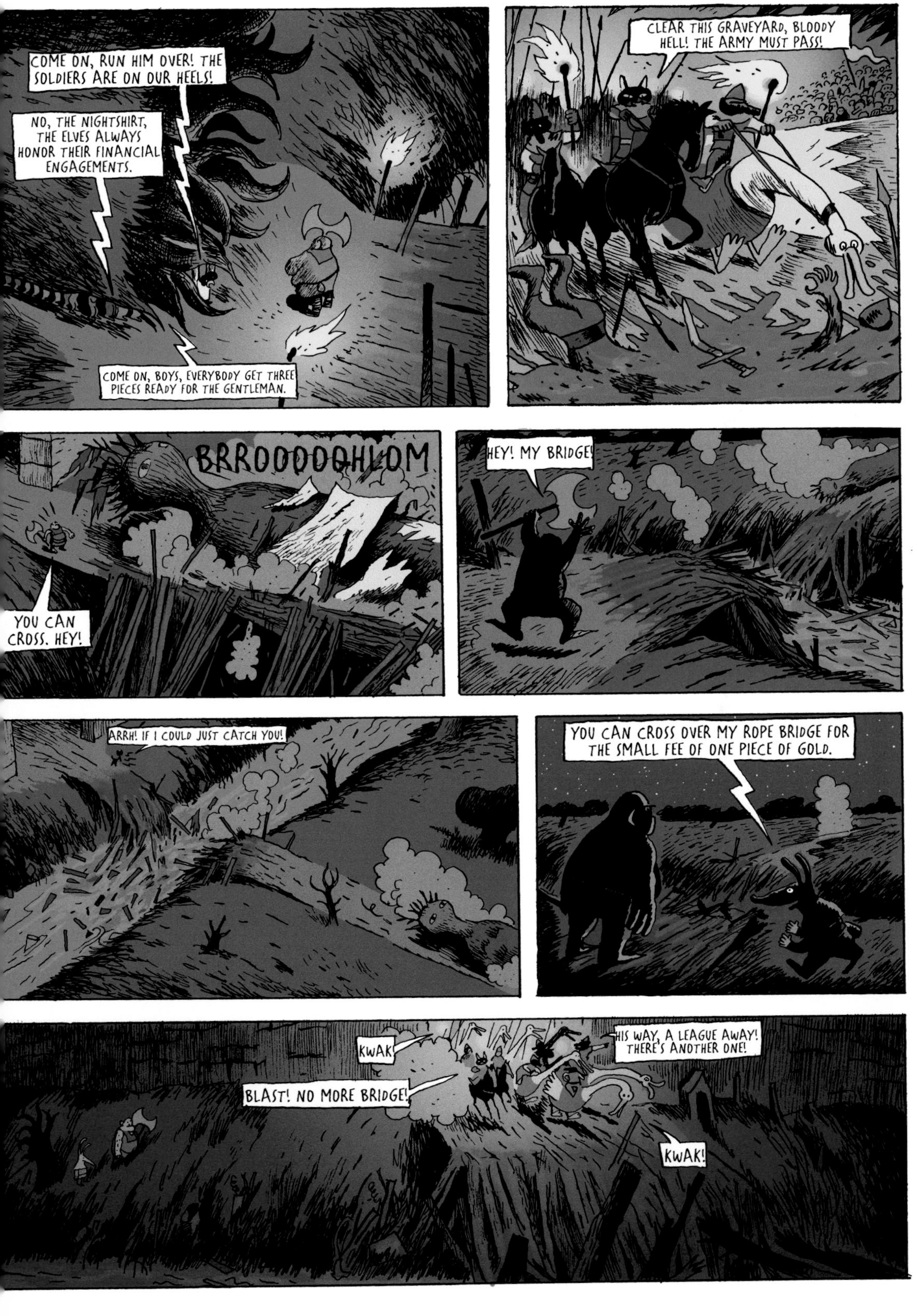
COME ON, RUN HIM OVER! THE SOLDIERS ARE ON OUR HEELS!
NO, THE NIGHTSHIRT, THE ELVES ALWAYS HONOR THEIR FINANCIAL ENGAGEMENTS.
COME ON, BOYS, EVERYBODY GET THREE PIECES READY FOR THE GENTLEMAN.
CLEAR THIS GRAVEYARD, BLOODY HELL! THE ARMY MUST PASS!
BRROOOOOHLOM
YOU CAN CROSS. HEY!
HEY! MY BRIDGE!
ARRH! IF I COULD JUST CATCH YOU!
YOU CAN CROSS OVER MY ROPE BRIDGE FOR THE SMALL FEE OF ONE PIECE OF GOLD.
KWAK!
BLAST! NO MORE BRIDGE!
HIS WAY, A LEAGUE AWAY! THERE'S ANOTHER ONE!
KWAK!

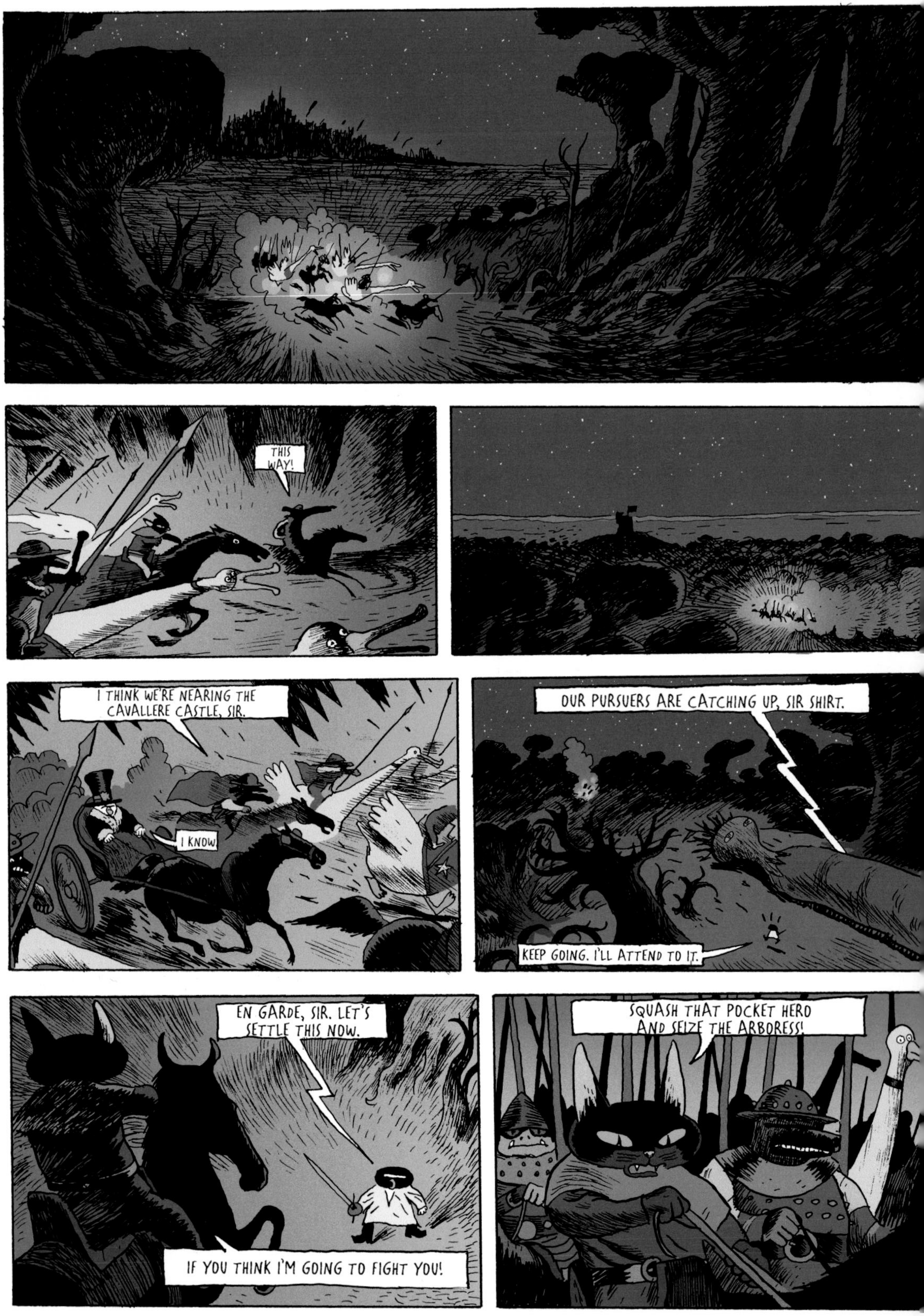
THIS WAY!
I THINK WE'RE NEARING THE CAVALLERE CASTLE, SIR.
I KNOW
OUR PURSUERS ARE CATCHING UP, SIR SHIRT.
KEEP GOING. I'LL ATTEND TO IT.
EN GARDE, SIR. LET'S SETTLE THIS NOW.
IF YOU THINK I'M GOING TO FIGHT YOU!
SQUASH THAT POCKET HERO AND SEIZE THE ARBORESS!

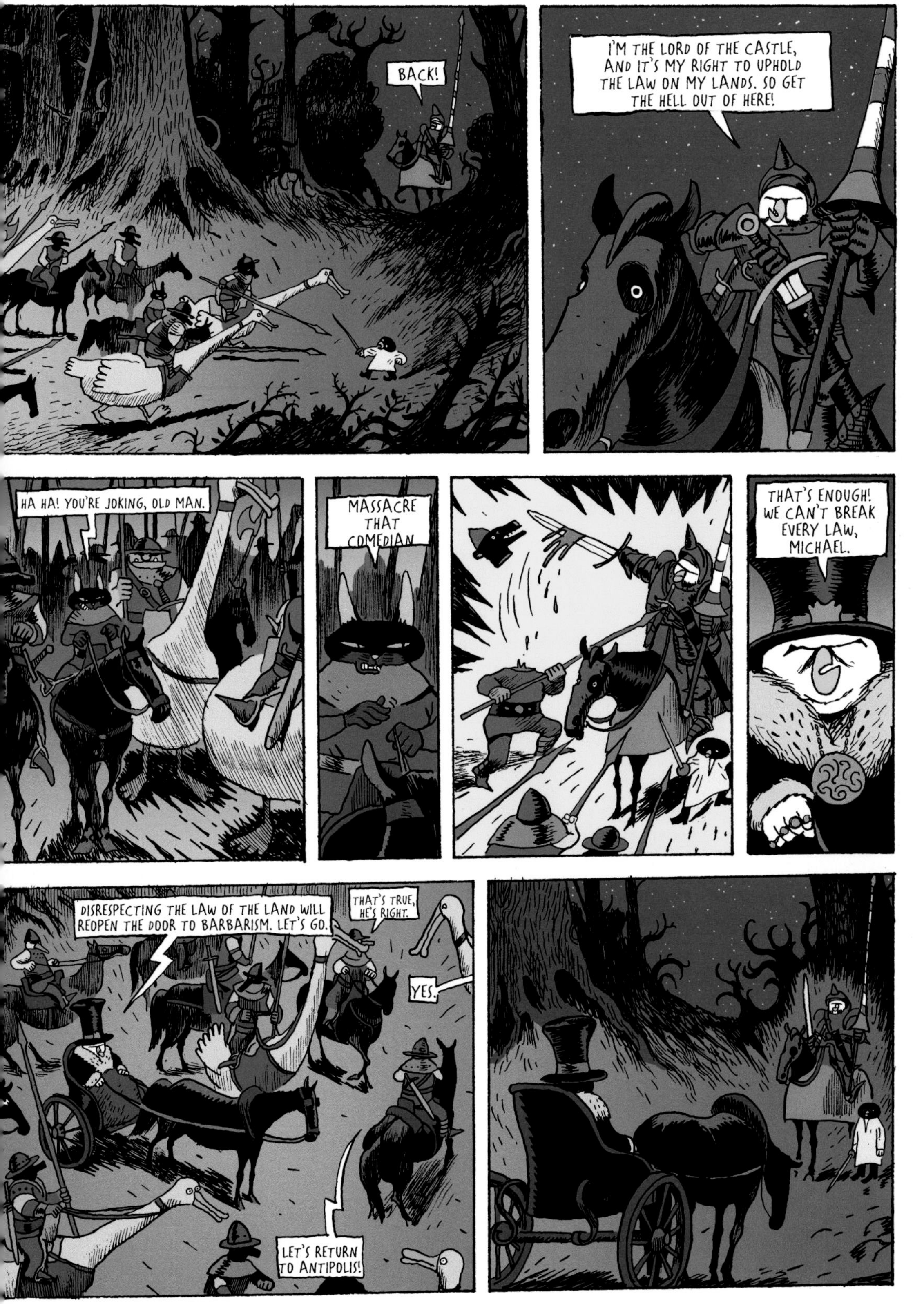
BACK!
I'M THE LORD OF THE CASTLE, AND IT'S MY RIGHT TO UPHOLD THE LAW ON MY LANDS. SO GET THE HELL OUT OF HERE!
HA HA! YOU'RE JOKING, OLD MAN.
MASSACRE THAT COMEDIAN
THAT'S ENOUGH! WE CAN'T BREAK EVERY LAW, MICHAEL.
DISRESPECTING THE LAW OF THE LAND WILL REOPEN THE DOOR TO BARBARISM. LET'S GO.
THAT'S TRUE, HE'S RIGHT.
YES.
LET'S RETURN TO ANTIPOLIS!

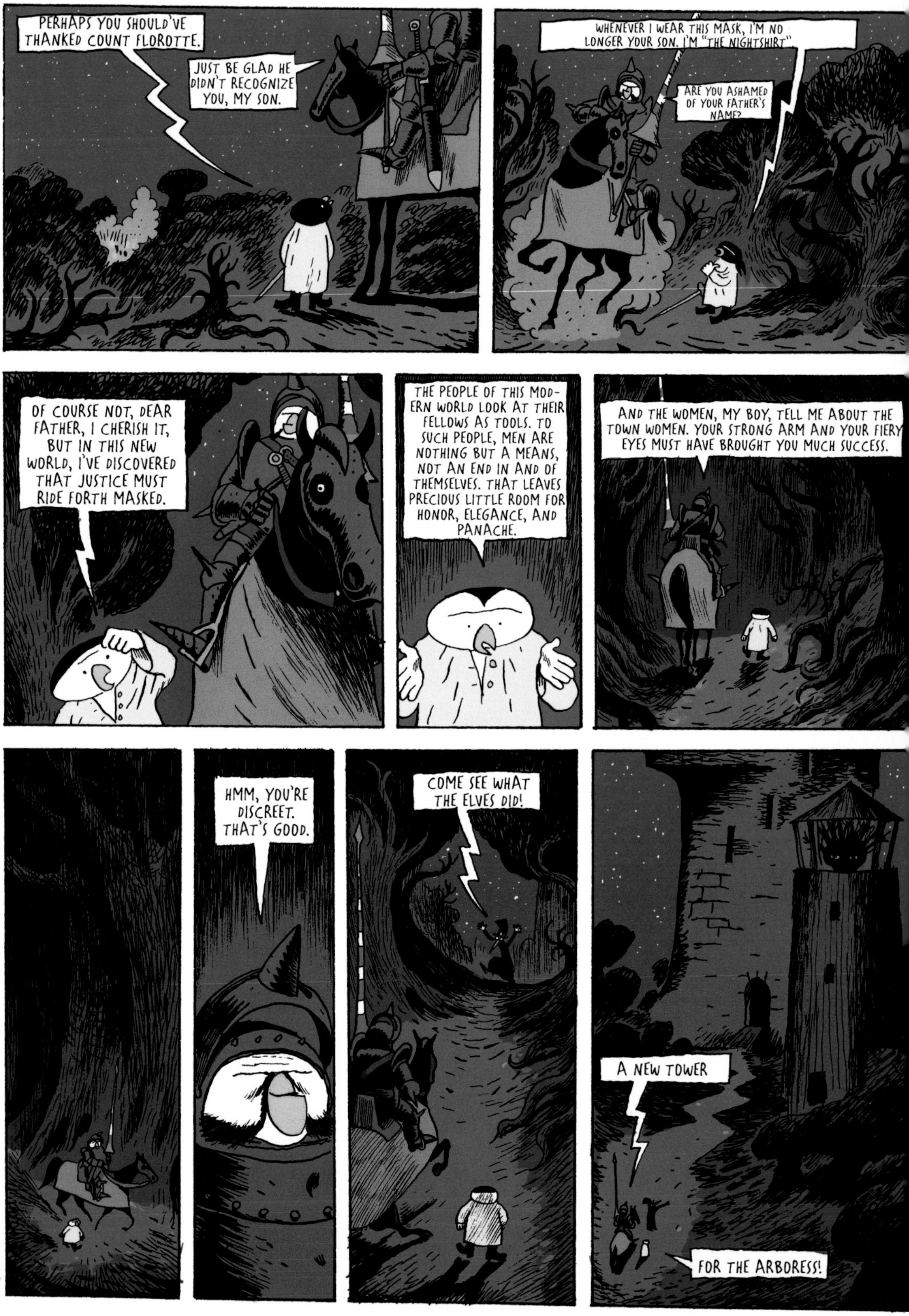
PERHAPS YOU SHOULD'VE THANKED COUNT FLOROTTE.
JUST BE GLAD HE DIDN'T RECOGNIZE YOU, MY SON.
WHENEVER I WEAR THIS MASK, I'M NO LONGER YOUR SON. I'M "THE NIGHTSHIRT"
ARE YOU ASHAMED OF YOUR FATHER'S NAME?
OF COURSE NOT, DEAR FATHER, I CHERISH IT, BUT IN THIS NEW WORLD, I'VE DISCOVERED THAT JUSTICE MUST RIDE FORTH MASKED.
THE PEOPLE OF THIS MODERN WORLD LOOK AT THEIR FELLOWS AS TOOLS. TO SUCH PEOPLE, MEN ARE NOTHING BUT A MEANS, NOT AN END IN AND OF THEMSELVES. THAT LEAVES PRECIOUS LITTLE ROOM FOR HONOR, ELEGANCE, AND PANACHE.
AND THE WOMEN, MY BOY, TELL ME ABOUT THE TOWN WOMEN. YOUR STRONG ARM AND YOUR FIERY EYES MUST HAVE BROUGHT YOU MUCH SUCCESS.
HMM, YOU'RE DISCREET. THAT'S GOOD.
COME SEE WHAT THE ELVES DID!
A NEW TOWER
FOR THE ARBORESS!

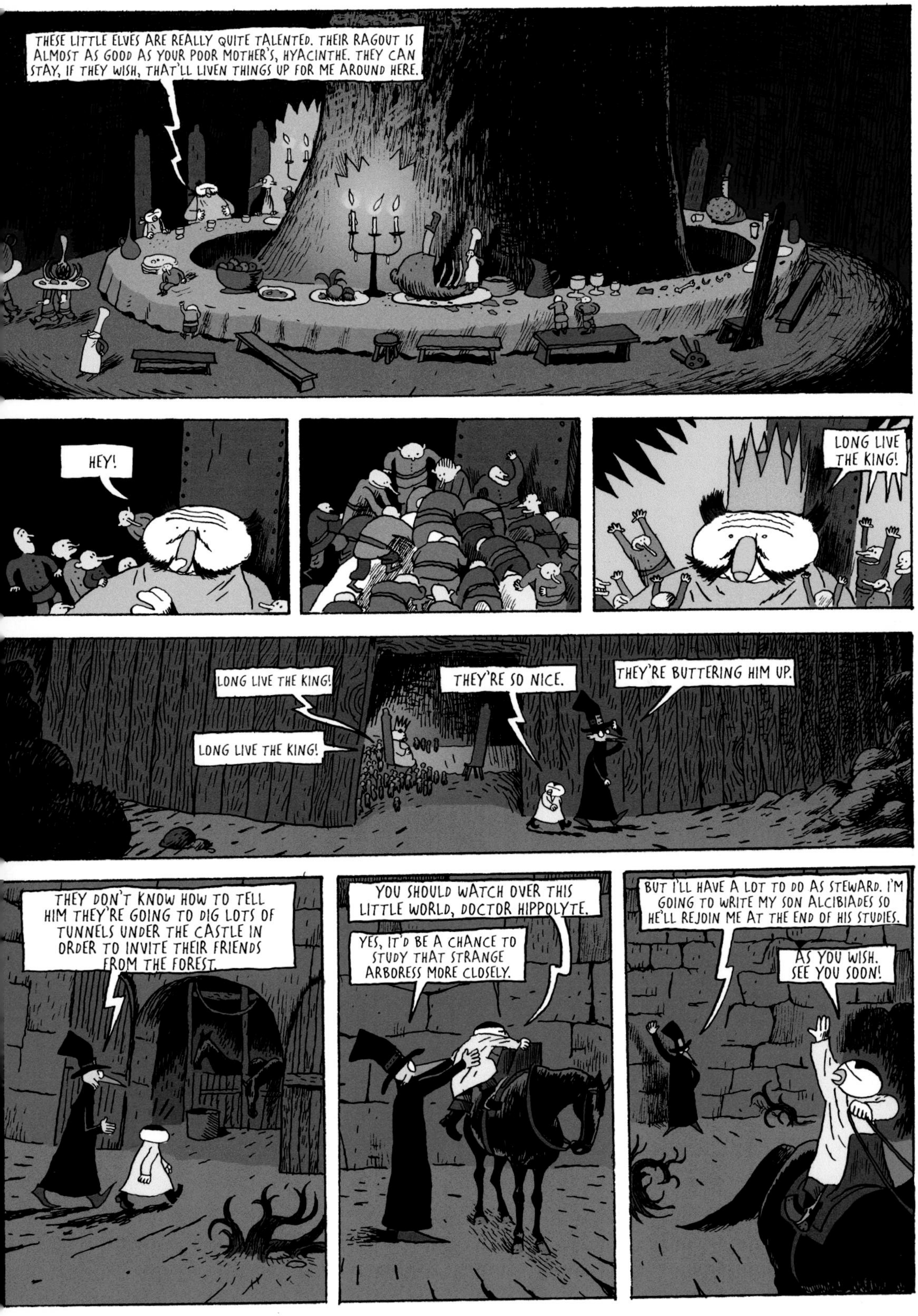
THESE LITTLE ELVES ARE REALLY QUITE TALENTED. THEIR RAGOUT IS ALMOST AS GOOD AS YOUR POOR MOTHER'S, HYACINTHE. THEY CAN STAY, IF THEY WISH, THAT'LL LIVEN THINGS UP FOR ME AROUND HERE.
HEY!
LONG LIVE THE KING!
LONG LIVE THE KING!
LONG LIVE THE KING!
THEY'RE SO NICE.
THEY'RE BUTTERING HIM UP.
THEY DON'T KNOW HOW TO TELL HIM THEY'RE GOING TO DIG LOTS OF TUNNELS UNDER THE CASTLE IN ORDER TO INVITE THEIR FRIENDS FROM THE FOREST.
YOU SHOULD WATCH OVER THIS LITTLE WORLD, DOCTOR HIPPOLYTE.
YES, IT'D BE A CHANCE TO STUDY THAT STRANGE ARBORESS MORE CLOSELY.
BUT I'LL HAVE A LOT TO DO AS STEWARD. I'M GOING TO WRITE MY SON ALCIBIADES SO HE'LL REJOIN ME AT THE END OF HIS STUDIES.
AS YOU WISH. SEE YOU SOON!

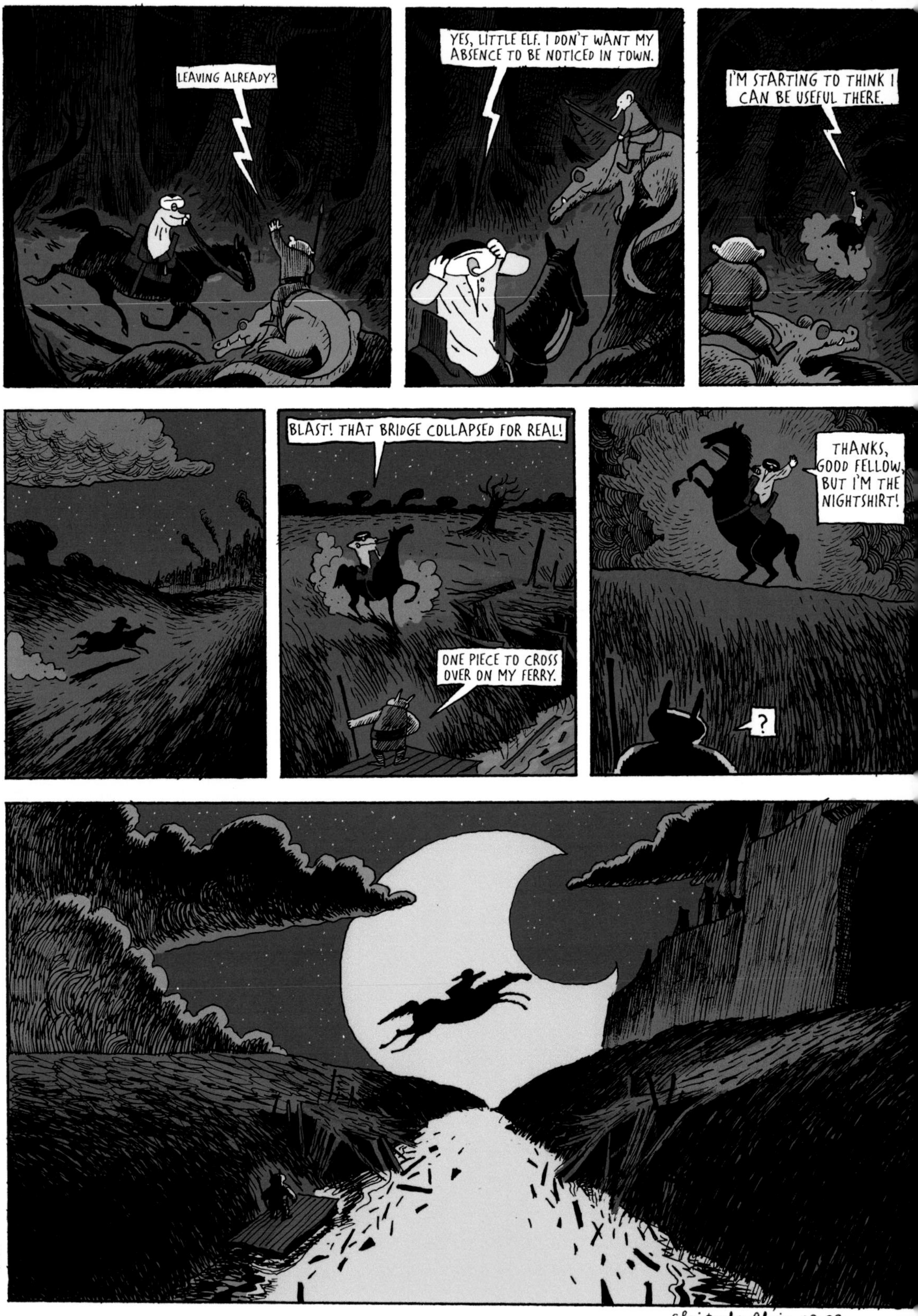
LEAVING ALREADY?
YES, LITTLE ELF. I DON'T WANT MY ABSENCE TO BE NOTICED IN TOWN.
I'M STARTING TO THINK I CAN BE USEFUL THERE.
BLAST! THAT BRIDGE COLLAPSED FOR REAL!
ONE PIECE TO CROSS OVER ON MY FERRY.
THANKS, GOOD FELLOW, BUT I'M THE NIGHTSHIRT!
?

Christophe Blain 09.99

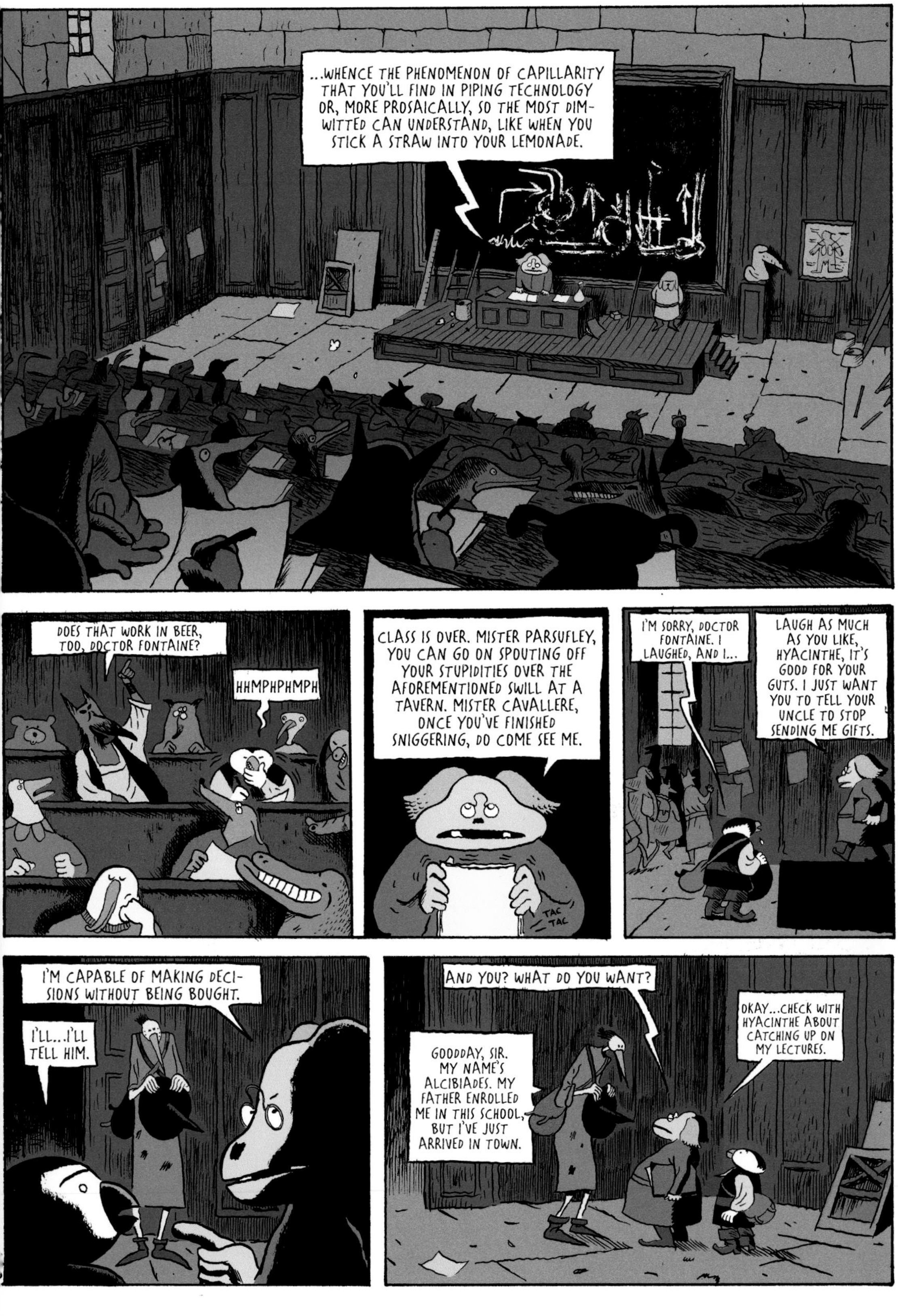
...WHENCE THE PHENOMENON OF CAPILLARITY THAT YOU'LL FIND IN PIPING TECHNOLOGY OR, MORE PROSAICALLY, SO THE MOST DIM-WITTED CAN UNDERSTAND, LIKE WHEN YOU STICK A STRAW INTO YOUR LEMONADE.
DOES THAT WORK IN BEER, TOO, DOCTOR FONTAINE?
HHMPHPHMPH
CLASS IS OVER. MISTER PARSUFLEY, YOU CAN GO ON SPOUTING OFF YOUR STUPIDITIES OVER THE AFOREMENTIONED SWILL AT A TAVERN. MISTER CAVALLERE, ONCE YOU'VE FINISHED SNIGGERING, DO COME SEE ME.
TAC TAC
I'M SORRY, DOCTOR FONTAINE. I LAUGHED, AND I...
LAUGH AS MUCH AS YOU LIKE, HYACINTHE, IT'S GOOD FOR YOUR GUTS. I JUST WANT YOU TO TELL YOUR UNCLE TO STOP SENDING ME GIFTS.
I'M CAPABLE OF MAKING DECISIONS WITHOUT BEING BOUGHT.
I'LL...I'LL TELL HIM.
AND YOU? WHAT DO YOU WANT?
GOODDAY, SIR. MY NAME'S ALCIBIADES. MY FATHER ENROLLED ME IN THIS SCHOOL, BUT I'VE JUST ARRIVED IN TOWN.
OKAY...CHECK WITH HYACINTHE ABOUT CATCHING UP ON MY LECTURES.

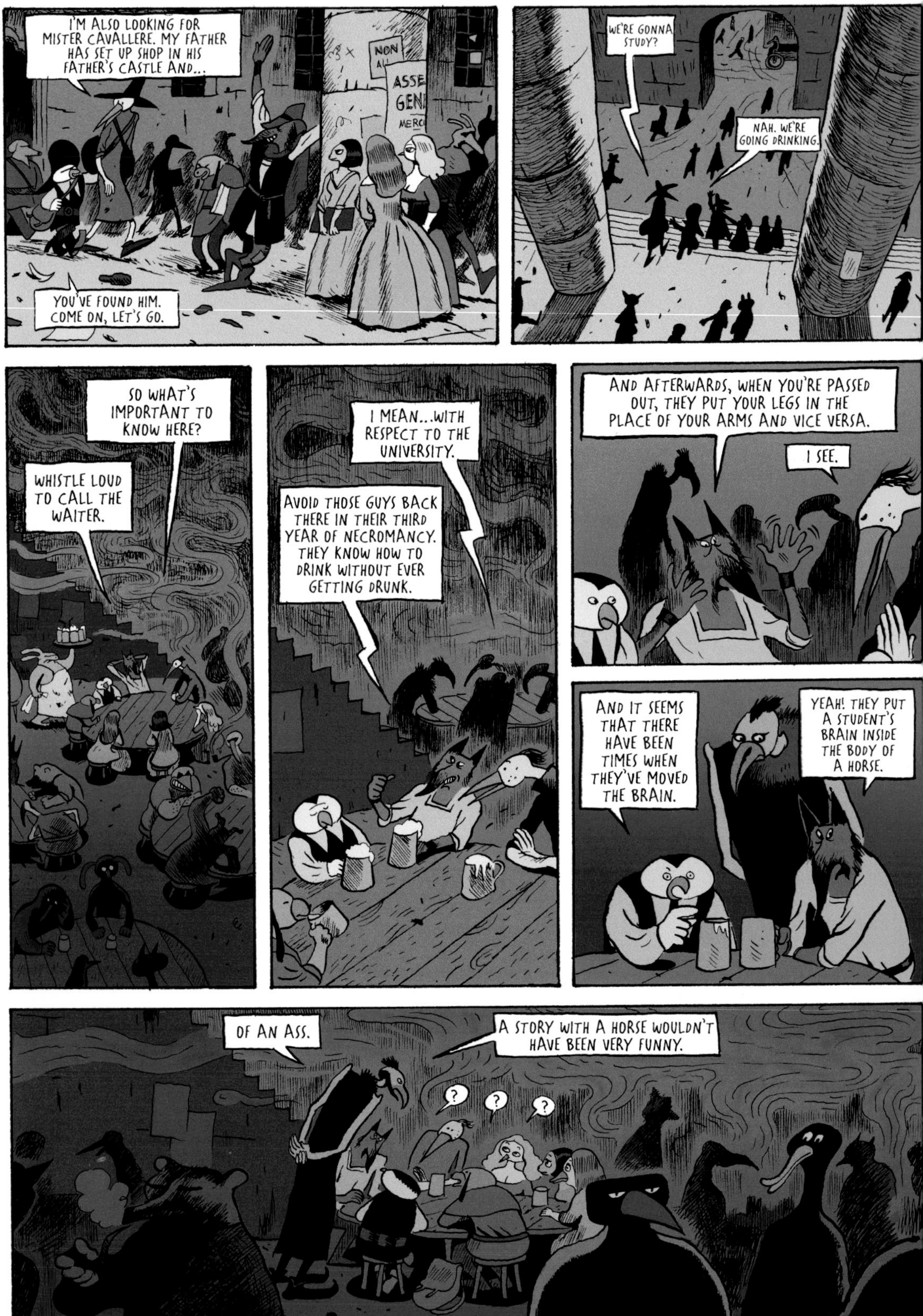
I'M ALSO LOOKING FOR MISTER CAVALLERE. MY FATHER HAS SET UP SHOP IN HIS FATHER'S CASTLE AND...
NON
ASSE GEN
MERC
YOU'VE FOUND HIM. COME ON, LET'S GO.
WE'RE GONNA STUDY?
NAH. WE'RE GOING DRINKING.
SO WHAT'S IMPORTANT TO KNOW HERE?
WHISTLE LOUD TO CALL THE WAITER.
I MEAN...WITH RESPECT TO THE UNIVERSITY.
AVOID THOSE GUYS BACK THERE IN THEIR THIRD YEAR OF NECROMANCY. THEY KNOW HOW TO DRINK WITHOUT EVER GETTING DRUNK.
AND AFTERWARDS, WHEN YOU'RE PASSED OUT, THEY PUT YOUR LEGS IN THE PLACE OF YOUR ARMS AND VICE VERSA.
I SEE.
AND IT SEEMS THAT THERE HAVE BEEN TIMES WHEN THEY'VE MOVED THE BRAIN.
YEAH! THEY PUT A STUDENT'S BRAIN INSIDE THE BODY OF A HORSE.
OF AN ASS.
A STORY WITH A HORSE WOULDN'T HAVE BEEN VERY FUNNY.
?
?
?

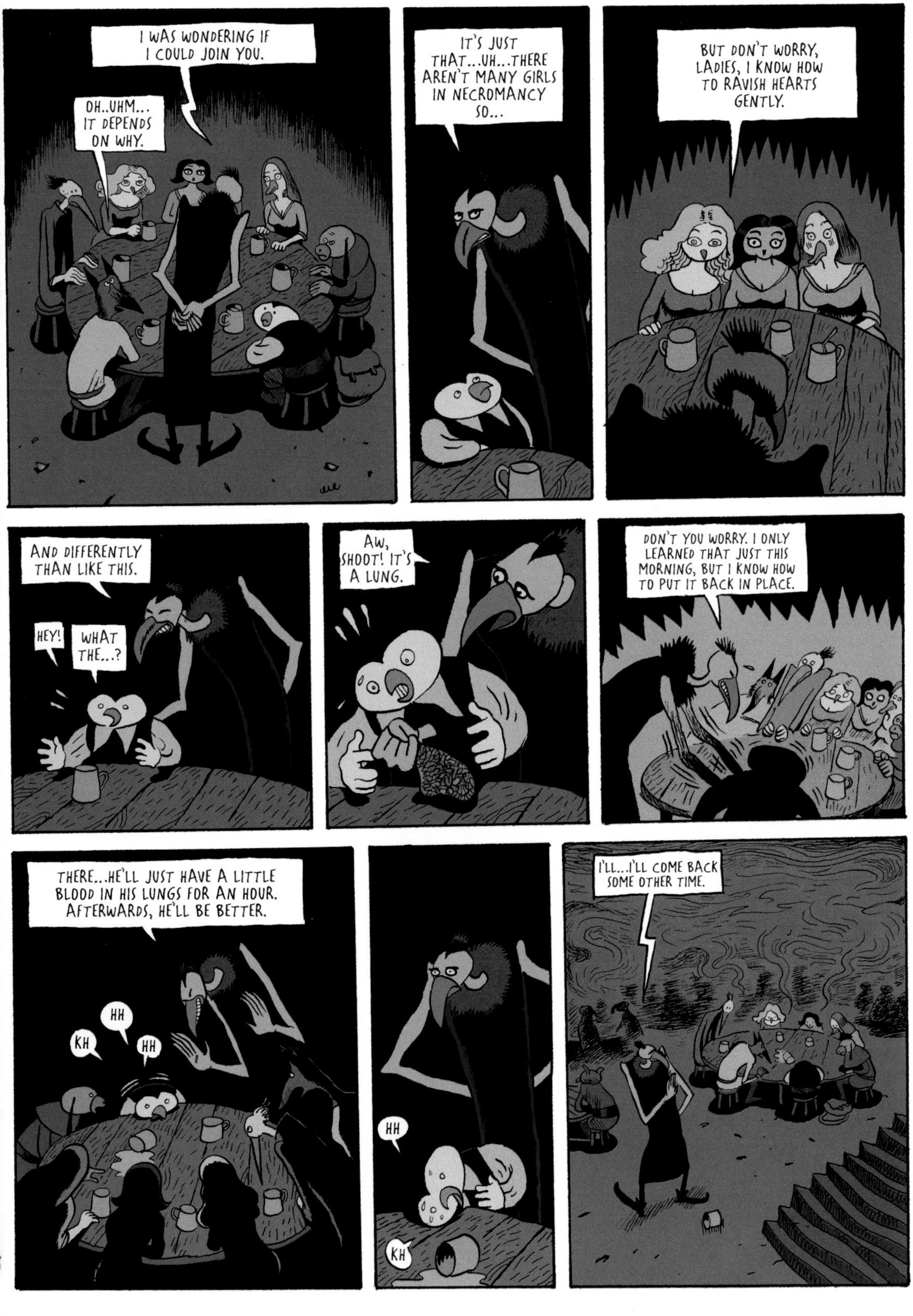
I WAS WONDERING IF I COULD JOIN YOU.
OH..UHM... IT DEPENDS ON WHY.
IT'S JUST THAT...UH...THERE AREN'T MANY GIRLS IN NECROMANCY SO...
BUT DON'T WORRY, LADIES, I KNOW HOW TO RAVISH HEARTS GENTLY.
AND DIFFERENTLY THAN LIKE THIS.
HEY!
WHAT THE...?
AW, SHOOT! IT'S A LUNG.
DON'T YOU WORRY. I ONLY LEARNED THAT JUST THIS MORNING, BUT I KNOW HOW TO PUT IT BACK IN PLACE.
THERE...HE'LL JUST HAVE A LITTLE BLOOD IN HIS LUNGS FOR AN HOUR. AFTERWARDS, HE'LL BE BETTER.
KH
HH
HH
HH
KH
I'LL...I'LL COME BACK SOME OTHER TIME.

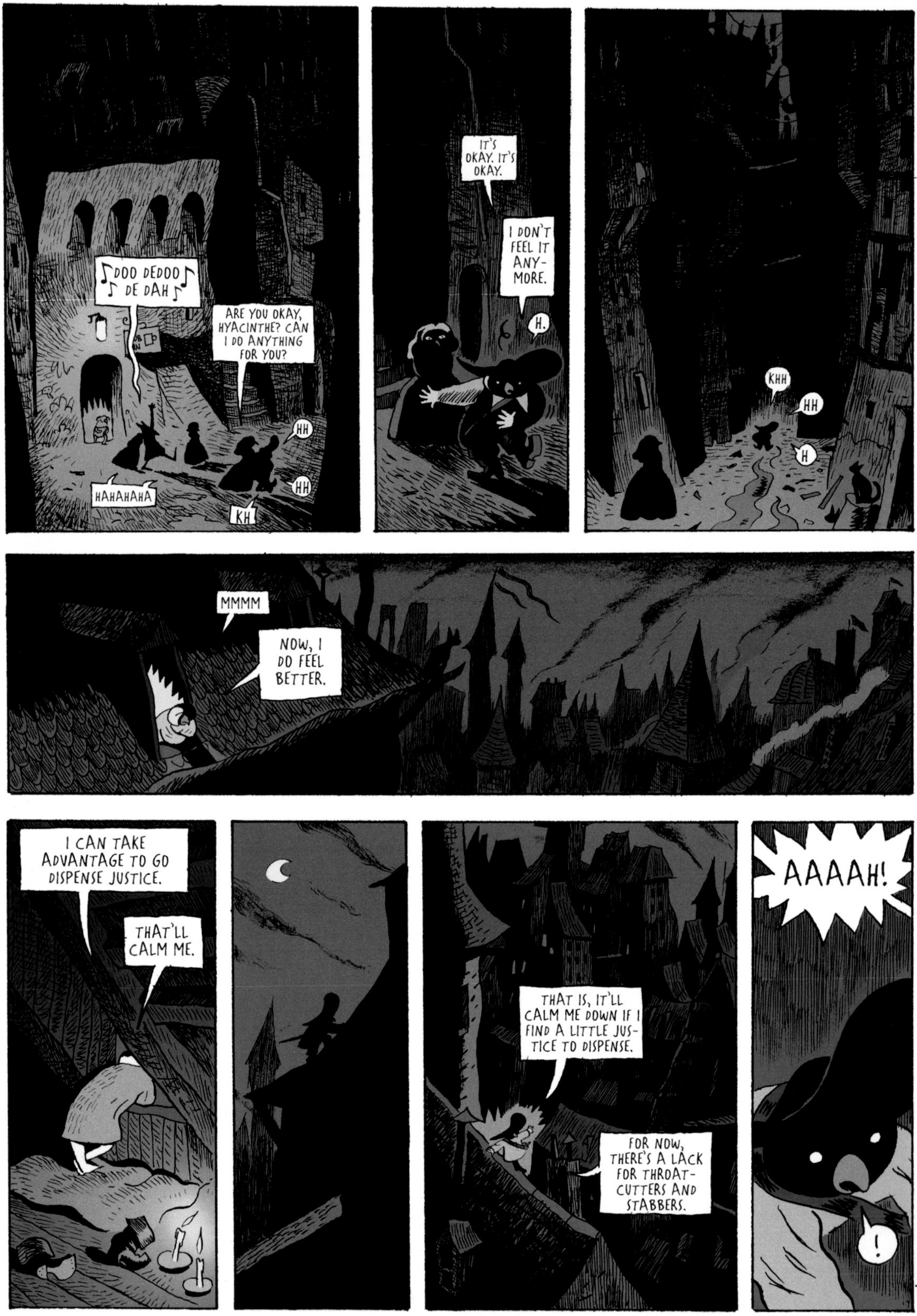
DOO DEDOO DE DAH
ARE YOU OKAY, HYACINTHE? CAN I DO ANYTHING FOR YOU?
HH
HAHAHAHA
HH
KH
IT'S OKAY. IT'S OKAY.
I DON'T FEEL IT ANY-MORE.
H.
KHH
HH
H
MMMM
NOW, I DO FEEL BETTER.
I CAN TAKE ADVANTAGE TO GO DISPENSE JUSTICE.
THAT'LL CALM ME.
THAT IS, IT'LL CALM ME DOWN IF I FIND A LITTLE JUS-TICE TO DISPENSE.
FOR NOW, THERE'S A LACK FOR THROAT-CUTTERS AND STABBERS.
AAAAH!
!

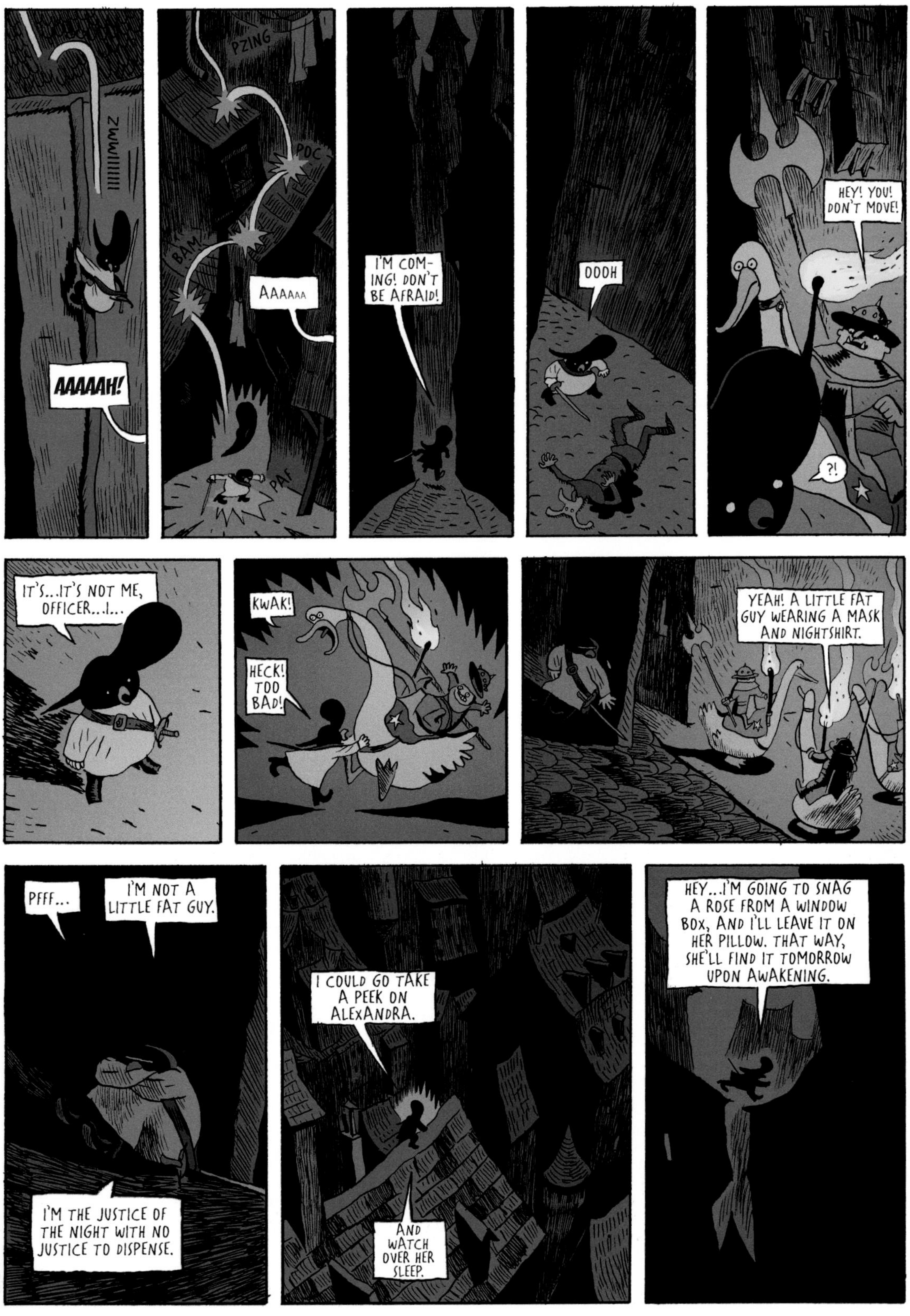
ZWIIIIIIIII
AAAAAH!
PZING
POC
BAM
AAAAAA
PAF
I'M COMING! DON'T BE AFRAID!
OOOH
HEY! YOU! DON'T MOVE!
?!
IT'S...IT'S NOT ME, OFFICER...I...
KWAK!
HECK! TOO BAD!
YEAH! A LITTLE FAT GUY WEARING A MASK AND NIGHTSHIRT.
PFFF...
I'M NOT A LITTLE FAT GUY.
I'M THE JUSTICE OF THE NIGHT WITH NO JUSTICE TO DISPENSE.
I COULD GO TAKE A PEEK ON ALEXANDRA.
AND WATCH OVER HER SLEEP.
HEY...I'M GOING TO SNAG A ROSE FROM A WINDOW BOX, AND I'LL LEAVE IT ON HER PILLOW. THAT WAY, SHE'LL FIND IT TOMORROW UPON AWAKENING.

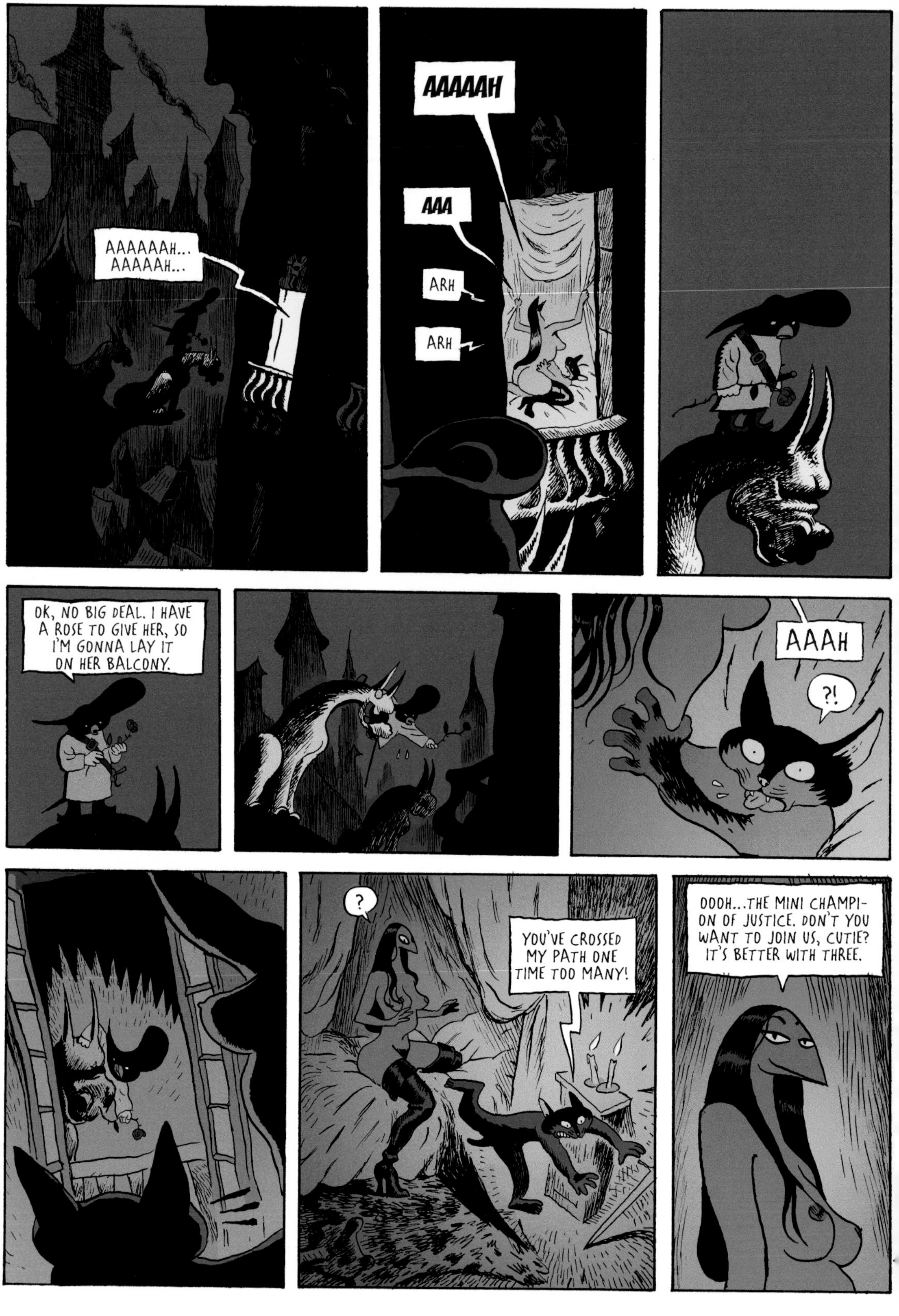

AAAAAAH...
AAAAAH...
AAAAAH
AAA
ARH
ARH
OK, NO BIG DEAL. I HAVE A ROSE TO GIVE HER, SO I'M GONNA LAY IT ON HER BALCONY.
AAAH
?!
?
YOU'VE CROSSED MY PATH ONE TIME TOO MANY!
OOOH...THE MINI CHAMPI-ON OF JUSTICE. DON'T YOU WANT TO JOIN US, CUTIE? IT'S BETTER WITH THREE.

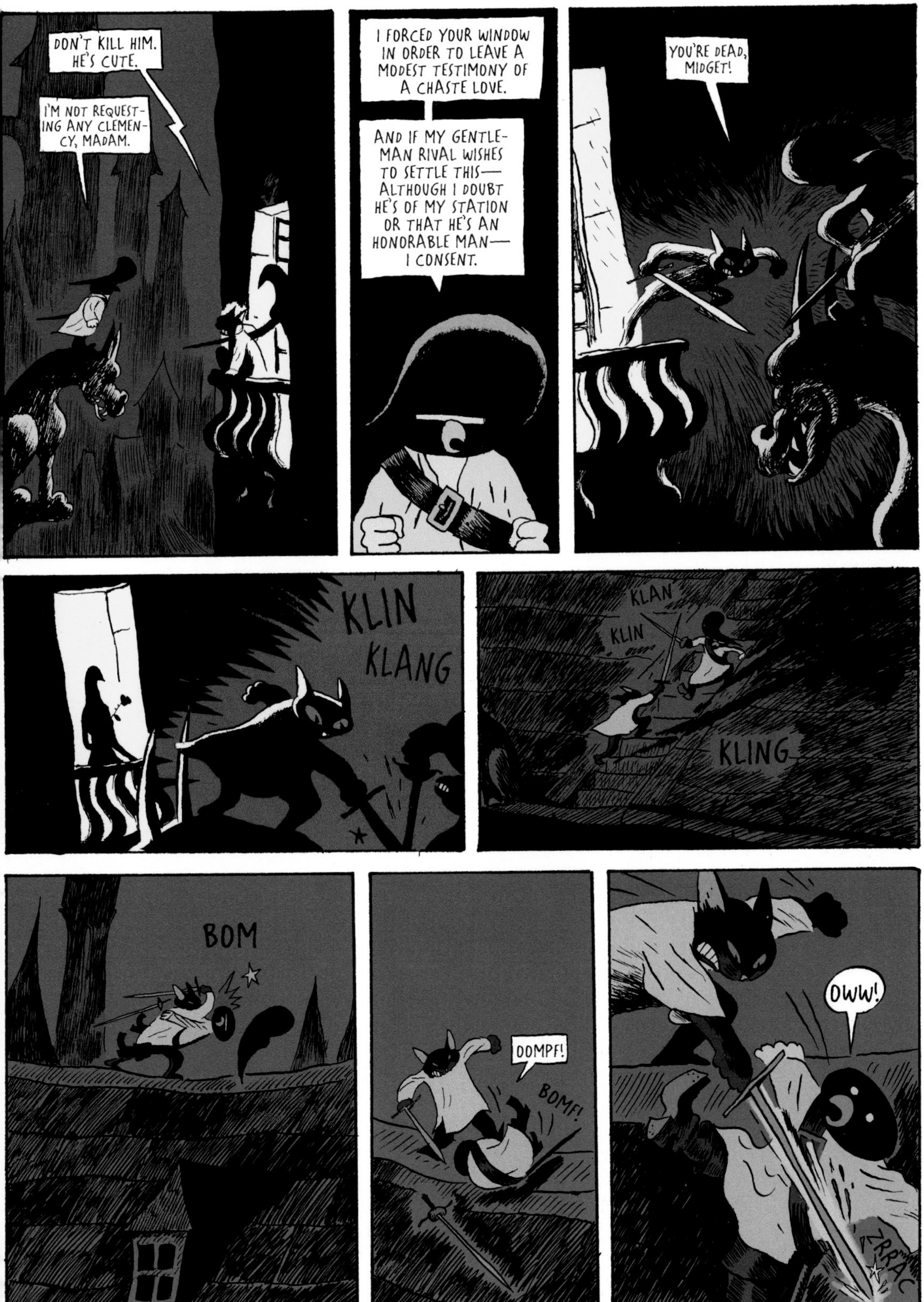

DON'T KILL HIM. HE'S CUTE.
I'M NOT REQUESTING ANY CLEMENCY, MADAM.
I FORCED YOUR WINDOW IN ORDER TO LEAVE A MODEST TESTIMONY OF A CHASTE LOVE.
AND IF MY GENTLEMAN RIVAL WISHES TO SETTLE THIS— ALTHOUGH I DOUBT HE'S OF MY STATION OR THAT HE'S AN HONORABLE MAN— I CONSENT.
YOU'RE DEAD, MIDGET!
KLIN
KLANG
KLAN
KLIN
KLING
BOM
DOMPF!
BOMF!
OWW!
ZRRAC

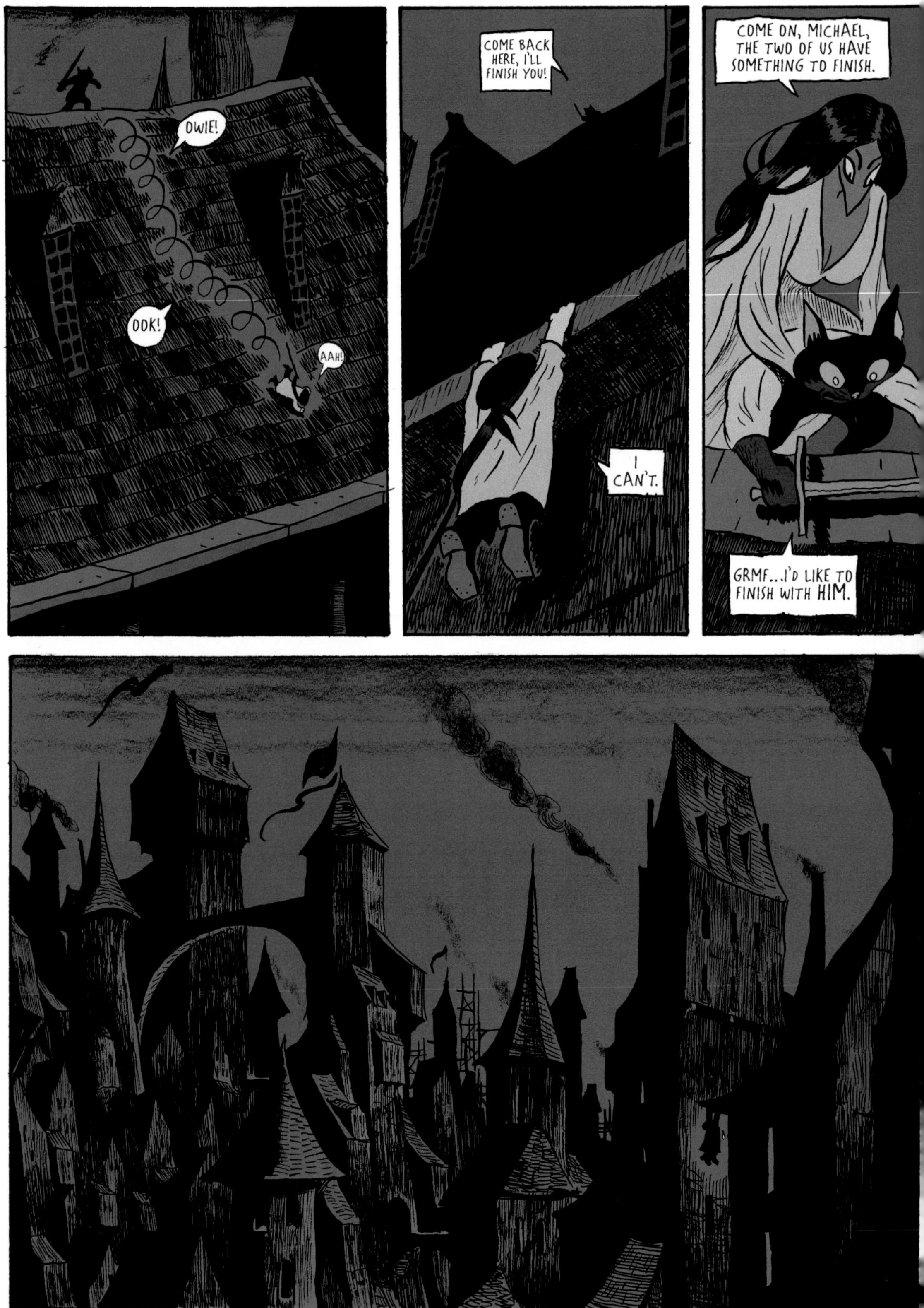
OWIE!
OOK!
AAH!
COME BACK HERE, I'LL FINISH YOU!
I CAN'T.
COME ON, MICHAEL, THE TWO OF US HAVE SOMETHING TO FINISH.
GRMF...I'D LIKE TO FINISH WITH HIM.

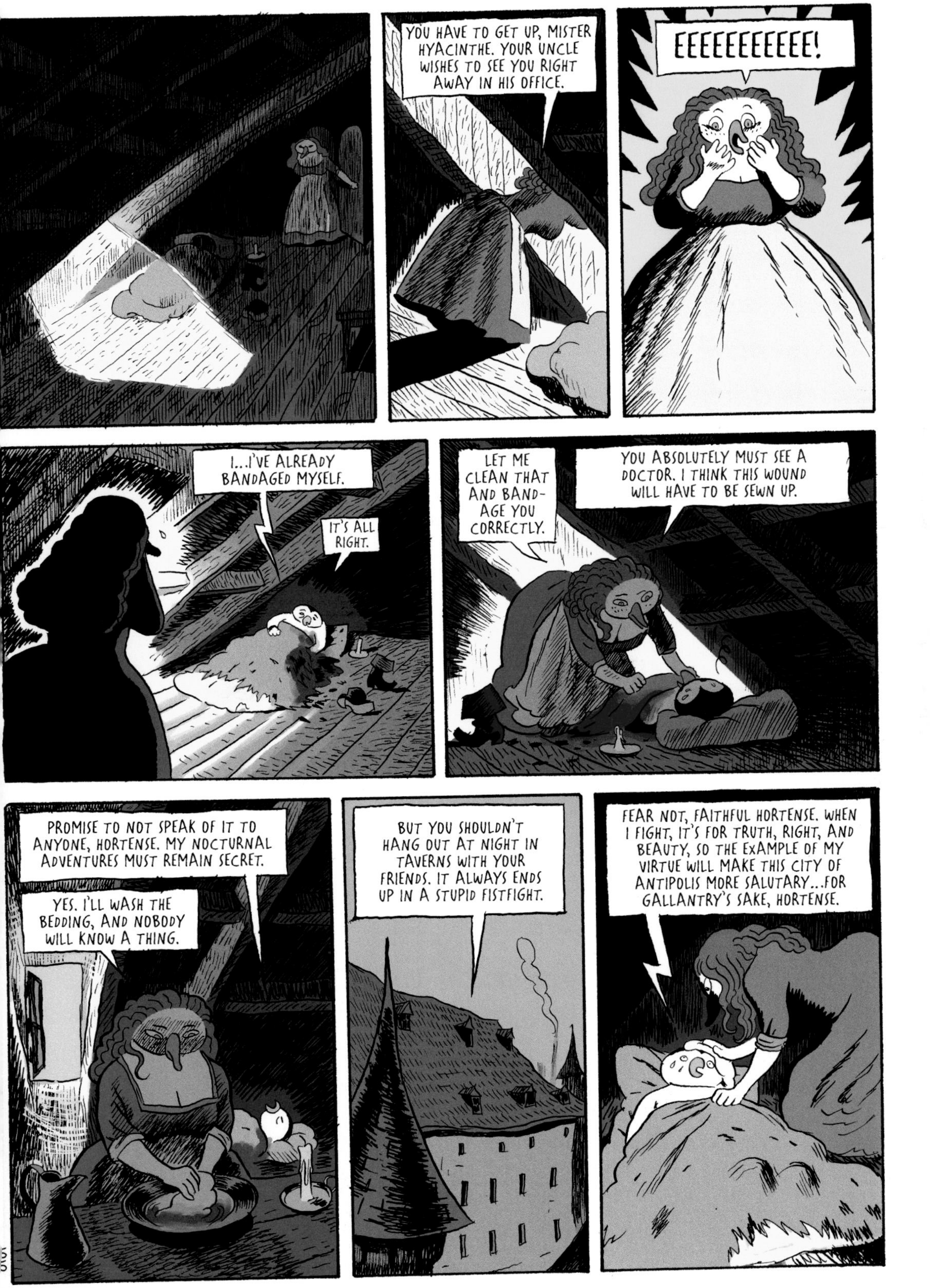
YOU HAVE TO GET UP, MISTER HYACINTHE. YOUR UNCLE WISHES TO SEE YOU RIGHT AWAY IN HIS OFFICE.
EEEEEEEEEEE!
I...I'VE ALREADY BANDAGED MYSELF.
IT'S ALL RIGHT.
LET ME CLEAN THAT AND BANDAGE YOU CORRECTLY.
YOU ABSOLUTELY MUST SEE A DOCTOR. I THINK THIS WOUND WILL HAVE TO BE SEWN UP.
PROMISE TO NOT SPEAK OF IT TO ANYONE, HORTENSE. MY NOCTURNAL ADVENTURES MUST REMAIN SECRET.
YES. I'LL WASH THE BEDDING, AND NOBODY WILL KNOW A THING.
BUT YOU SHOULDN'T HANG OUT AT NIGHT IN TAVERNS WITH YOUR FRIENDS. IT ALWAYS ENDS UP IN A STUPID FISTFIGHT.
FEAR NOT, FAITHFUL HORTENSE. WHEN I FIGHT, IT'S FOR TRUTH, RIGHT, AND BEAUTY, SO THE EXAMPLE OF MY VIRTUE WILL MAKE THIS CITY OF ANTIPOLIS MORE SALUTARY...FOR GALLANTRY'S SAKE, HORTENSE.

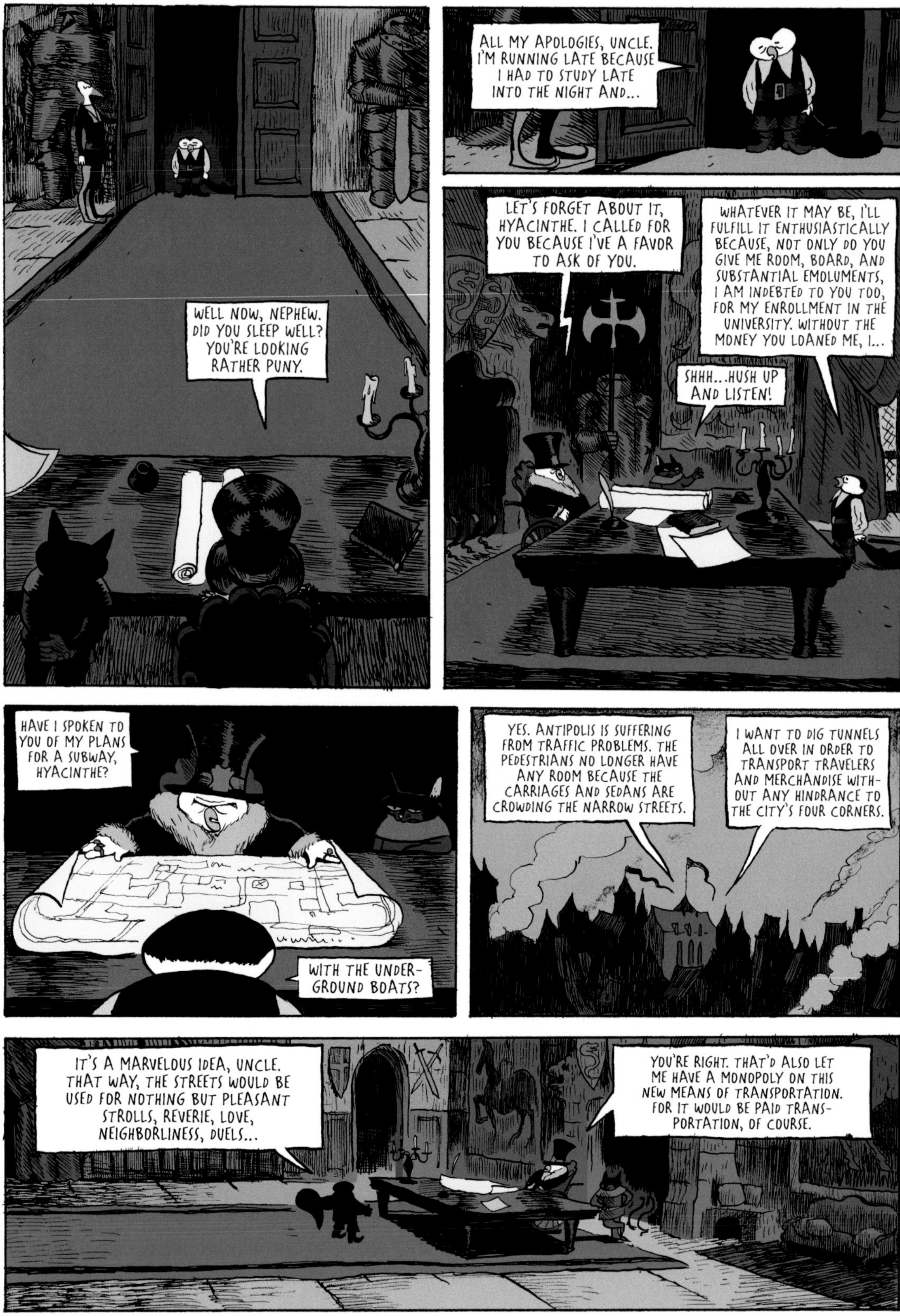
WELL NOW, NEPHEW. DID YOU SLEEP WELL? YOU'RE LOOKING RATHER PUNY.
ALL MY APOLOGIES, UNCLE. I'M RUNNING LATE BECAUSE I HAD TO STUDY LATE INTO THE NIGHT AND...
LET'S FORGET ABOUT IT, HYACINTHE. I CALLED FOR YOU BECAUSE I'VE A FAVOR TO ASK OF YOU.
WHATEVER IT MAY BE, I'LL FULFILL IT ENTHUSIASTICALLY BECAUSE, NOT ONLY DO YOU GIVE ME ROOM, BOARD, AND SUBSTANTIAL EMOLUMENTS, I AM INDEBTED TO YOU TOO, FOR MY ENROLLMENT IN THE UNIVERSITY. WITHOUT THE MONEY YOU LOANED ME, I...
SHHH...HUSH UP AND LISTEN!
HAVE I SPOKEN TO YOU OF MY PLANS FOR A SUBWAY, HYACINTHE?
WITH THE UNDERGROUND BOATS?
YES. ANTIPOLIS IS SUFFERING FROM TRAFFIC PROBLEMS. THE PEDESTRIANS NO LONGER HAVE ANY ROOM BECAUSE THE CARRIAGES AND SEDANS ARE CROWDING THE NARROW STREETS.
I WANT TO DIG TUNNELS ALL OVER IN ORDER TO TRANSPORT TRAVELERS AND MERCHANDISE WITHOUT ANY HINDRANCE TO THE CITY'S FOUR CORNERS.
IT'S A MARVELOUS IDEA, UNCLE. THAT WAY, THE STREETS WOULD BE USED FOR NOTHING BUT PLEASANT STROLLS, REVERIE, LOVE, NEIGHBORLINESS, DUELS...
YOU'RE RIGHT. THAT'D ALSO LET ME HAVE A MONOPOLY ON THIS NEW MEANS OF TRANSPORTATION. FOR IT WOULD BE PAID TRANSPORTATION, OF COURSE.

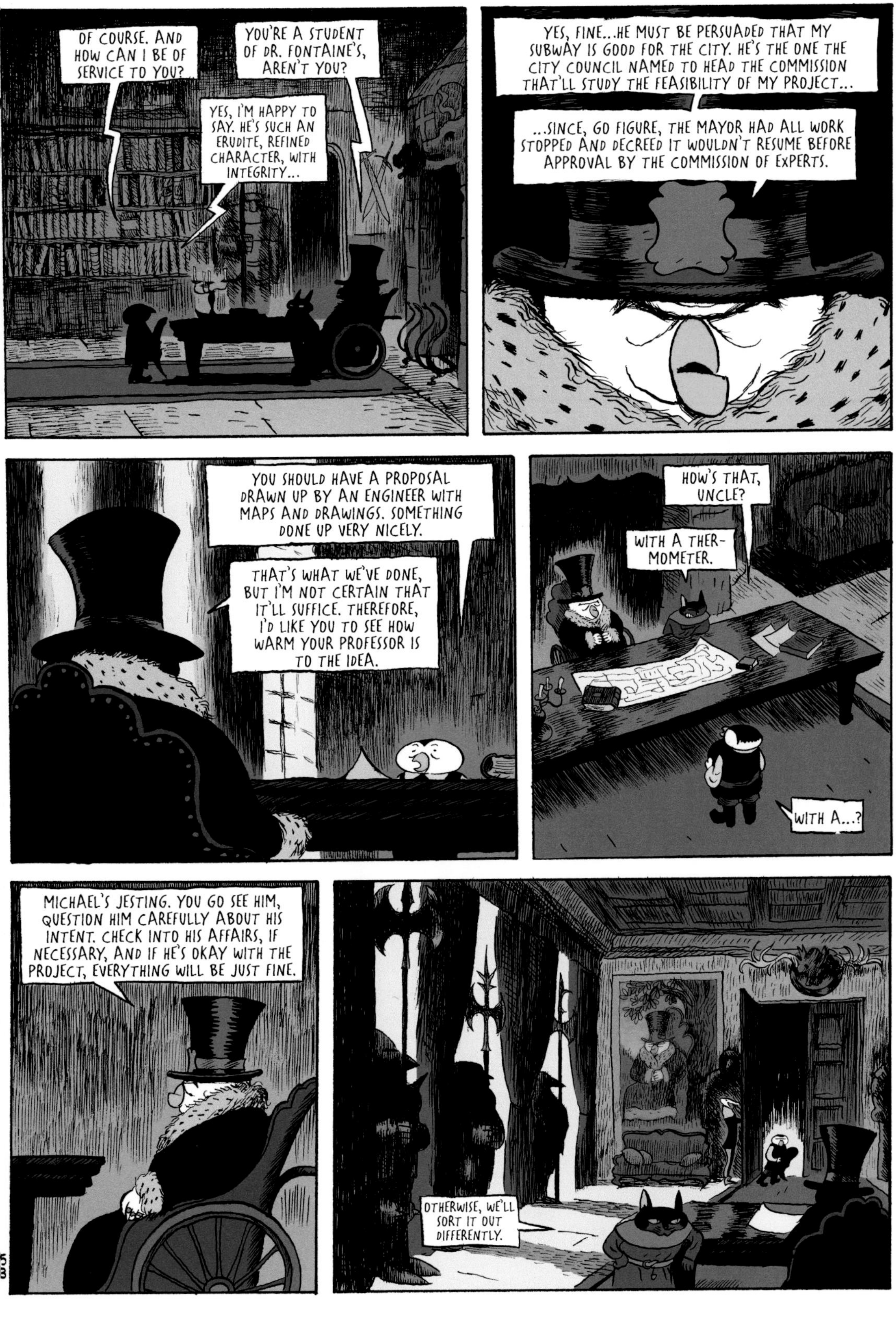
OF COURSE. AND HOW CAN I BE OF SERVICE TO YOU?
YOU'RE A STUDENT OF DR. FONTAINE'S, AREN'T YOU?
YES, I'M HAPPY TO SAY. HE'S SUCH AN ERUDITE, REFINED CHARACTER, WITH INTEGRITY...
YES, FINE...HE MUST BE PERSUADED THAT MY SUBWAY IS GOOD FOR THE CITY. HE'S THE ONE THE CITY COUNCIL NAMED TO HEAD THE COMMISSION THAT'LL STUDY THE FEASIBILITY OF MY PROJECT...
...SINCE, GO FIGURE, THE MAYOR HAD ALL WORK STOPPED AND DECREED IT WOULDN'T RESUME BEFORE APPROVAL BY THE COMMISSION OF EXPERTS.
YOU SHOULD HAVE A PROPOSAL DRAWN UP BY AN ENGINEER WITH MAPS AND DRAWINGS. SOMETHING DONE UP VERY NICELY.
THAT'S WHAT WE'VE DONE, BUT I'M NOT CERTAIN THAT IT'LL SUFFICE. THEREFORE, I'D LIKE YOU TO SEE HOW WARM YOUR PROFESSOR IS TO THE IDEA.
HOW'S THAT, UNCLE?
WITH A THER-MOMETER.
WITH A...?
MICHAEL'S JESTING. YOU GO SEE HIM, QUESTION HIM CAREFULLY ABOUT HIS INTENT. CHECK INTO HIS AFFAIRS, IF NECESSARY, AND IF HE'S OKAY WITH THE PROJECT, EVERYTHING WILL BE JUST FINE.
OTHERWISE, WE'LL SORT IT OUT DIFFERENTLY.

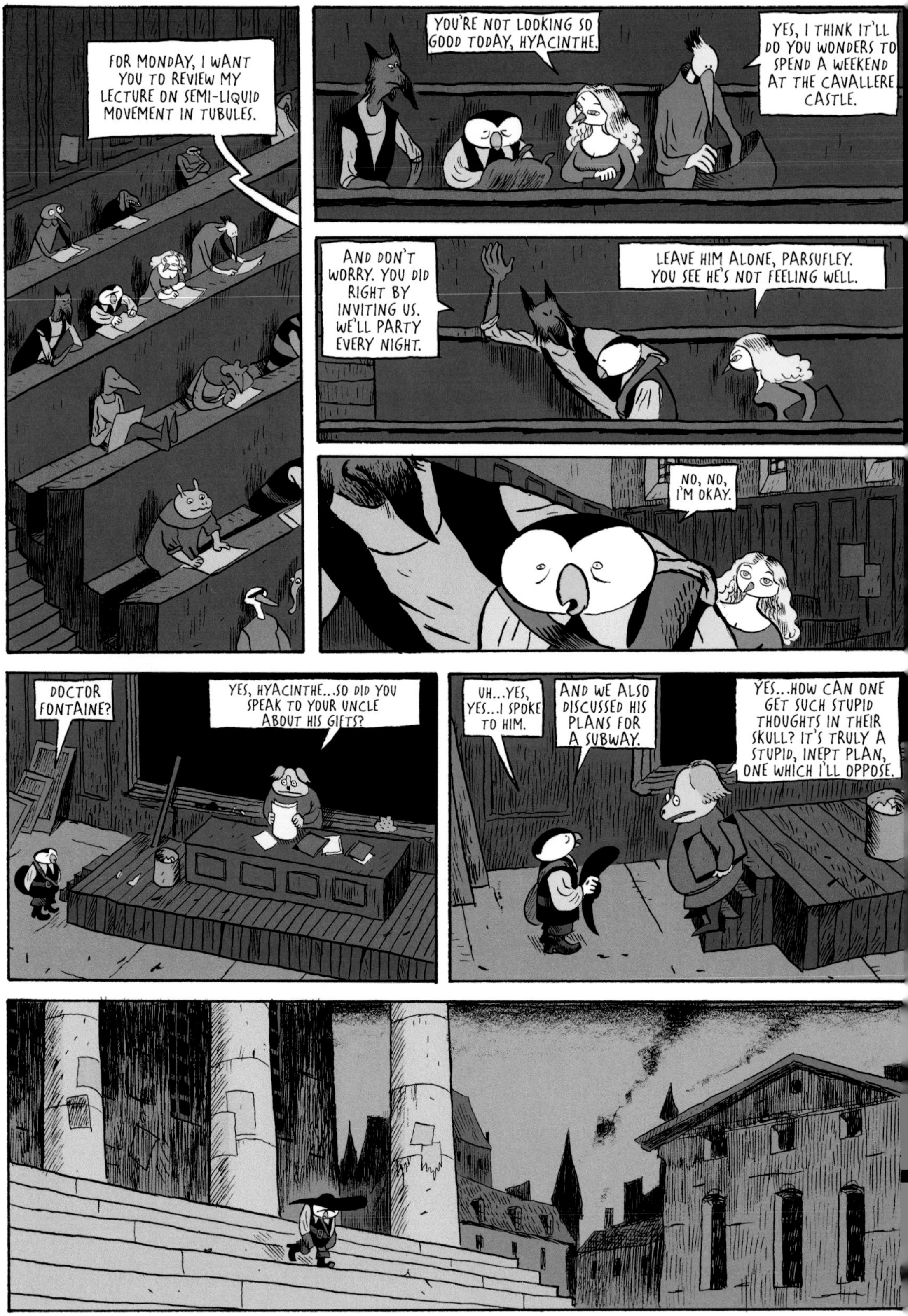
FOR MONDAY, I WANT YOU TO REVIEW MY LECTURE ON SEMI-LIQUID MOVEMENT IN TUBULES.
YOU'RE NOT LOOKING SO GOOD TODAY, HYACINTHE.
YES, I THINK IT'LL DO YOU WONDERS TO SPEND A WEEKEND AT THE CAVALLERE CASTLE.
AND DON'T WORRY. YOU DID RIGHT BY INVITING US. WE'LL PARTY EVERY NIGHT.
LEAVE HIM ALONE, PARSUFLEY. YOU SEE HE'S NOT FEELING WELL.
NO, NO, I'M OKAY.
DOCTOR FONTAINE?
YES, HYACINTHE...SO DID YOU SPEAK TO YOUR UNCLE ABOUT HIS GIFTS?
UH...YES, YES...I SPOKE TO HIM.
AND WE ALSO DISCUSSED HIS PLANS FOR A SUBWAY.
YES...HOW CAN ONE GET SUCH STUPID THOUGHTS IN THEIR SKULL? IT'S TRULY A STUPID, INEPT PLAN, ONE WHICH I'LL OPPOSE.

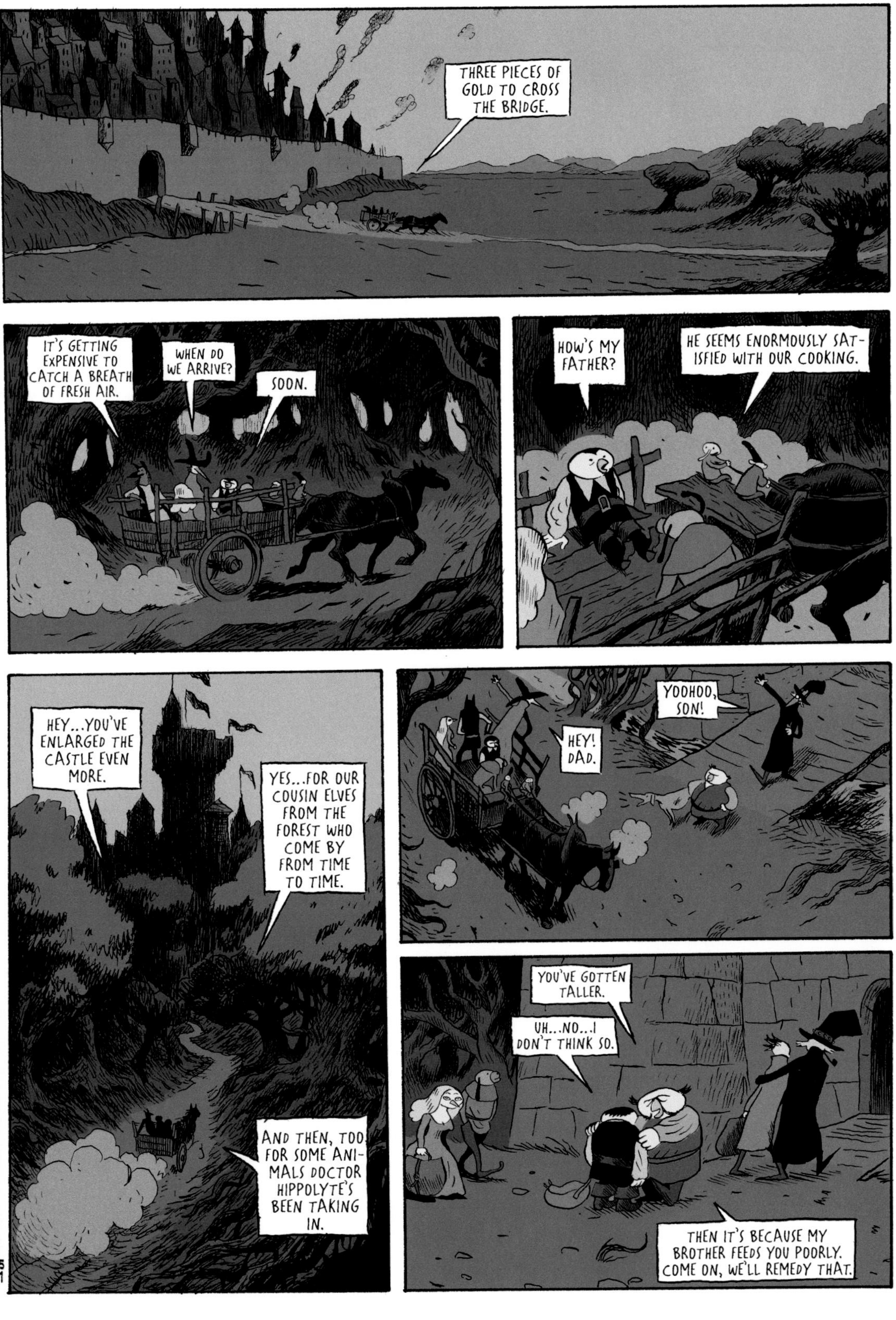

THREE PIECES OF GOLD TO CROSS THE BRIDGE.
IT'S GETTING EXPENSIVE TO CATCH A BREATH OF FRESH AIR.
WHEN DO WE ARRIVE?
SOON.
HOW'S MY FATHER?
HE SEEMS ENORMOUSLY SAT-ISFIED WITH OUR COOKING.
HEY...YOU'VE ENLARGED THE CASTLE EVEN MORE.
YES...FOR OUR COUSIN ELVES FROM THE FOREST WHO COME BY FROM TIME TO TIME.
AND THEN, TOO FOR SOME ANI-MALS DOCTOR HIPPOLYTE'S BEEN TAKING IN.
YOOHOO, SON!
HEY! DAD.
YOU'VE GOTTEN TALLER.
UH...NO...I DON'T THINK SO.
THEN IT'S BECAUSE MY BROTHER FEEDS YOU POORLY. COME ON, WE'LL REMEDY THAT.

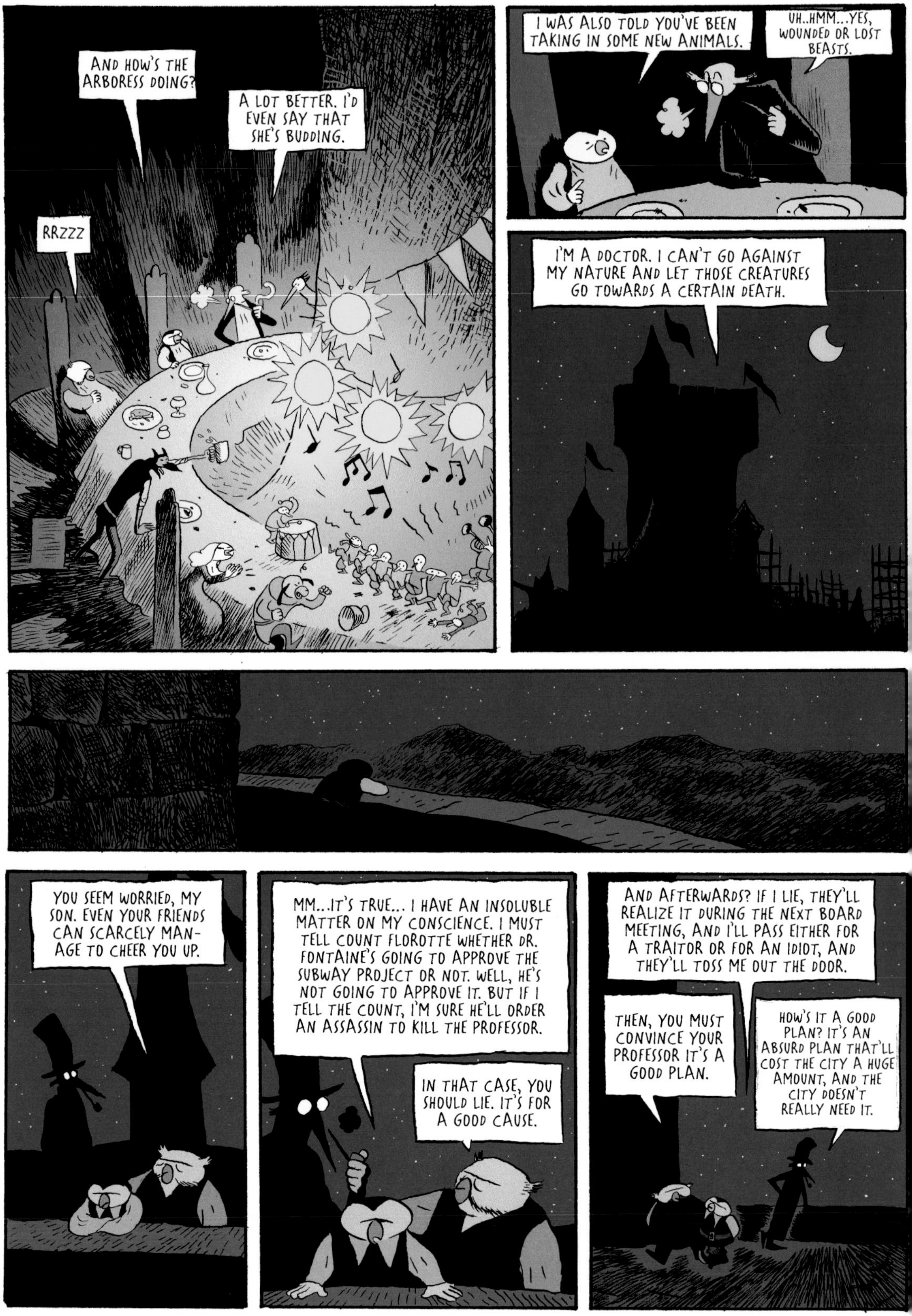
AND HOW'S THE ARBORESS DOING?
A LOT BETTER. I'D EVEN SAY THAT SHE'S BUDDING.
RRZZZ
I WAS ALSO TOLD YOU'VE BEEN TAKING IN SOME NEW ANIMALS.
UH..HMM...YES, WOUNDED OR LOST BEASTS.
I'M A DOCTOR. I CAN'T GO AGAINST MY NATURE AND LET THOSE CREATURES GO TOWARDS A CERTAIN DEATH.
YOU SEEM WORRIED, MY SON. EVEN YOUR FRIENDS CAN SCARCELY MAN-AGE TO CHEER YOU UP.
MM...IT'S TRUE... I HAVE AN INSOLUBLE MATTER ON MY CONSCIENCE. I MUST TELL COUNT FLOROTTE WHETHER DR. FONTAINE'S GOING TO APPROVE THE SUBWAY PROJECT OR NOT. WELL, HE'S NOT GOING TO APPROVE IT. BUT IF I TELL THE COUNT, I'M SURE HE'LL ORDER AN ASSASSIN TO KILL THE PROFESSOR.
IN THAT CASE, YOU SHOULD LIE. IT'S FOR A GOOD CAUSE.
AND AFTERWARDS? IF I LIE, THEY'LL REALIZE IT DURING THE NEXT BOARD MEETING, AND I'LL PASS EITHER FOR A TRAITOR OR FOR AN IDIOT, AND THEY'LL TOSS ME OUT THE DOOR.
THEN, YOU MUST CONVINCE YOUR PROFESSOR IT'S A GOOD PLAN.
HOW'S IT A GOOD PLAN? IT'S AN ABSURD PLAN THAT'LL COST THE CITY A HUGE AMOUNT, AND THE CITY DOESN'T REALLY NEED IT.

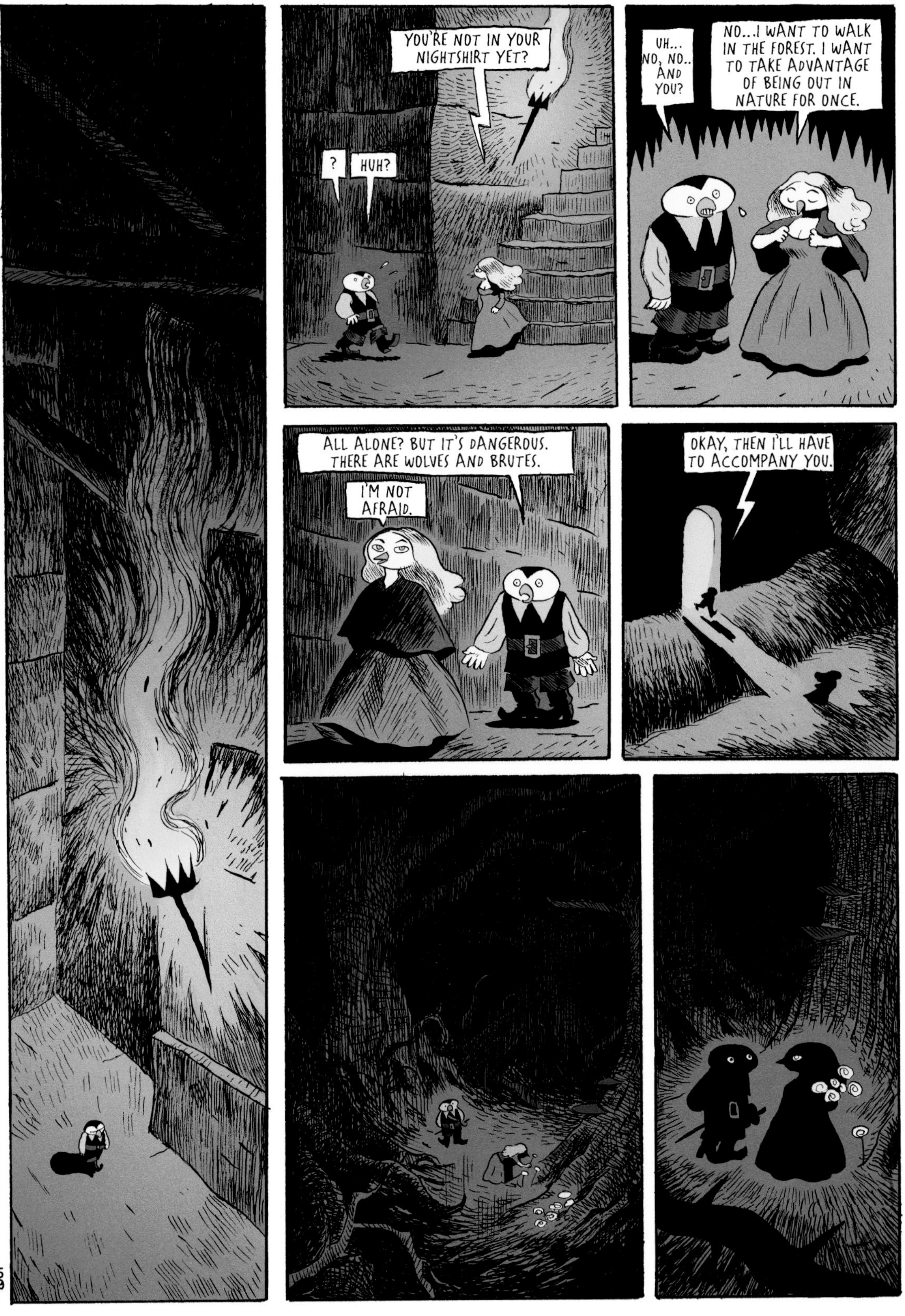
YOU'RE NOT IN YOUR NIGHTSHIRT YET?
?
HUH?
UH... NO, NO.. AND YOU?
NO...I WANT TO WALK IN THE FOREST. I WANT TO TAKE ADVANTAGE OF BEING OUT IN NATURE FOR ONCE.
ALL ALONE? BUT IT'S DANGEROUS. THERE ARE WOLVES AND BRUTES.
I'M NOT AFRAID.
OKAY, THEN I'LL HAVE TO ACCOMPANY YOU.

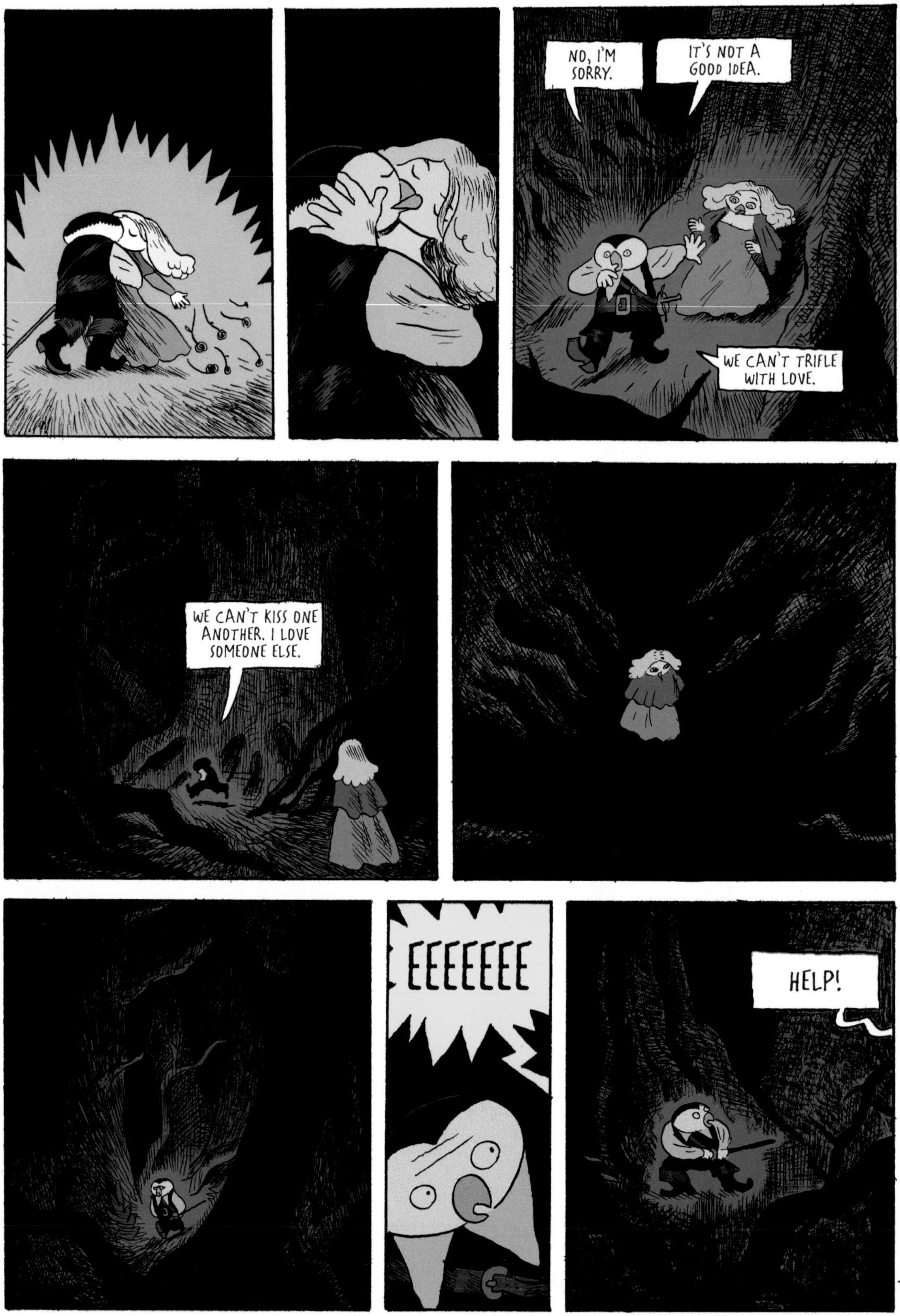
NO, I'M SORRY.
IT'S NOT A GOOD IDEA.
WE CAN'T TRIFLE WITH LOVE.
WE CAN'T KISS ONE ANOTHER. I LOVE SOMEONE ELSE.
EEEEEEE
HELP!

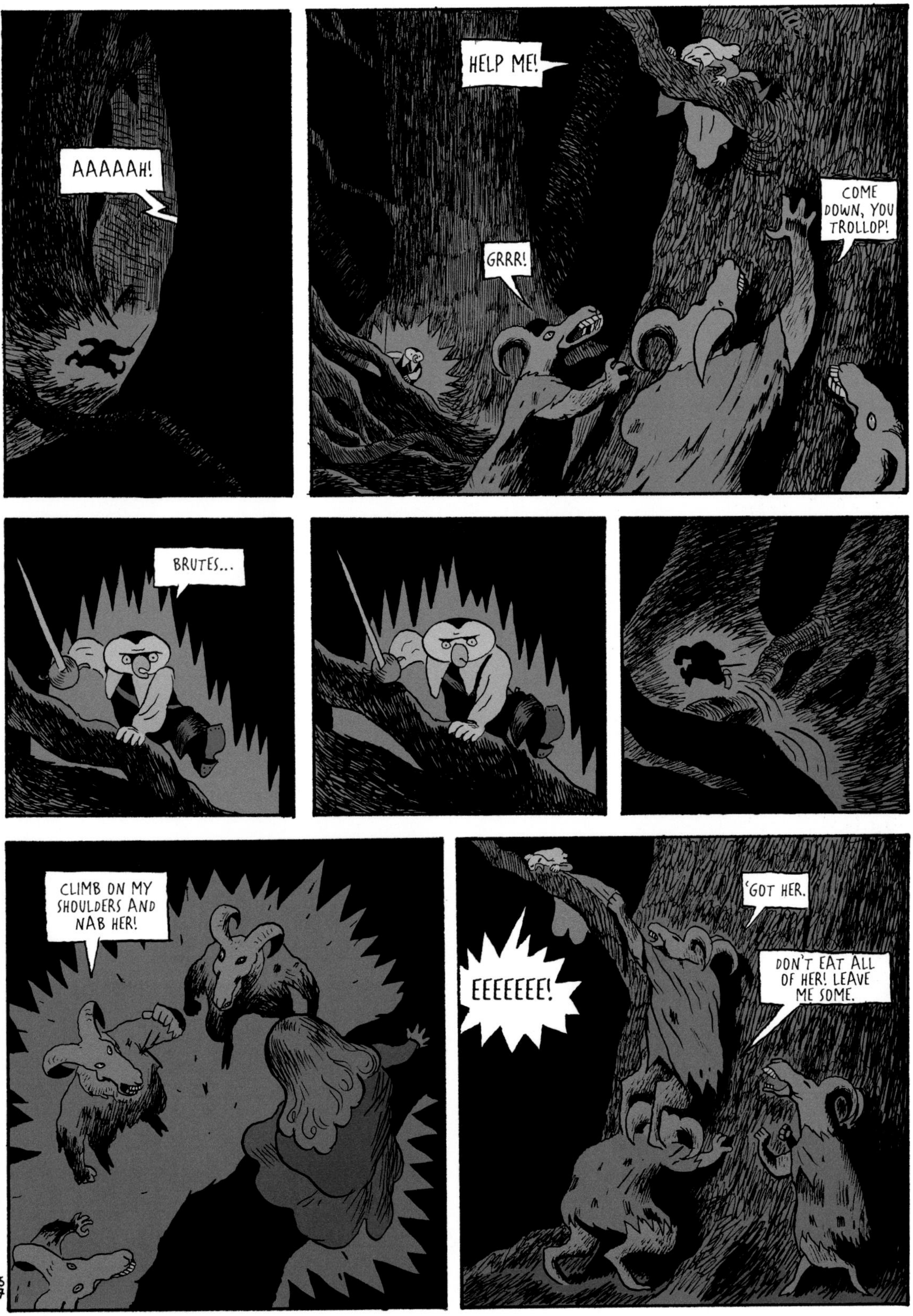
AAAAAH!
HELP ME!
GRRR!
COME DOWN, YOU TROLLOP!
BRUTES...
CLIMB ON MY SHOULDERS AND NAB HER!
EEEEEEE!
'GOT HER.
DON'T EAT ALL OF HER! LEAVE ME SOME.

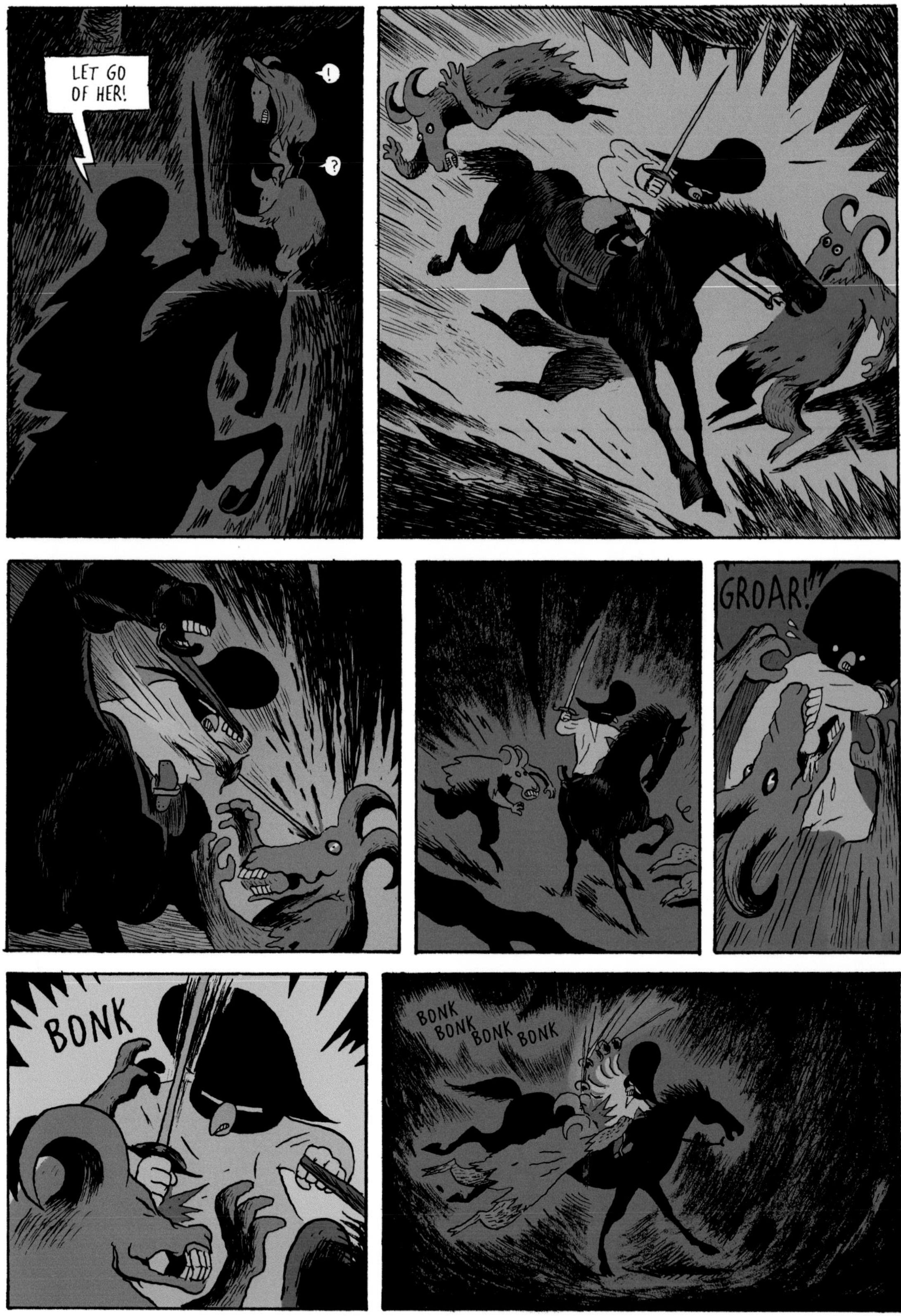
LET GO OF HER!
!
?
GROAR!
BONK
BONK
BONK
BONK
BONK

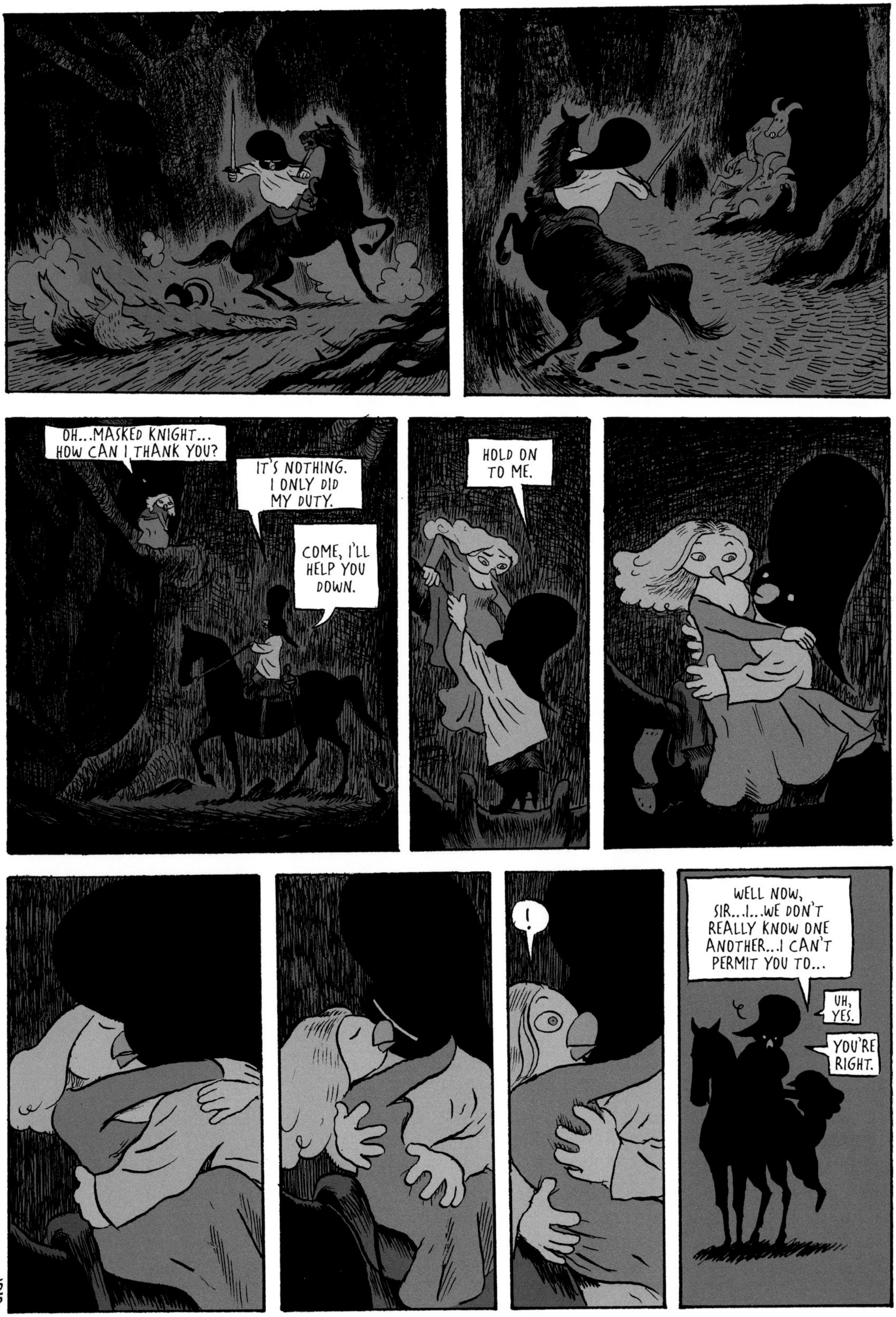
OH...MASKED KNIGHT... HOW CAN I THANK YOU?
IT'S NOTHING. I ONLY DID MY DUTY.
COME, I'LL HELP YOU DOWN.
HOLD ON TO ME.
!
WELL NOW, SIR...I...WE DON'T REALLY KNOW ONE ANOTHER...I CAN'T PERMIT YOU TO...
UH, YES.
YOU'RE RIGHT.

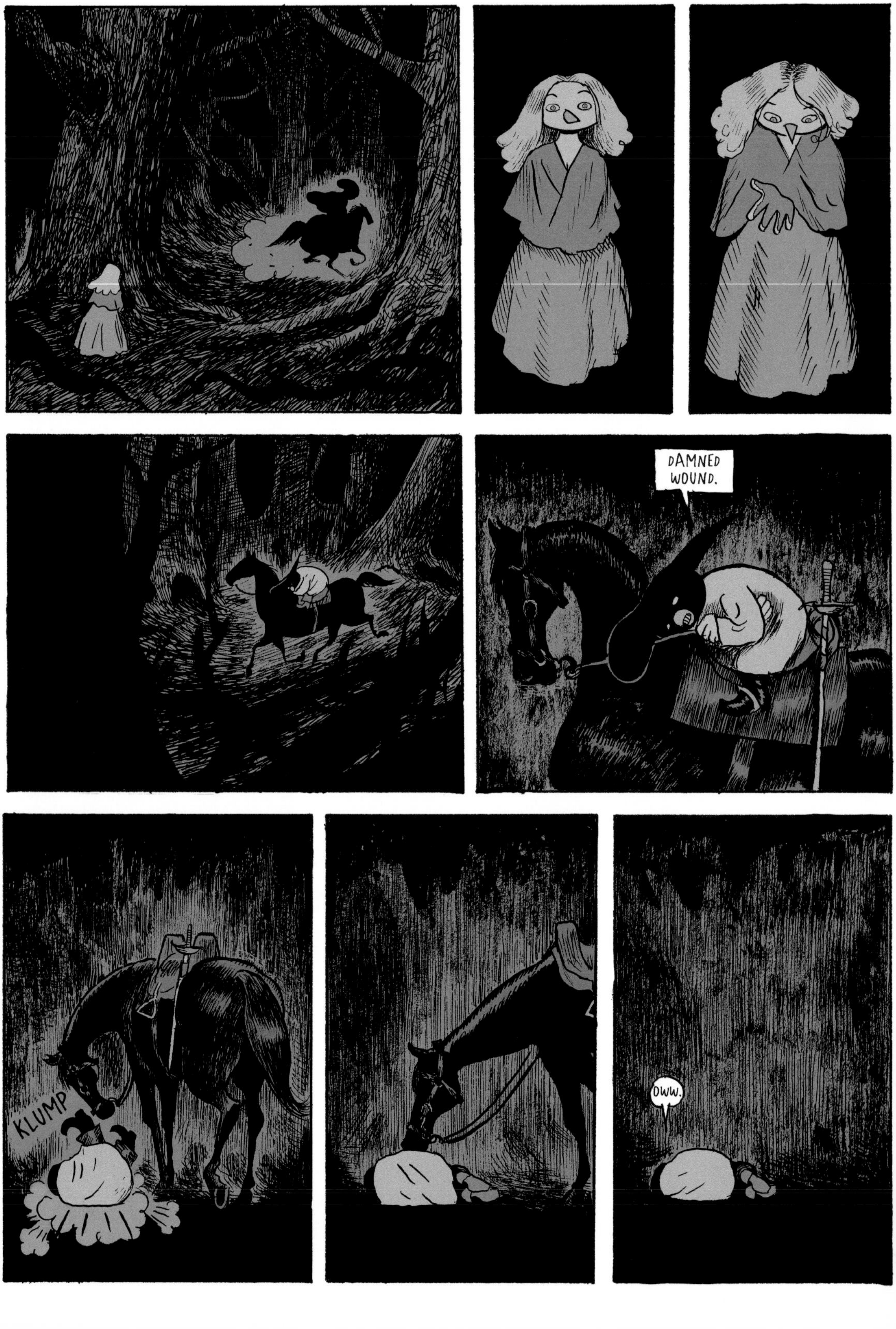
DAMNED WOUND.
KLUMP
OWW.

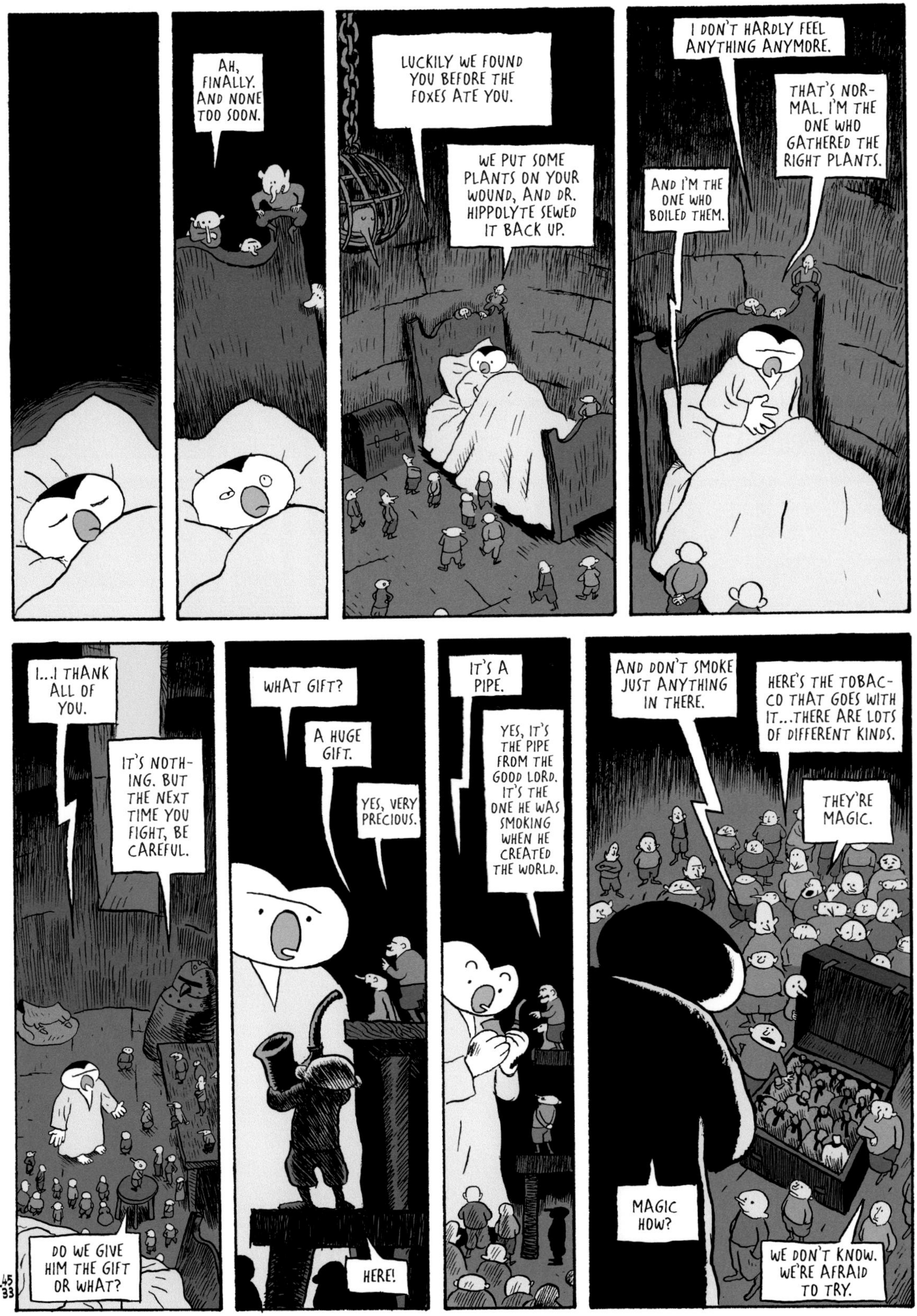
AH, FINALLY. AND NONE TOO SOON.
LUCKILY WE FOUND YOU BEFORE THE FOXES ATE YOU.
WE PUT SOME PLANTS ON YOUR WOUND, AND DR. HIPPOLYTE SEWED IT BACK UP.
I DON'T HARDLY FEEL ANYTHING ANYMORE.
THAT'S NOR-MAL. I'M THE ONE WHO GATHERED THE RIGHT PLANTS.
AND I'M THE ONE WHO BOILED THEM.
I...I THANK ALL OF YOU.
IT'S NOTH-ING. BUT THE NEXT TIME YOU FIGHT, BE CAREFUL.
DO WE GIVE HIM THE GIFT OR WHAT?
WHAT GIFT?
A HUGE GIFT.
YES, VERY PRECIOUS.
HERE!
IT'S A PIPE.
YES, IT'S THE PIPE FROM THE GOOD LORD. IT'S THE ONE HE WAS SMOKING WHEN HE CREATED THE WORLD.
AND DON'T SMOKE JUST ANYTHING IN THERE.
HERE'S THE TOBAC-CO THAT GOES WITH IT...THERE ARE LOTS OF DIFFERENT KINDS.
THEY'RE MAGIC.
MAGIC HOW?
WE DON'T KNOW. WE'RE AFRAID TO TRY.

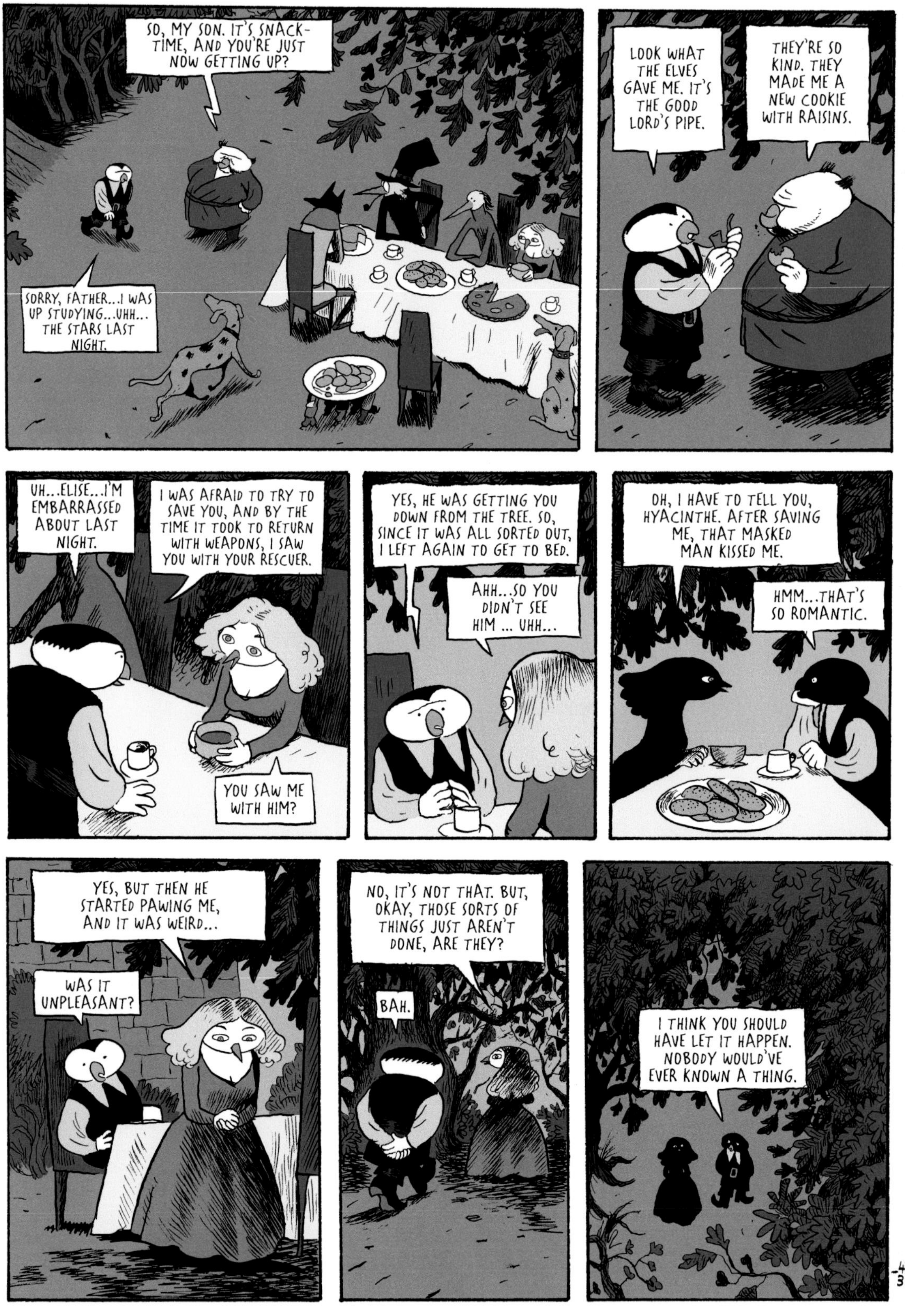
SO, MY SON. IT'S SNACK-TIME, AND YOU'RE JUST NOW GETTING UP?
SORRY, FATHER...I WAS UP STUDYING...UHH... THE STARS LAST NIGHT.
LOOK WHAT THE ELVES GAVE ME. IT'S THE GOOD LORD'S PIPE.
THEY'RE SO KIND. THEY MADE ME A NEW COOKIE WITH RAISINS.
UH...ELISE...I'M EMBARRASSED ABOUT LAST NIGHT.
I WAS AFRAID TO TRY TO SAVE YOU, AND BY THE TIME IT TOOK TO RETURN WITH WEAPONS, I SAW YOU WITH YOUR RESCUER.
YOU SAW ME WITH HIM?
YES, HE WAS GETTING YOU DOWN FROM THE TREE. SO, SINCE IT WAS ALL SORTED OUT, I LEFT AGAIN TO GET TO BED.
AHH...SO YOU DIDN'T SEE HIM ... UHH...
OH, I HAVE TO TELL YOU, HYACINTHE. AFTER SAVING ME, THAT MASKED MAN KISSED ME.
HMM...THAT'S SO ROMANTIC.
YES, BUT THEN HE STARTED PAWING ME, AND IT WAS WEIRD...
WAS IT UNPLEASANT?
NO, IT'S NOT THAT. BUT, OKAY, THOSE SORTS OF THINGS JUST AREN'T DONE, ARE THEY?
BAH.
I THINK YOU SHOULD HAVE LET IT HAPPEN. NOBODY WOULD'VE EVER KNOWN A THING.

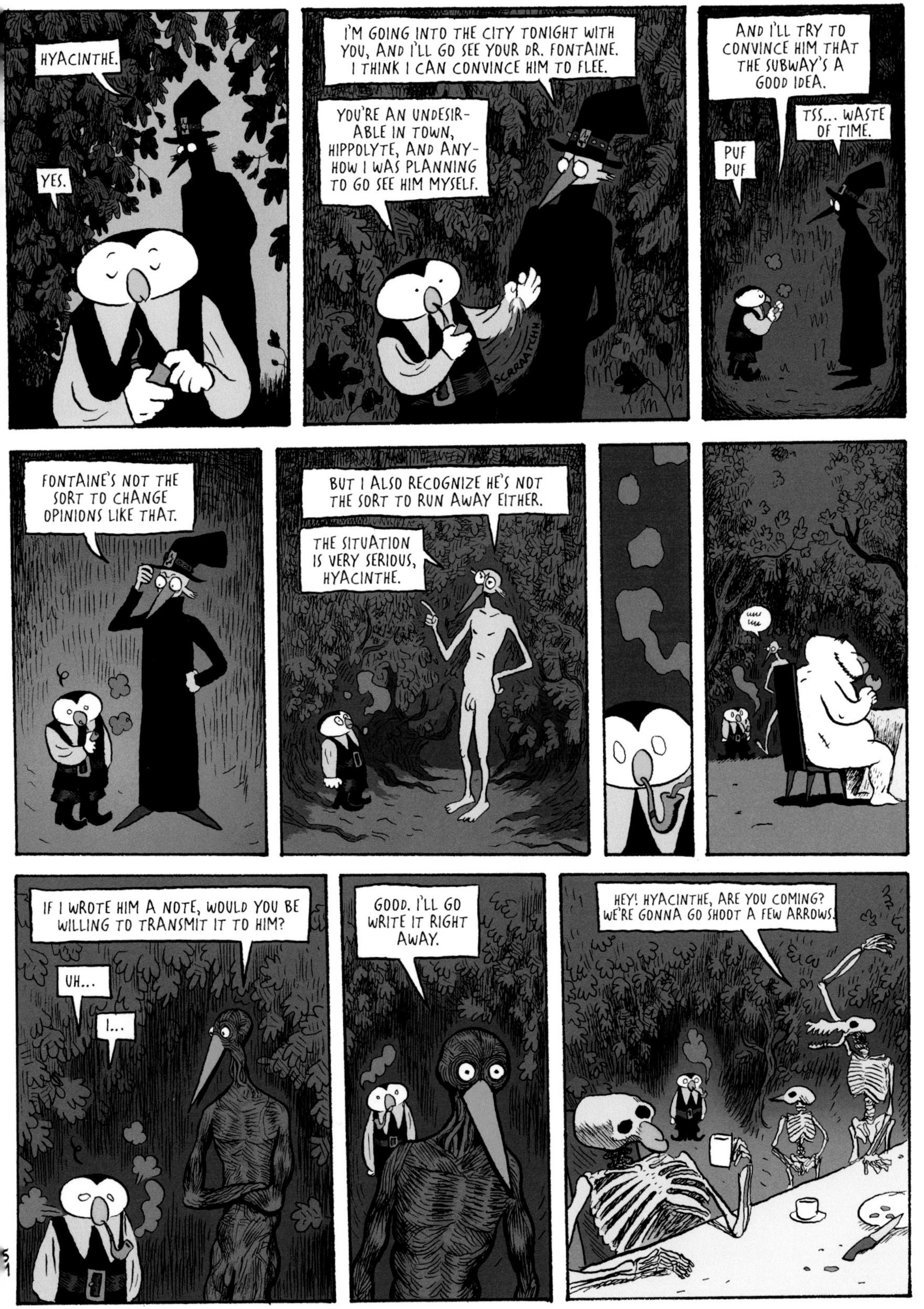
HYACINTHE.
YES.
I'M GOING INTO THE CITY TONIGHT WITH YOU, AND I'LL GO SEE YOUR DR. FONTAINE. I THINK I CAN CONVINCE HIM TO FLEE.
YOU'RE AN UNDESIRABLE IN TOWN, HIPPOLYTE, AND ANYHOW I WAS PLANNING TO GO SEE HIM MYSELF.
SCRRAATCHH
AND I'LL TRY TO CONVINCE HIM THAT THE SUBWAY'S A GOOD IDEA.
PUF PUF
TSS... WASTE OF TIME.
FONTAINE'S NOT THE SORT TO CHANGE OPINIONS LIKE THAT.
BUT I ALSO RECOGNIZE HE'S NOT THE SORT TO RUN AWAY EITHER.
THE SITUATION IS VERY SERIOUS, HYACINTHE.
IF I WROTE HIM A NOTE, WOULD YOU BE WILLING TO TRANSMIT IT TO HIM?
UH...
I...
GOOD. I'LL GO WRITE IT RIGHT AWAY.
HEY! HYACINTHE, ARE YOU COMING? WE'RE GONNA GO SHOOT A FEW ARROWS.

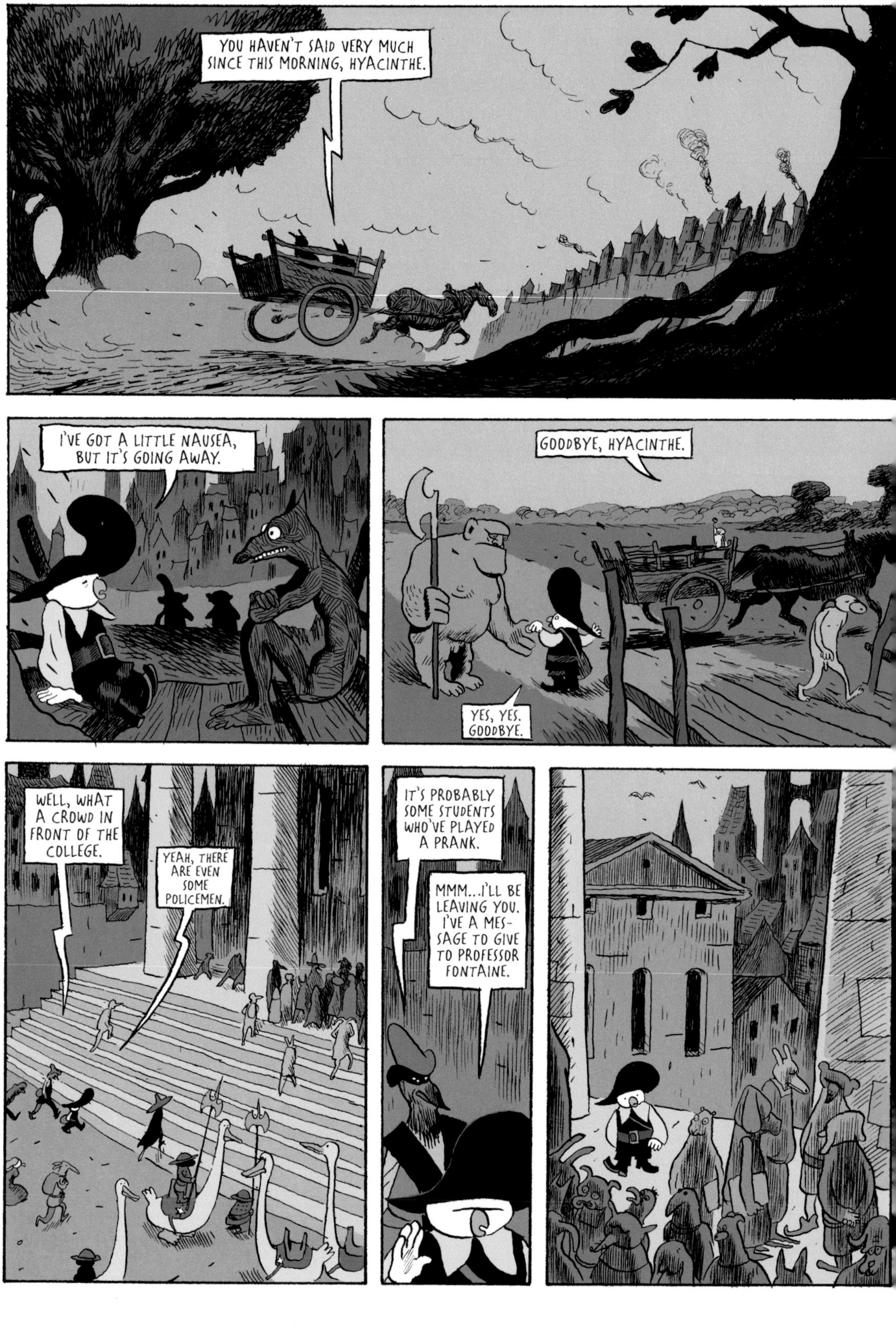
YOU HAVEN'T SAID VERY MUCH SINCE THIS MORNING, HYACINTHE.
I'VE GOT A LITTLE NAUSEA, BUT IT'S GOING AWAY.
GOODBYE, HYACINTHE.
YES, YES. GOODBYE.
WELL, WHAT A CROWD IN FRONT OF THE COLLEGE.
YEAH, THERE ARE EVEN SOME POLICEMEN.
IT'S PROBABLY SOME STUDENTS WHO'VE PLAYED A PRANK.
MMM...I'LL BE LEAVING YOU. I'VE A MES-SAGE TO GIVE TO PROFESSOR FONTAINE.

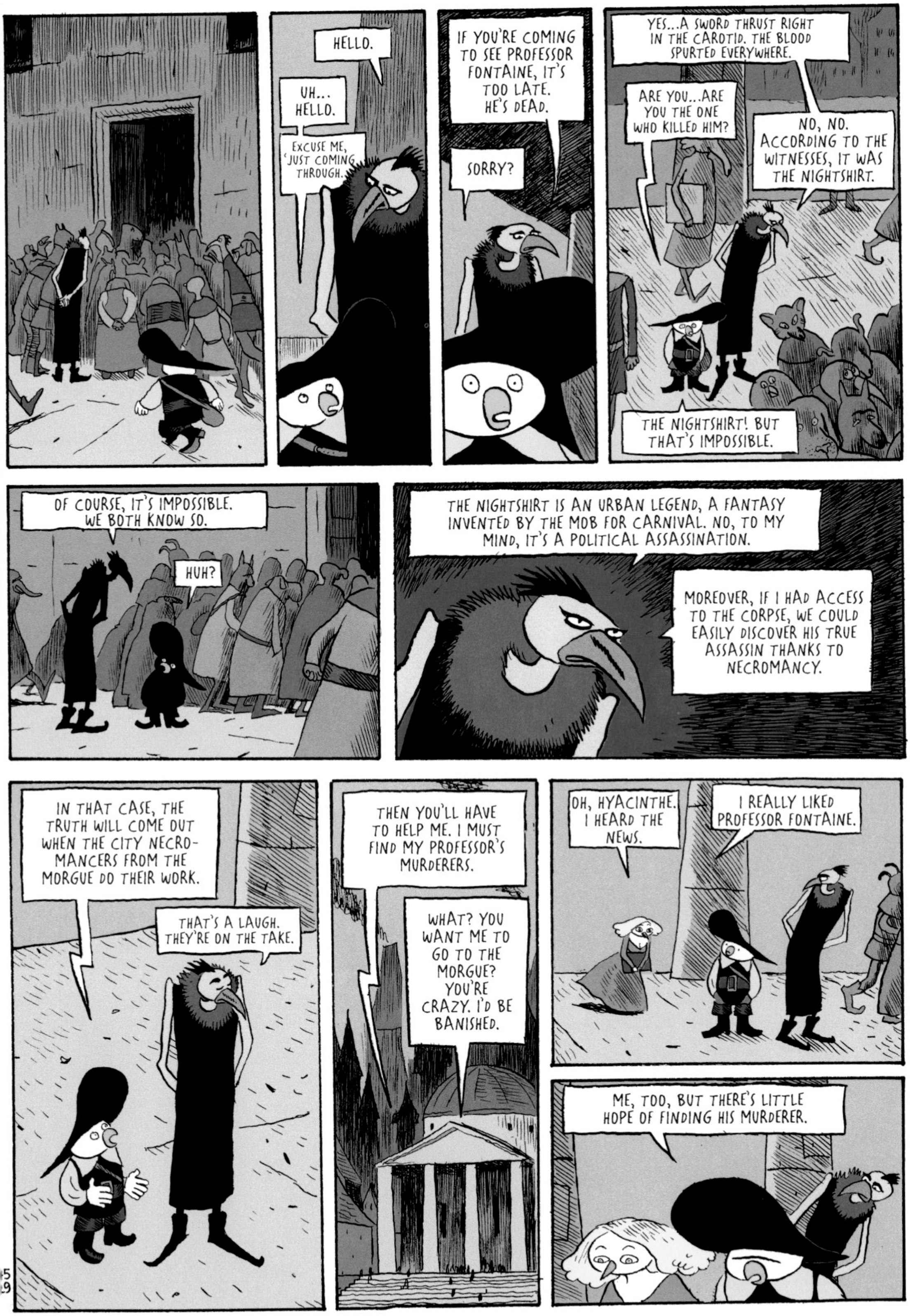
HELLO.
UH... HELLO.
EXCUSE ME, 'JUST COMING THROUGH.
IF YOU'RE COMING TO SEE PROFESSOR FONTAINE, IT'S TOO LATE. HE'S DEAD.
SORRY?
YES...A SWORD THRUST RIGHT IN THE CAROTID. THE BLOOD SPURTED EVERYWHERE.
ARE YOU...ARE YOU THE ONE WHO KILLED HIM?
NO, NO. ACCORDING TO THE WITNESSES, IT WAS THE NIGHTSHIRT.
THE NIGHTSHIRT! BUT THAT'S IMPOSSIBLE.
OF COURSE, IT'S IMPOSSIBLE. WE BOTH KNOW SO.
HUH?
THE NIGHTSHIRT IS AN URBAN LEGEND, A FANTASY INVENTED BY THE MOB FOR CARNIVAL. NO, TO MY MIND, IT'S A POLITICAL ASSASSINATION.
MOREOVER, IF I HAD ACCESS TO THE CORPSE, WE COULD EASILY DISCOVER HIS TRUE ASSASSIN THANKS TO NECROMANCY.
IN THAT CASE, THE TRUTH WILL COME OUT WHEN THE CITY NECRO-MANCERS FROM THE MORGUE DO THEIR WORK.
THAT'S A LAUGH. THEY'RE ON THE TAKE.
THEN YOU'LL HAVE TO HELP ME. I MUST FIND MY PROFESSOR'S MURDERERS.
WHAT? YOU WANT ME TO GO TO THE MORGUE? YOU'RE CRAZY. I'D BE BANISHED.
OH, HYACINTHE. I HEARD THE NEWS.
I REALLY LIKED PROFESSOR FONTAINE.
ME, TOO, BUT THERE'S LITTLE HOPE OF FINDING HIS MURDERER.

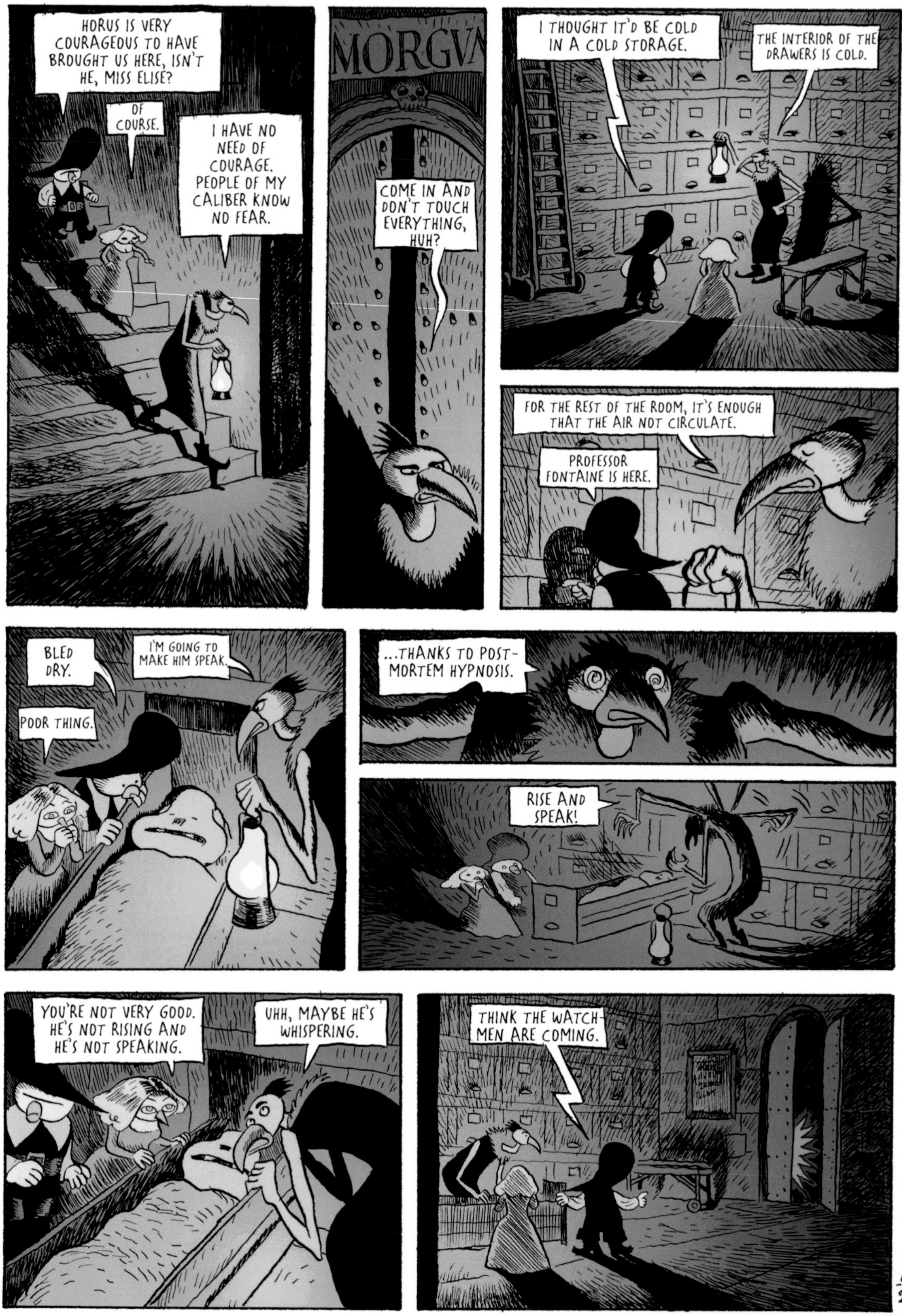
HORUS IS VERY COURAGEOUS TO HAVE BROUGHT US HERE, ISN'T HE, MISS ELISE?
OF COURSE.
I HAVE NO NEED OF COURAGE. PEOPLE OF MY CALIBER KNOW NO FEAR.
MORGV
COME IN AND DON'T TOUCH EVERYTHING, HUH?
I THOUGHT IT'D BE COLD IN A COLD STORAGE.
THE INTERIOR OF THE DRAWERS IS COLD.
FOR THE REST OF THE ROOM, IT'S ENOUGH THAT THE AIR NOT CIRCULATE.
PROFESSOR FONTAINE IS HERE.
BLED DRY.
I'M GOING TO MAKE HIM SPEAK.
POOR THING.
...THANKS TO POST-MORTEM HYPNOSIS.
RISE AND SPEAK!
YOU'RE NOT VERY GOOD. HE'S NOT RISING AND HE'S NOT SPEAKING.
UHH, MAYBE HE'S WHISPERING.
THINK THE WATCH-MEN ARE COMING.

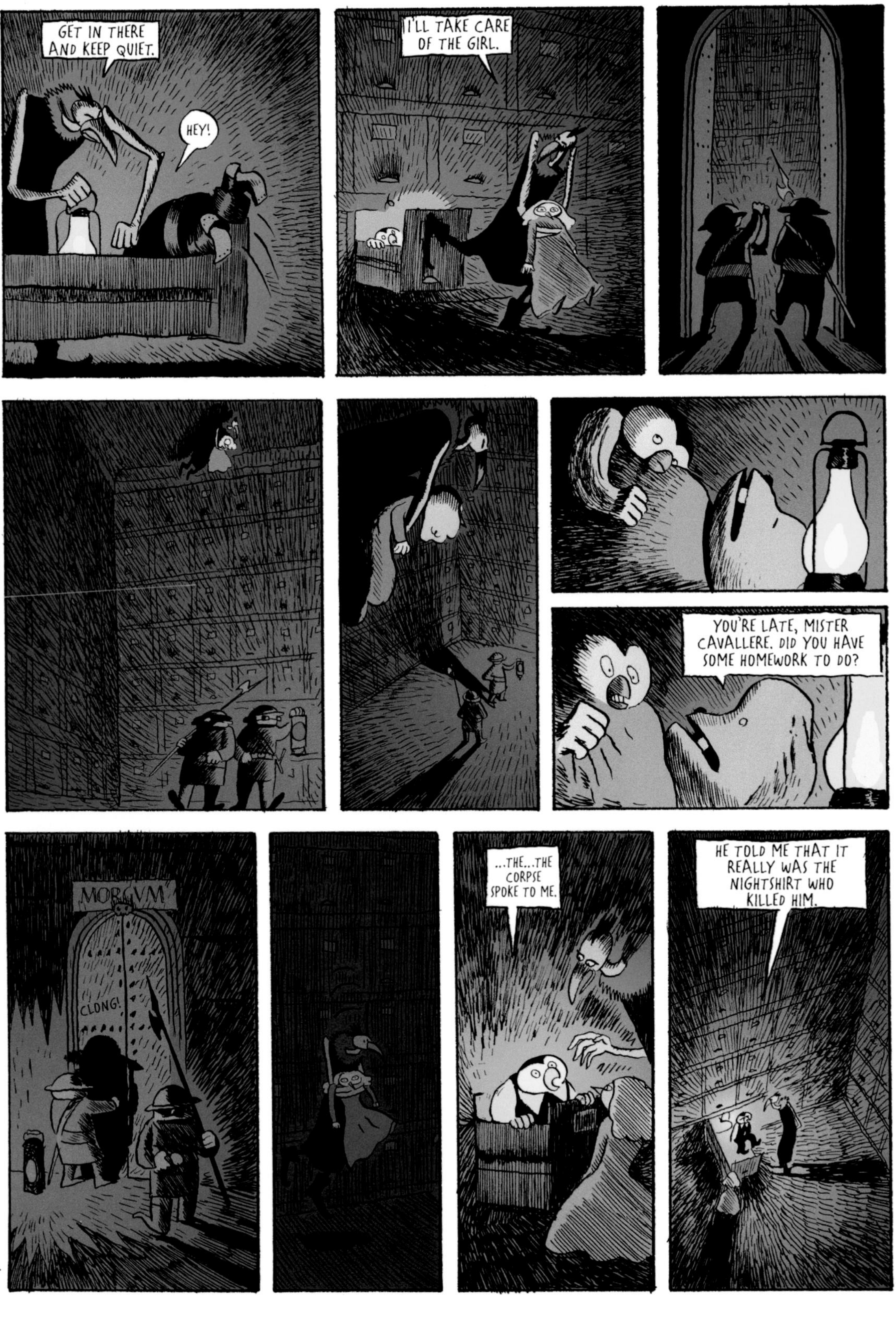
GET IN THERE AND KEEP QUIET.
HEY!
I'LL TAKE CARE OF THE GIRL.
YOU'RE LATE, MISTER CAVALLERE. DID YOU HAVE SOME HOMEWORK TO DO?
MORGVM
CLONG!
...THE...THE CORPSE SPOKE TO ME.
HE TOLD ME THAT IT REALLY WAS THE NIGHTSHIRT WHO KILLED HIM.

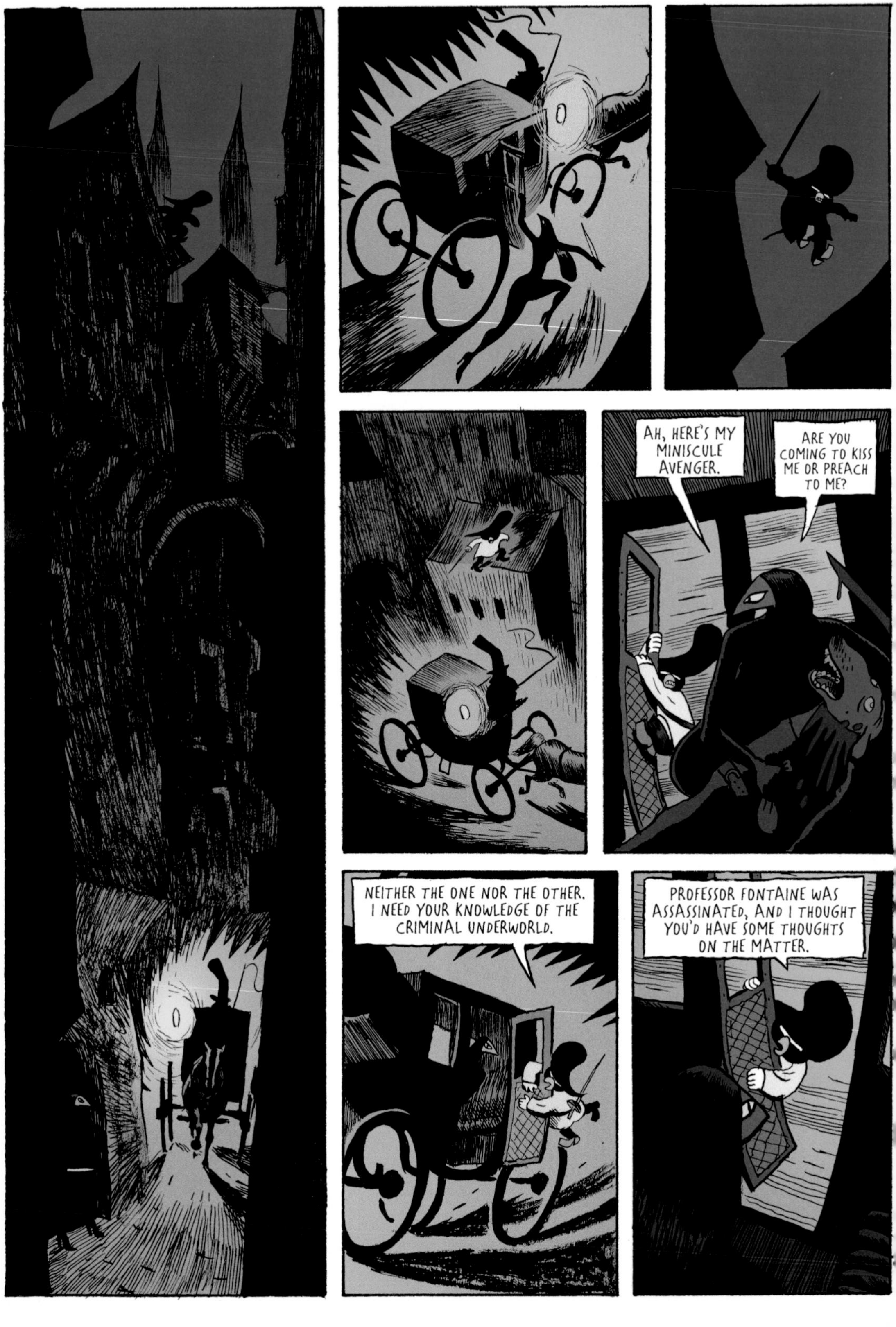
AH, HERE'S MY MINISCULE AVENGER.
ARE YOU COMING TO KISS ME OR PREACH TO ME?
NEITHER THE ONE NOR THE OTHER. I NEED YOUR KNOWLEDGE OF THE CRIMINAL UNDERWORLD.
PROFESSOR FONTAINE WAS ASSASSINATED, AND I THOUGHT YOU'D HAVE SOME THOUGHTS ON THE MATTER.

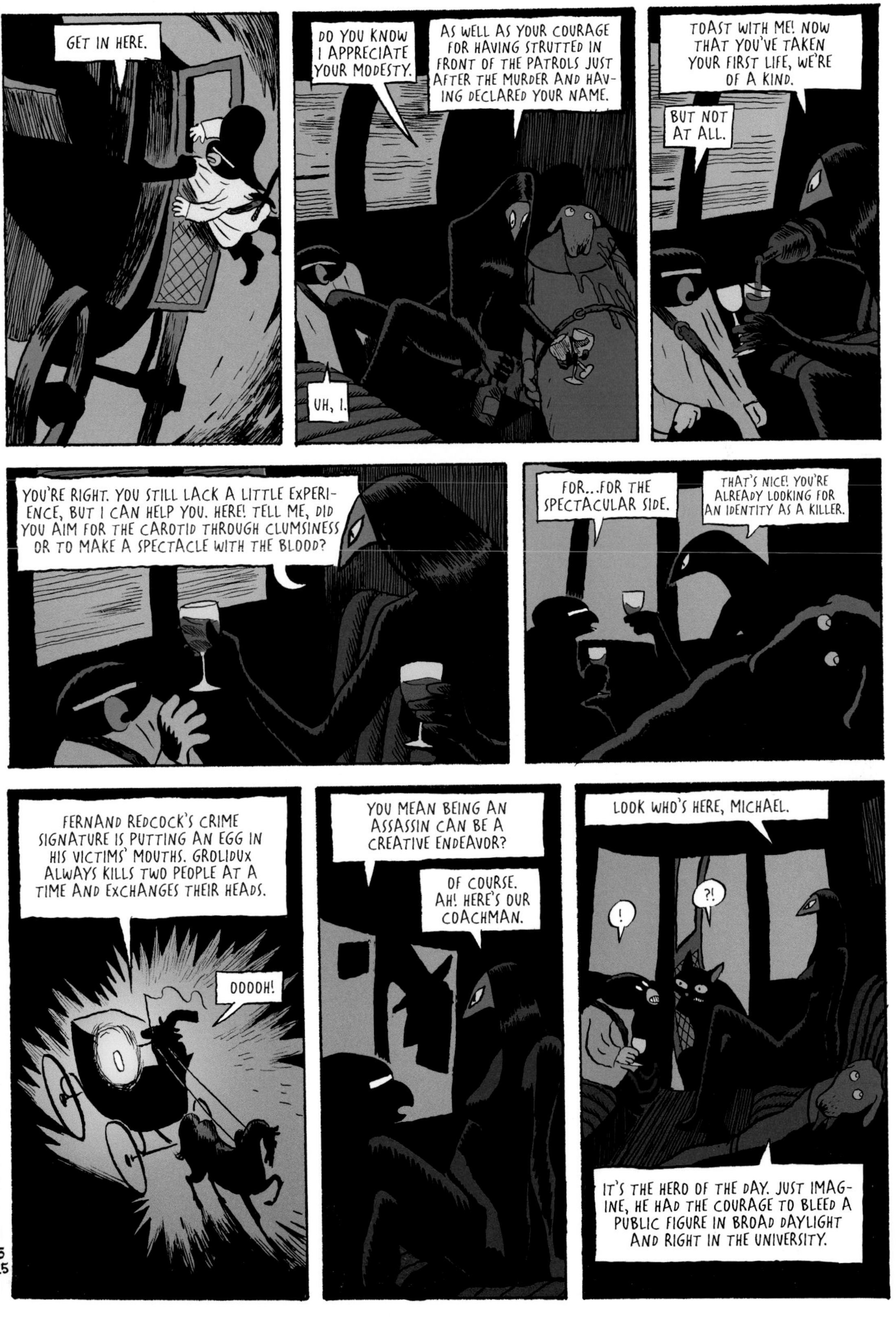
GET IN HERE.
DO YOU KNOW I APPRECIATE YOUR MODESTY.
AS WELL AS YOUR COURAGE FOR HAVING STRUTTED IN FRONT OF THE PATROLS JUST AFTER THE MURDER AND HAVING DECLARED YOUR NAME.
UH, I.
TOAST WITH ME! NOW THAT YOU'VE TAKEN YOUR FIRST LIFE, WE'RE OF A KIND.
BUT NOT AT ALL.
YOU'RE RIGHT. YOU STILL LACK A LITTLE EXPERIENCE, BUT I CAN HELP YOU. HERE! TELL ME, DID YOU AIM FOR THE CAROTID THROUGH CLUMSINESS OR TO MAKE A SPECTACLE WITH THE BLOOD?
FOR...FOR THE SPECTACULAR SIDE.
THAT'S NICE! YOU'RE ALREADY LOOKING FOR AN IDENTITY AS A KILLER.
FERNAND REDCOCK'S CRIME SIGNATURE IS PUTTING AN EGG IN HIS VICTIMS' MOUTHS. GROLIDUX ALWAYS KILLS TWO PEOPLE AT A TIME AND EXCHANGES THEIR HEADS.
OOOOH!
YOU MEAN BEING AN ASSASSIN CAN BE A CREATIVE ENDEAVOR?
OF COURSE. AH! HERE'S OUR COACHMAN.
LOOK WHO'S HERE, MICHAEL.
!
?!
IT'S THE HERO OF THE DAY. JUST IMAGINE, HE HAD THE COURAGE TO BLEED A PUBLIC FIGURE IN BROAD DAYLIGHT AND RIGHT IN THE UNIVERSITY.

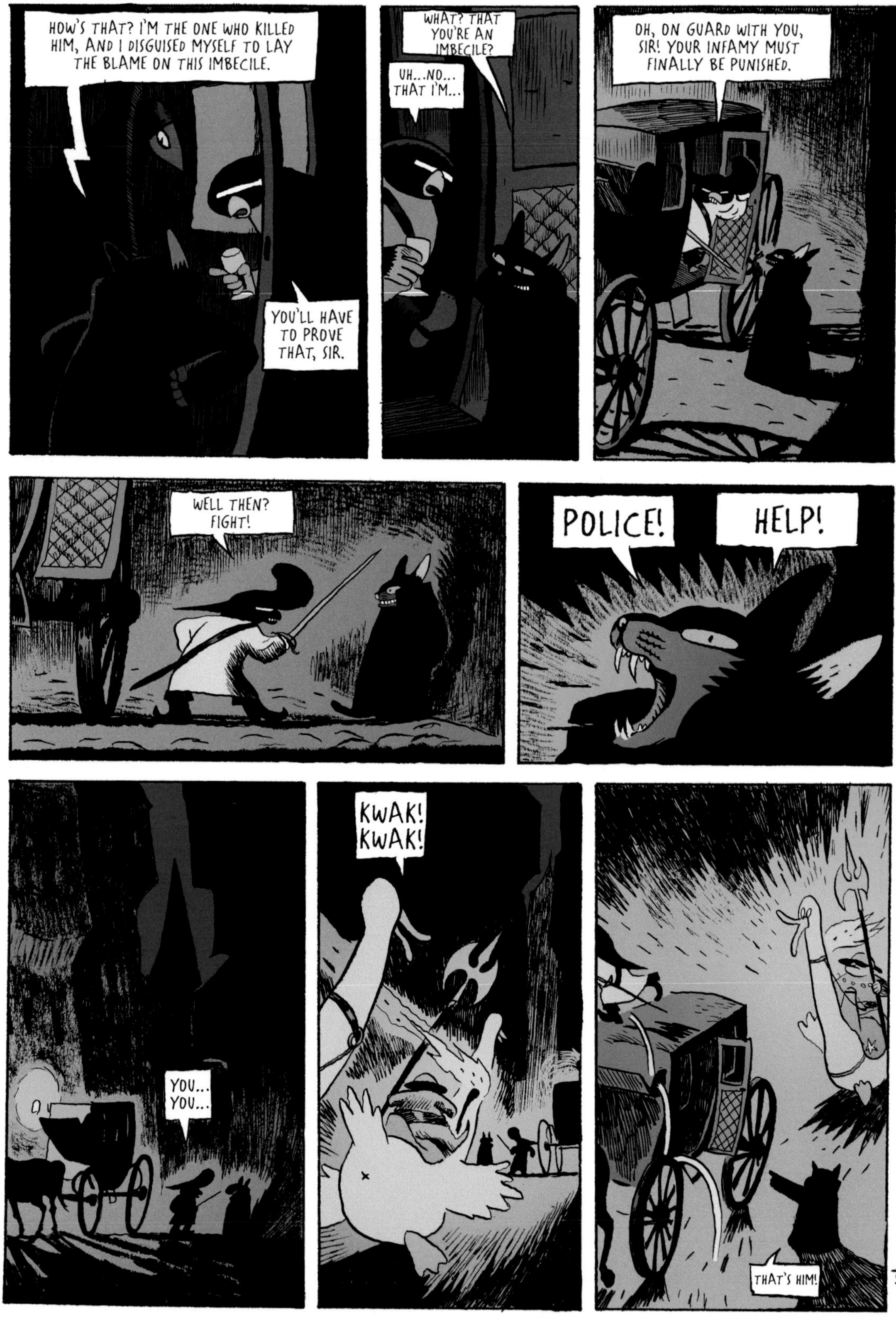
HOW'S THAT? I'M THE ONE WHO KILLED HIM, AND I DISGUISED MYSELF TO LAY THE BLAME ON THIS IMBECILE.
YOU'LL HAVE TO PROVE THAT, SIR.
WHAT? THAT YOU'RE AN IMBECILE?
UH...NO... THAT I'M...
OH, ON GUARD WITH YOU, SIR! YOUR INFAMY MUST FINALLY BE PUNISHED.
WELL THEN? FIGHT!
POLICE!
HELP!
YOU... YOU...
KWAK! KWAK!
THAT'S HIM!

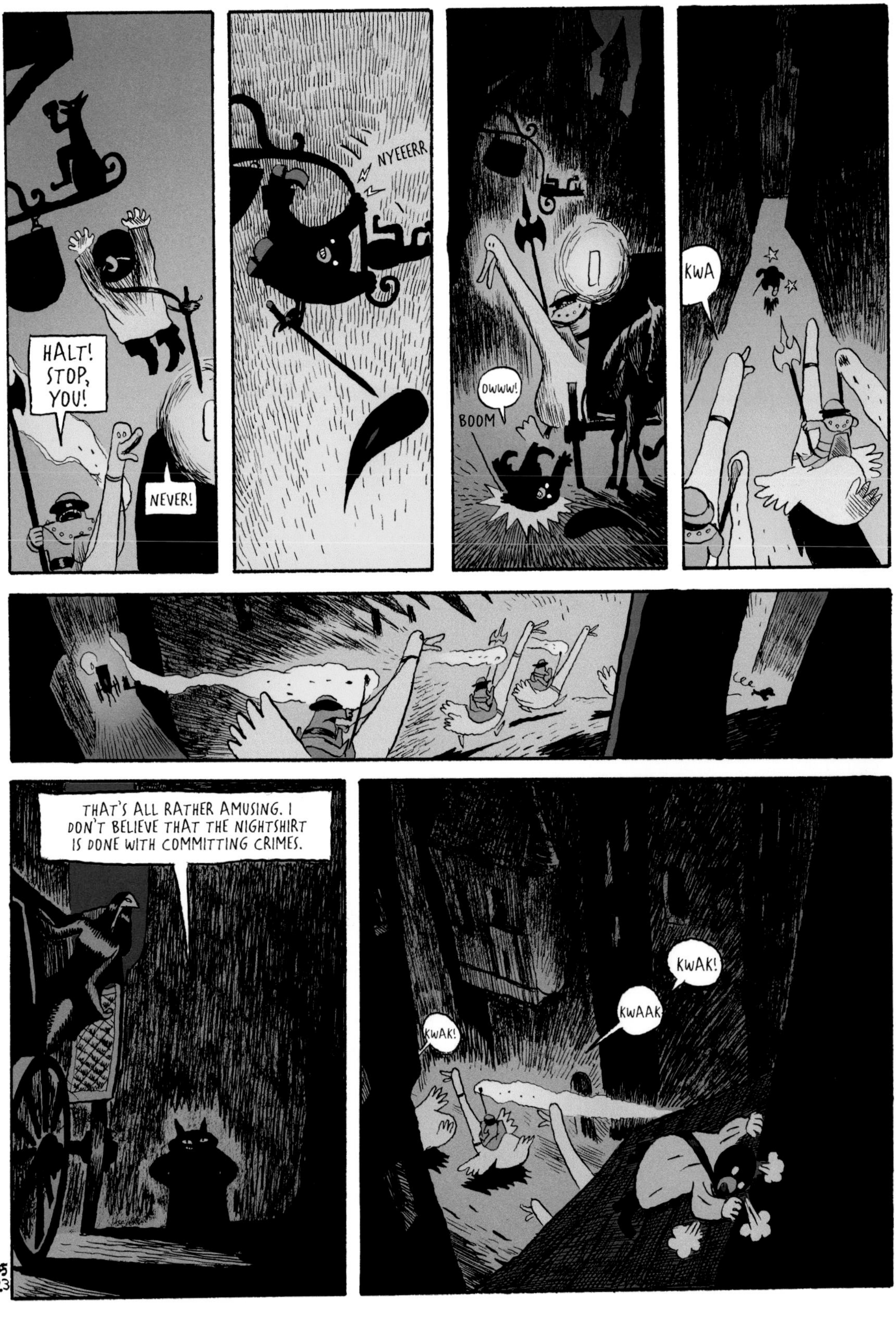

HALT! STOP, YOU!
NEVER!
NYEEERR
OWWW!
BOOM
KWA
THAT'S ALL RATHER AMUSING. I DON'T BELIEVE THAT THE NIGHTSHIRT IS DONE WITH COMMITTING CRIMES.
KWAK!
KWAAK
KWAK!

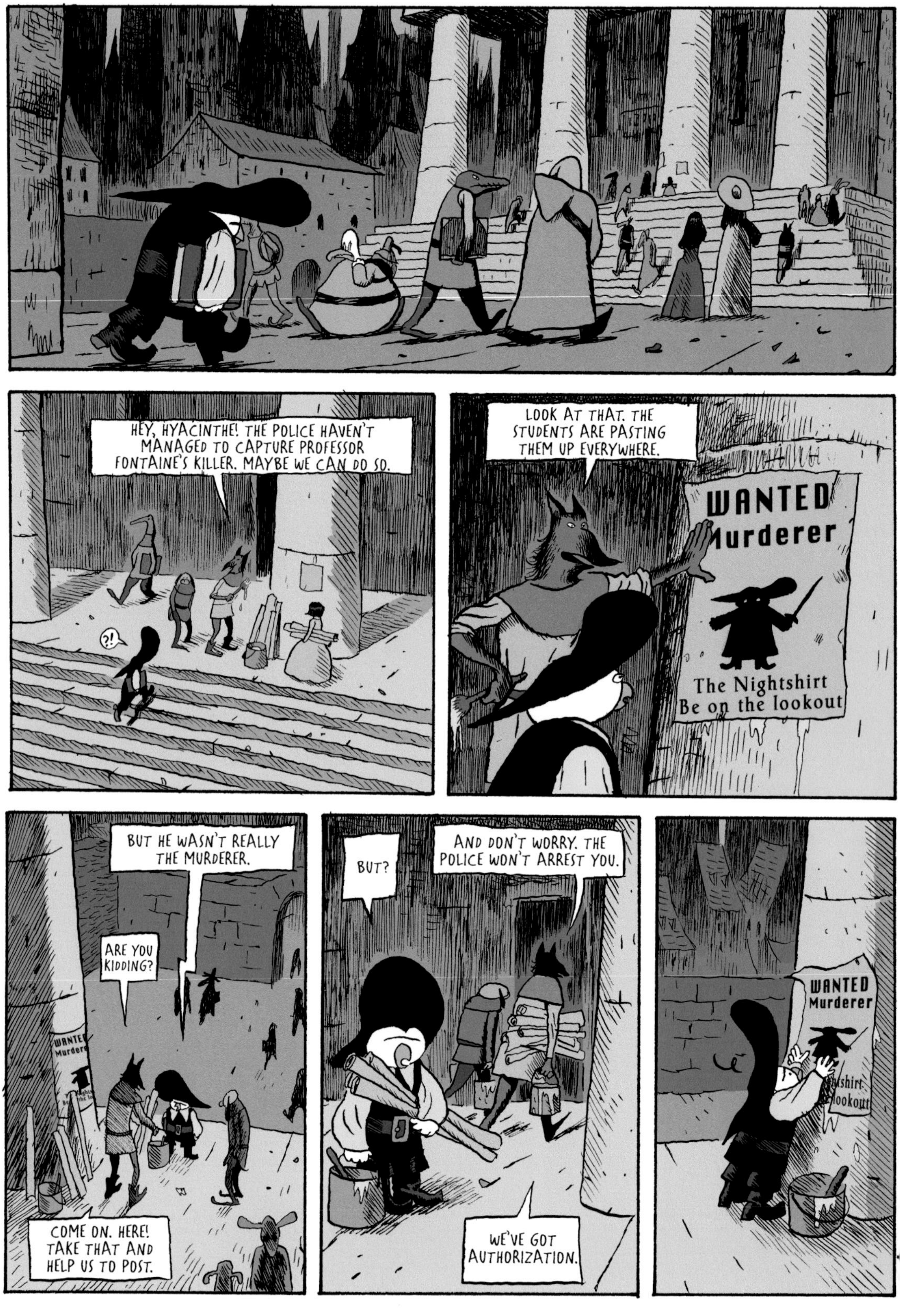
HEY, HYACINTHE! THE POLICE HAVEN'T MANAGED TO CAPTURE PROFESSOR FONTAINE'S KILLER. MAYBE WE CAN DO SO.
?!
LOOK AT THAT. THE STUDENTS ARE PASTING THEM UP EVERYWHERE.
WANTED
Murderer
The Nightshirt
Be on the lookout
BUT HE WASN'T REALLY THE MURDERER.
ARE YOU KIDDING?
COME ON. HERE! TAKE THAT AND HELP US TO POST.
BUT?
AND DON'T WORRY. THE POLICE WON'T ARREST YOU.
WE'VE GOT AUTHORIZATION.
WANTED
Murderer

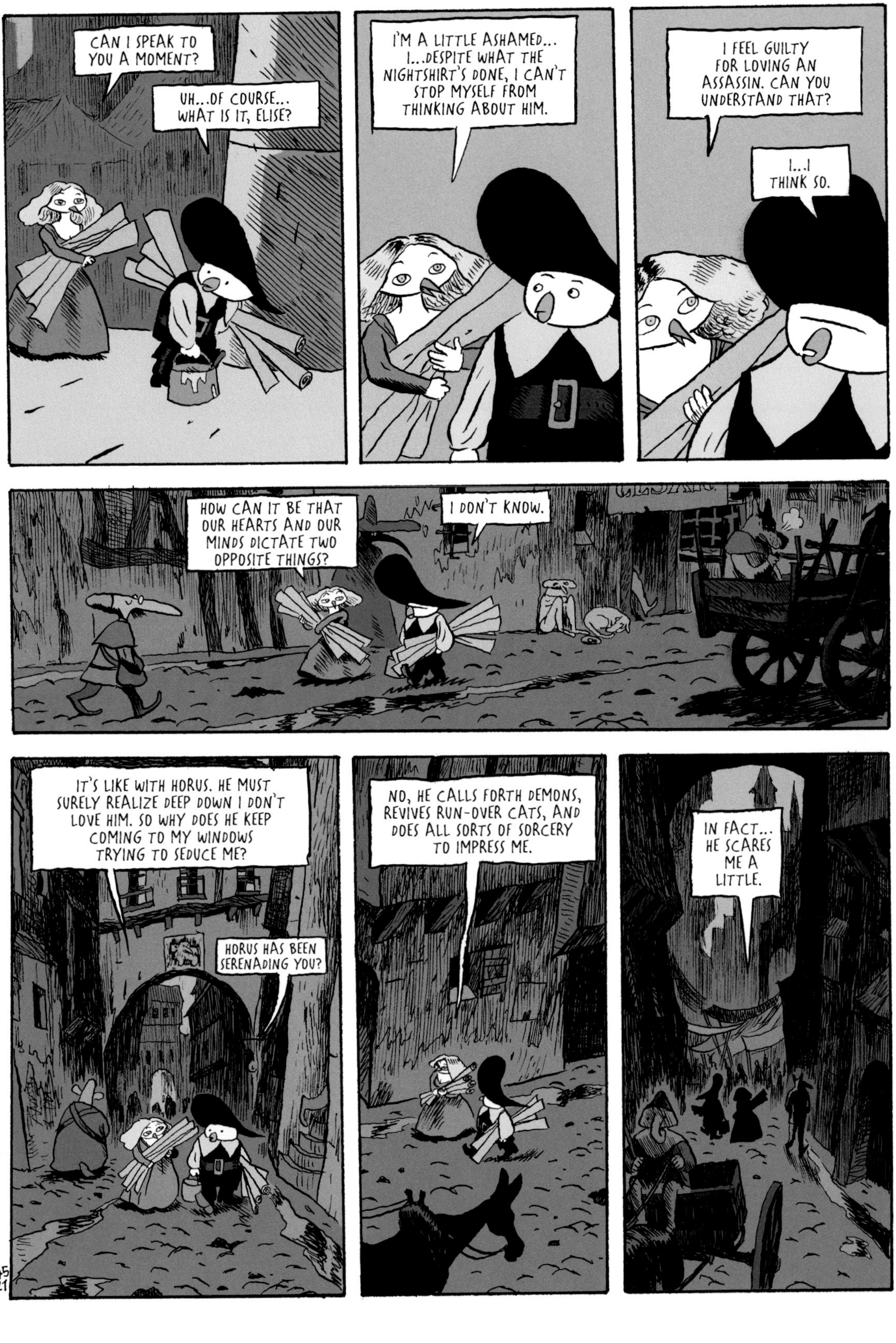
CAN I SPEAK TO YOU A MOMENT?
UH...OF COURSE... WHAT IS IT, ELISE?
I'M A LITTLE ASHAMED... I...DESPITE WHAT THE NIGHTSHIRT'S DONE, I CAN'T STOP MYSELF FROM THINKING ABOUT HIM.
I FEEL GUILTY FOR LOVING AN ASSASSIN. CAN YOU UNDERSTAND THAT?
I...I THINK SO.
HOW CAN IT BE THAT OUR HEARTS AND OUR MINDS DICTATE TWO OPPOSITE THINGS?
I DON'T KNOW.
IT'S LIKE WITH HORUS. HE MUST SURELY REALIZE DEEP DOWN I DON'T LOVE HIM. SO WHY DOES HE KEEP COMING TO MY WINDOWS TRYING TO SEDUCE ME?
HORUS HAS BEEN SERENADING YOU?
NO, HE CALLS FORTH DEMONS, REVIVES RUN-OVER CATS, AND DOES ALL SORTS OF SORCERY TO IMPRESS ME.
IN FACT... HE SCARES ME A LITTLE.

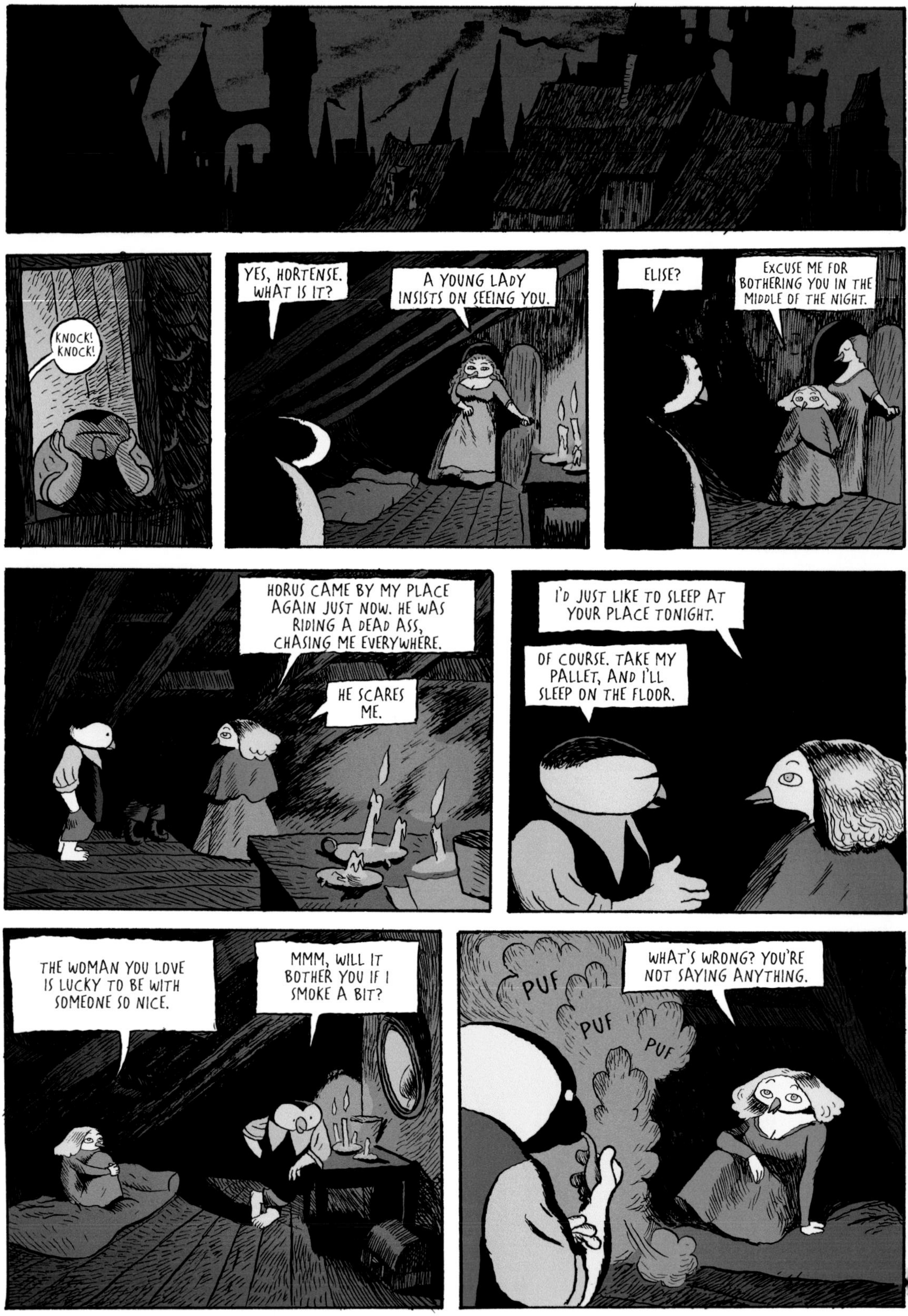
KNOCK! KNOCK!
YES, HORTENSE. WHAT IS IT?
A YOUNG LADY INSISTS ON SEEING YOU.
ELISE?
EXCUSE ME FOR BOTHERING YOU IN THE MIDDLE OF THE NIGHT.
HORUS CAME BY MY PLACE AGAIN JUST NOW. HE WAS RIDING A DEAD ASS, CHASING ME EVERYWHERE.
HE SCARES ME.
I'D JUST LIKE TO SLEEP AT YOUR PLACE TONIGHT.
OF COURSE. TAKE MY PALLET, AND I'LL SLEEP ON THE FLOOR.
THE WOMAN YOU LOVE IS LUCKY TO BE WITH SOMEONE SO NICE.
MMM, WILL IT BOTHER YOU IF I SMOKE A BIT?
PUF
PUF
PUF
WHAT'S WRONG? YOU'RE NOT SAYING ANYTHING.

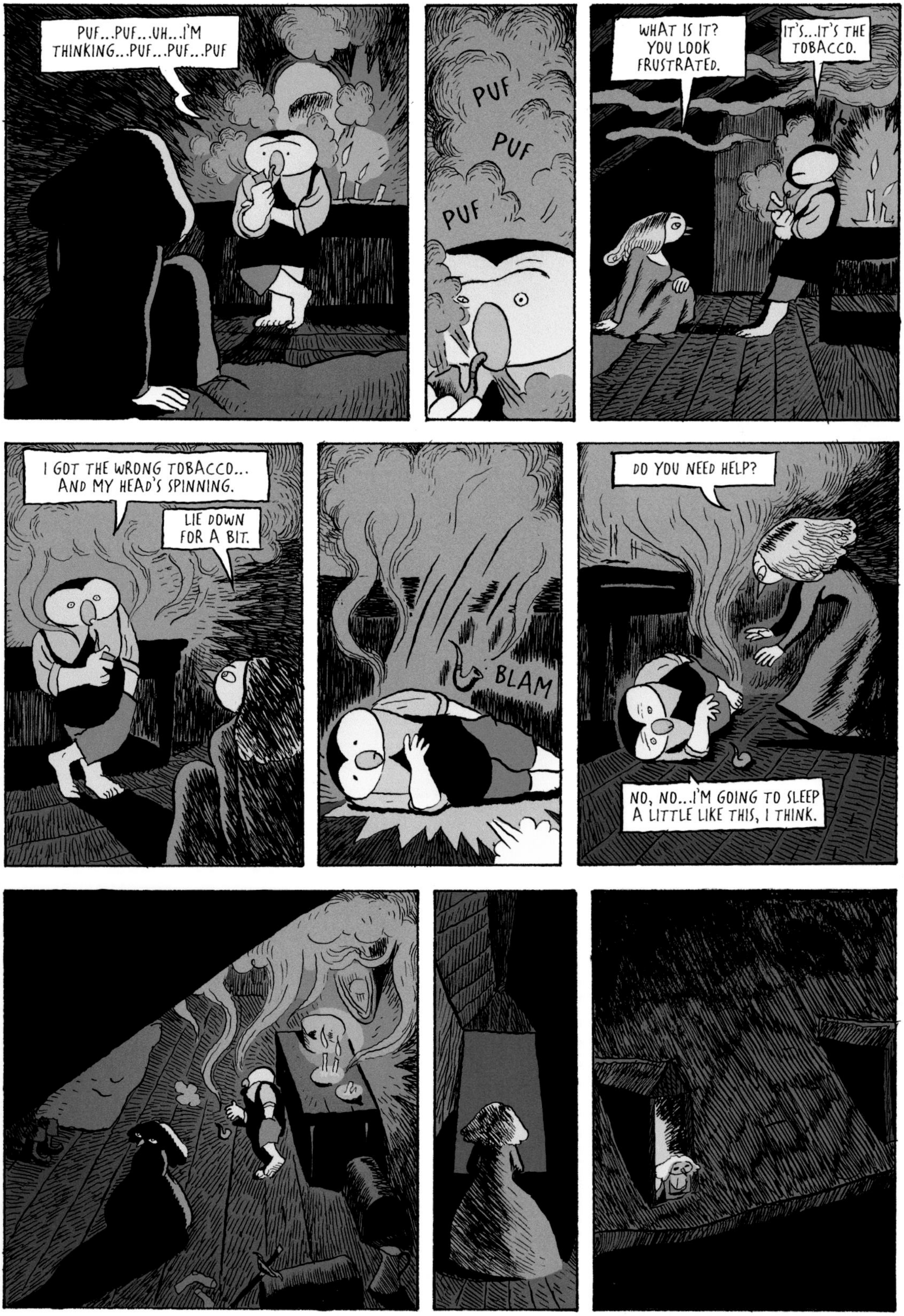
PUF...PUF...UH...I'M THINKING...PUF...PUF...PUF
PUF
PUF
PUF
WHAT IS IT? YOU LOOK FRUSTRATED.
IT'S...IT'S THE TOBACCO.
I GOT THE WRONG TOBACCO... AND MY HEAD'S SPINNING.
LIE DOWN FOR A BIT.
BLAM
DO YOU NEED HELP?
NO, NO...I'M GOING TO SLEEP A LITTLE LIKE THIS, I THINK.

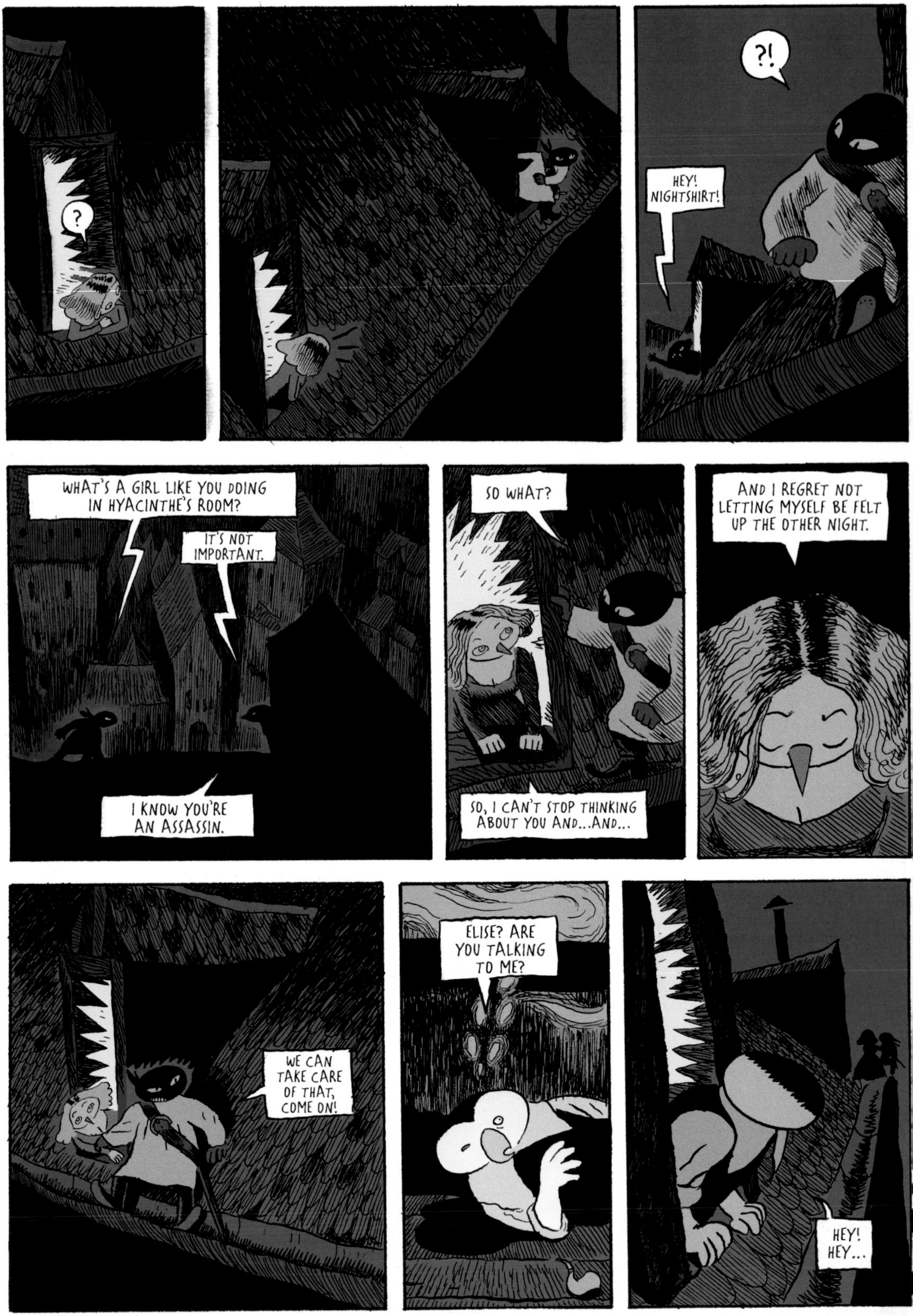
?
?!
HEY! NIGHTSHIRT!
WHAT'S A GIRL LIKE YOU DOING IN HYACINTHE'S ROOM?
IT'S NOT IMPORTANT.
I KNOW YOU'RE AN ASSASSIN.
SO WHAT?
SO, I CAN'T STOP THINKING ABOUT YOU AND...AND...
AND I REGRET NOT LETTING MYSELF BE FELT UP THE OTHER NIGHT.
WE CAN TAKE CARE OF THAT, COME ON!
ELISE? ARE YOU TALKING TO ME?
HEY! HEY...

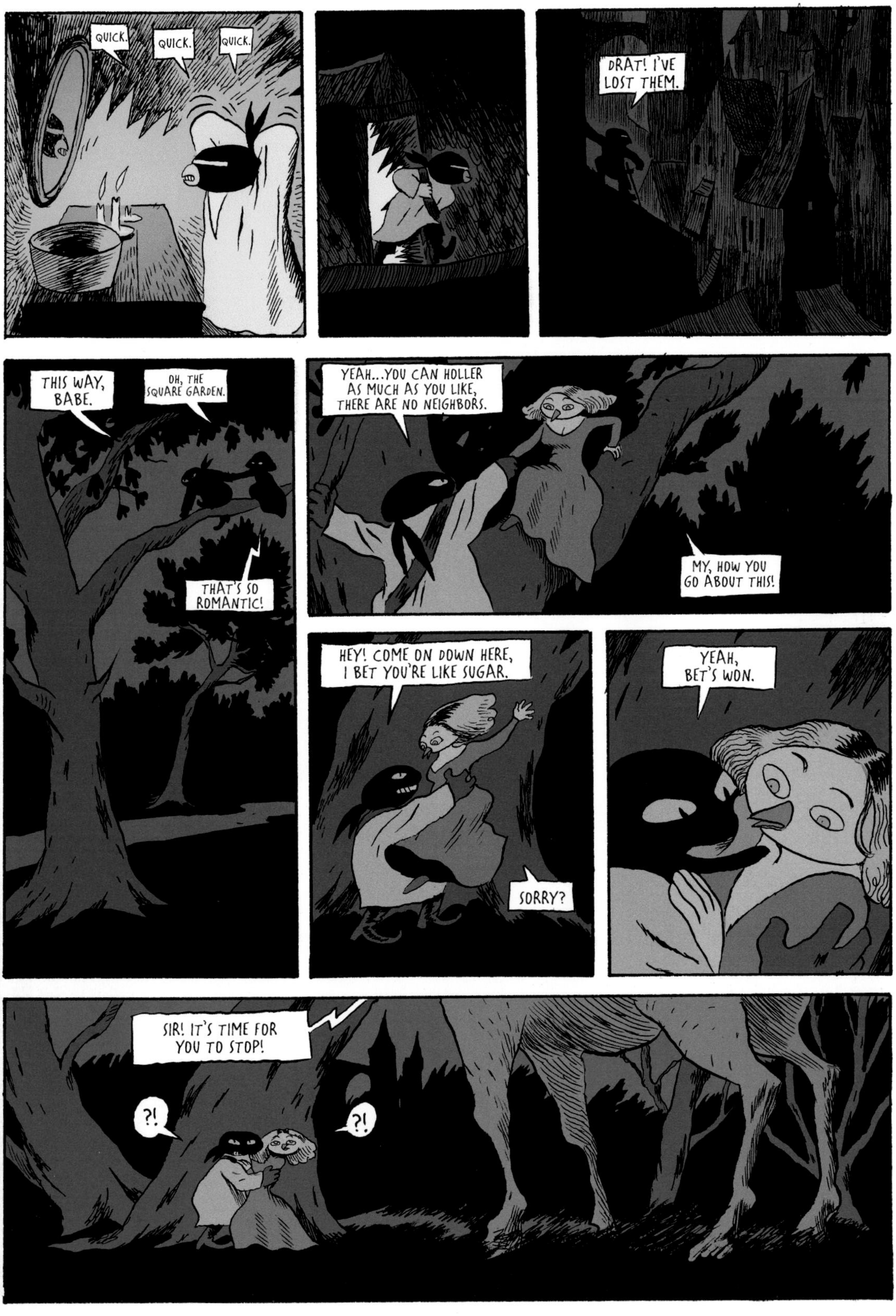
QUICK.
QUICK.
QUICK.
DRAT! I'VE LOST THEM.
THIS WAY, BABE.
OH, THE SQUARE GARDEN.
THAT'S SO ROMANTIC!
YEAH...YOU CAN HOLLER AS MUCH AS YOU LIKE, THERE ARE NO NEIGHBORS.
MY, HOW YOU GO ABOUT THIS!
HEY! COME ON DOWN HERE, I BET YOU'RE LIKE SUGAR.
SORRY?
YEAH, BET'S WON.
SIR! IT'S TIME FOR YOU TO STOP!
?!
?!

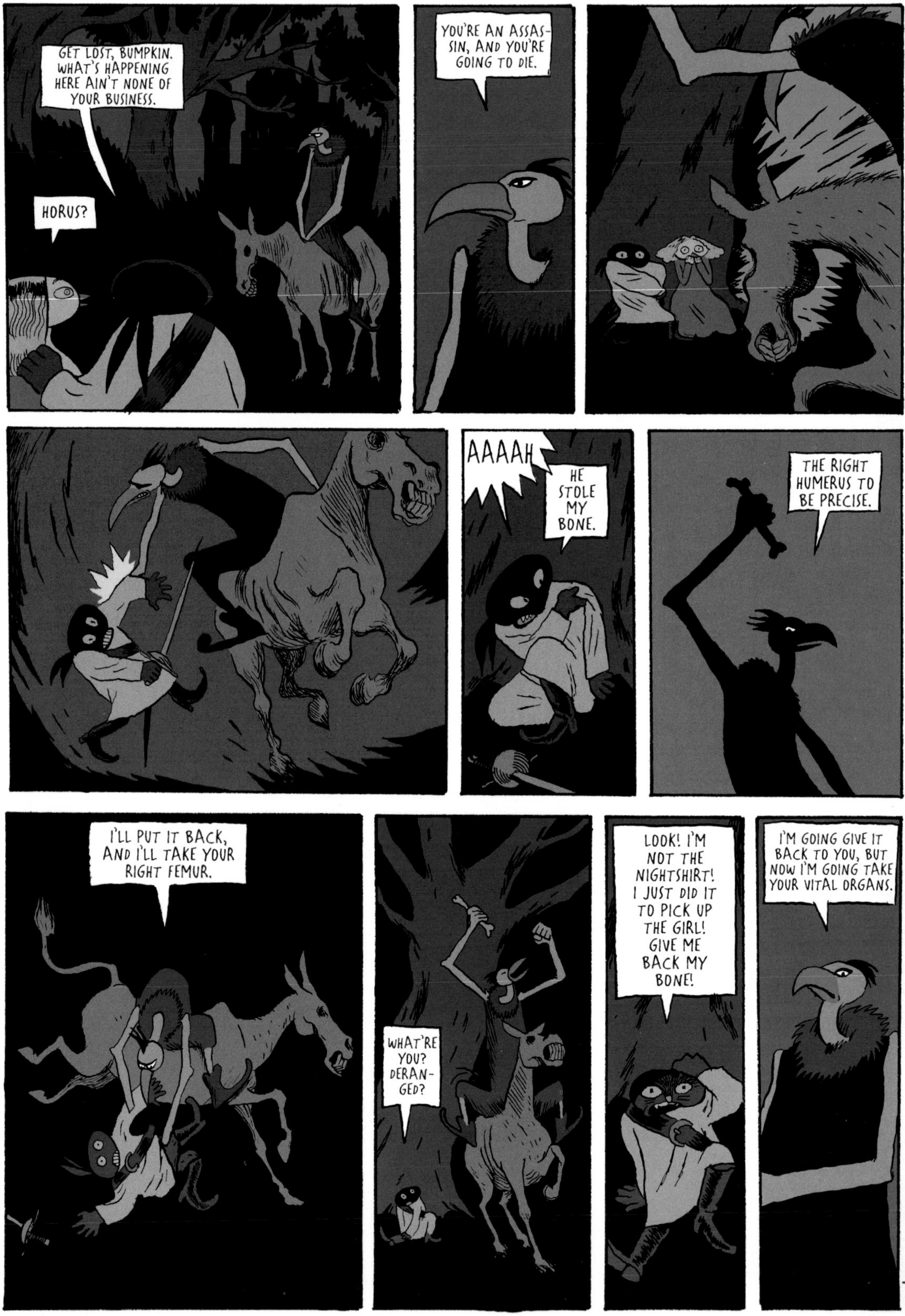
GET LOST, BUMPKIN. WHAT'S HAPPENING HERE AIN'T NONE OF YOUR BUSINESS.
HORUS?
YOU'RE AN ASSASSIN, AND YOU'RE GOING TO DIE.
AAAAH
HE STOLE MY BONE.
THE RIGHT HUMERUS TO BE PRECISE.
I'LL PUT IT BACK, AND I'LL TAKE YOUR RIGHT FEMUR.
WHAT'RE YOU? DERANGED?
LOOK! I'M NOT THE NIGHTSHIRT! I JUST DID IT TO PICK UP THE GIRL! GIVE ME BACK MY BONE!
I'M GOING GIVE IT BACK TO YOU, BUT NOW I'M GOING TAKE YOUR VITAL ORGANS.

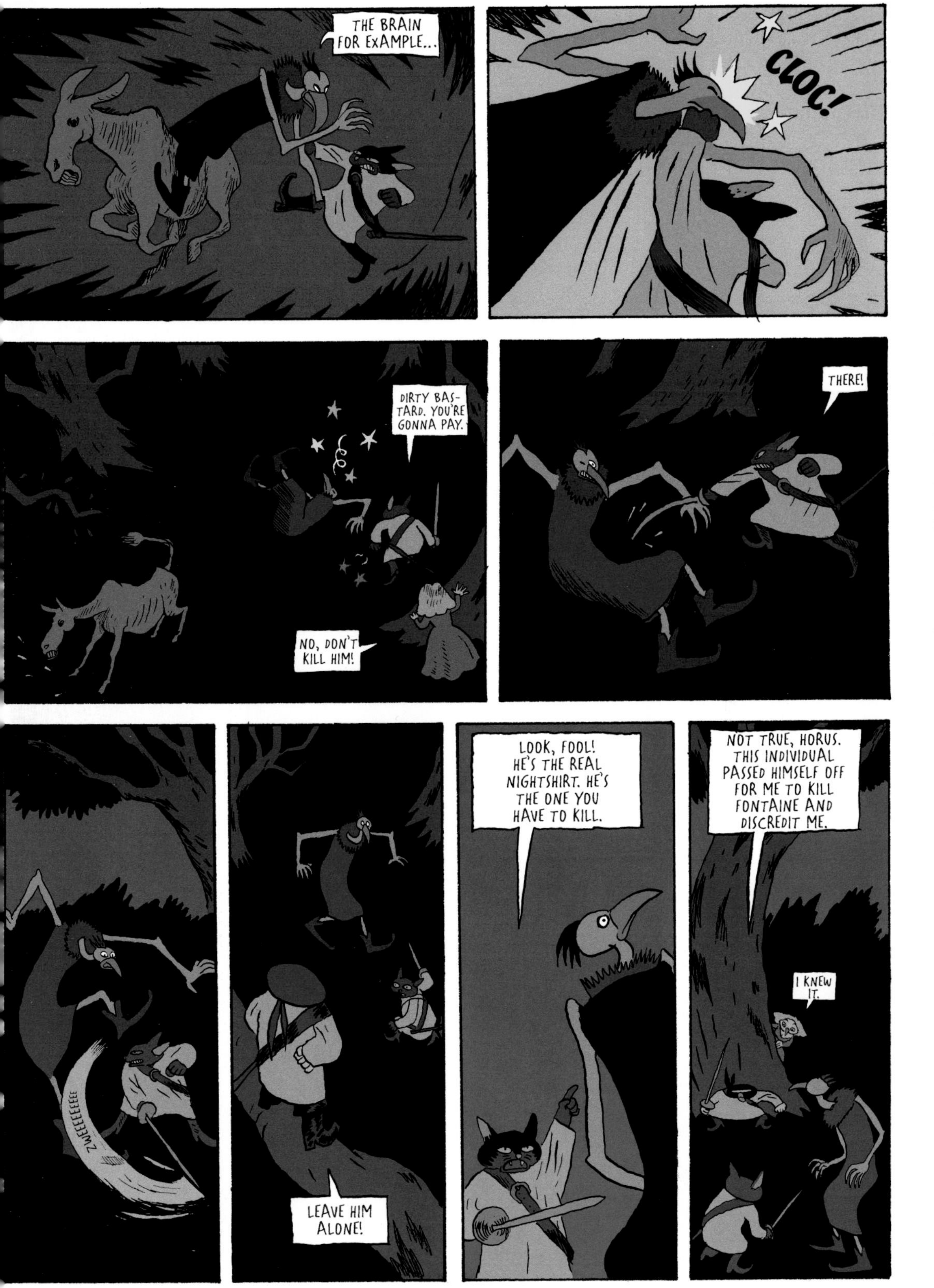
THE BRAIN FOR EXAMPLE...
CLOC!
DIRTY BASTARD. YOU'RE GONNA PAY.
NO, DON'T KILL HIM!
THERE!
ZWEEEEEEEEE
LEAVE HIM ALONE!
LOOK, FOOL! HE'S THE REAL NIGHTSHIRT. HE'S THE ONE YOU HAVE TO KILL.
NOT TRUE, HORUS. THIS INDIVIDUAL PASSED HIMSELF OFF FOR ME TO KILL FONTAINE AND DISCREDIT ME.
I KNEW IT.

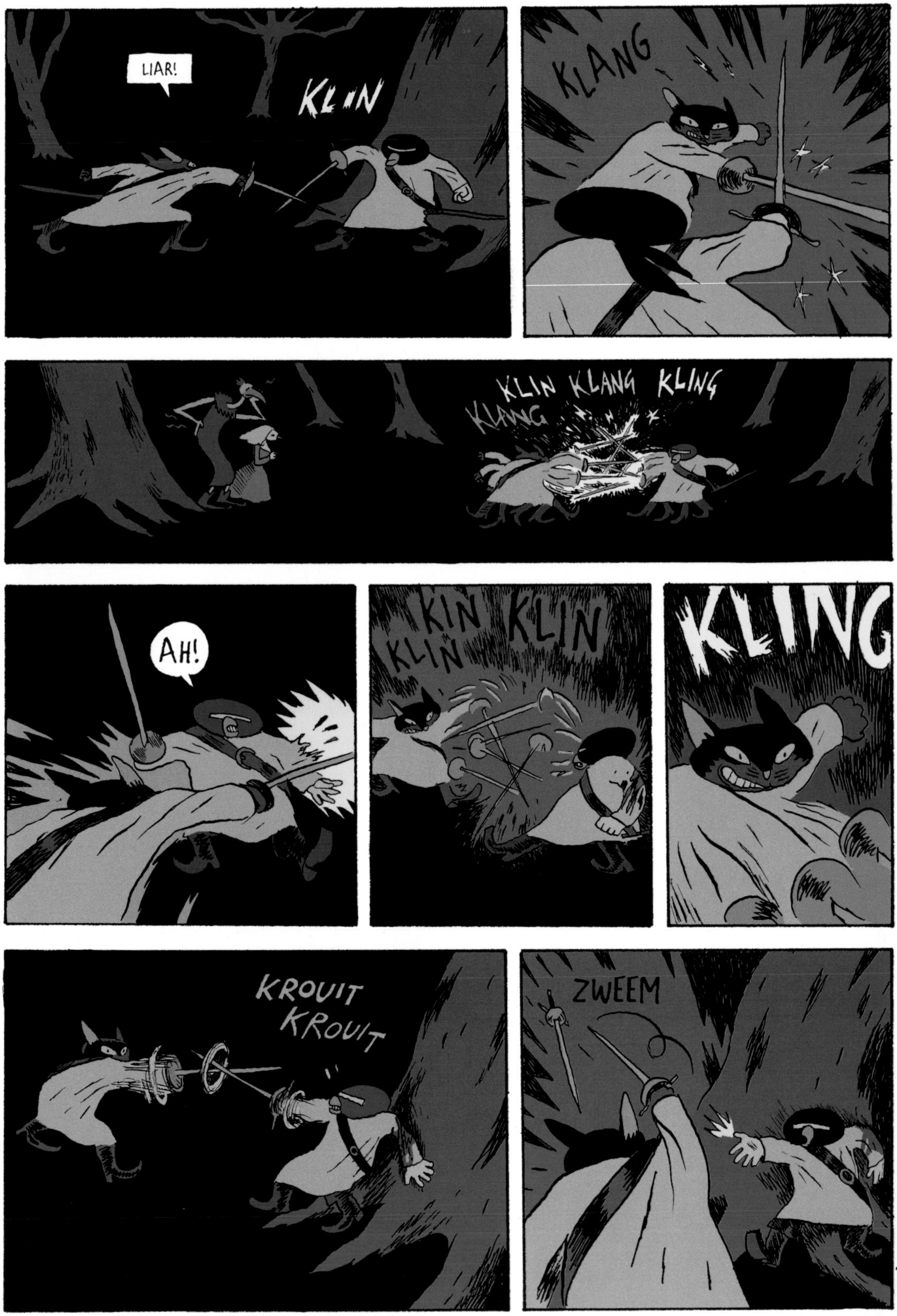
LIAR!
KLIN
KLANG
KLIN KLANG KLING
KLANG
AH!
KIN KLIN
KLIN
KLING
KROUIT
KROUIT
ZWEEM

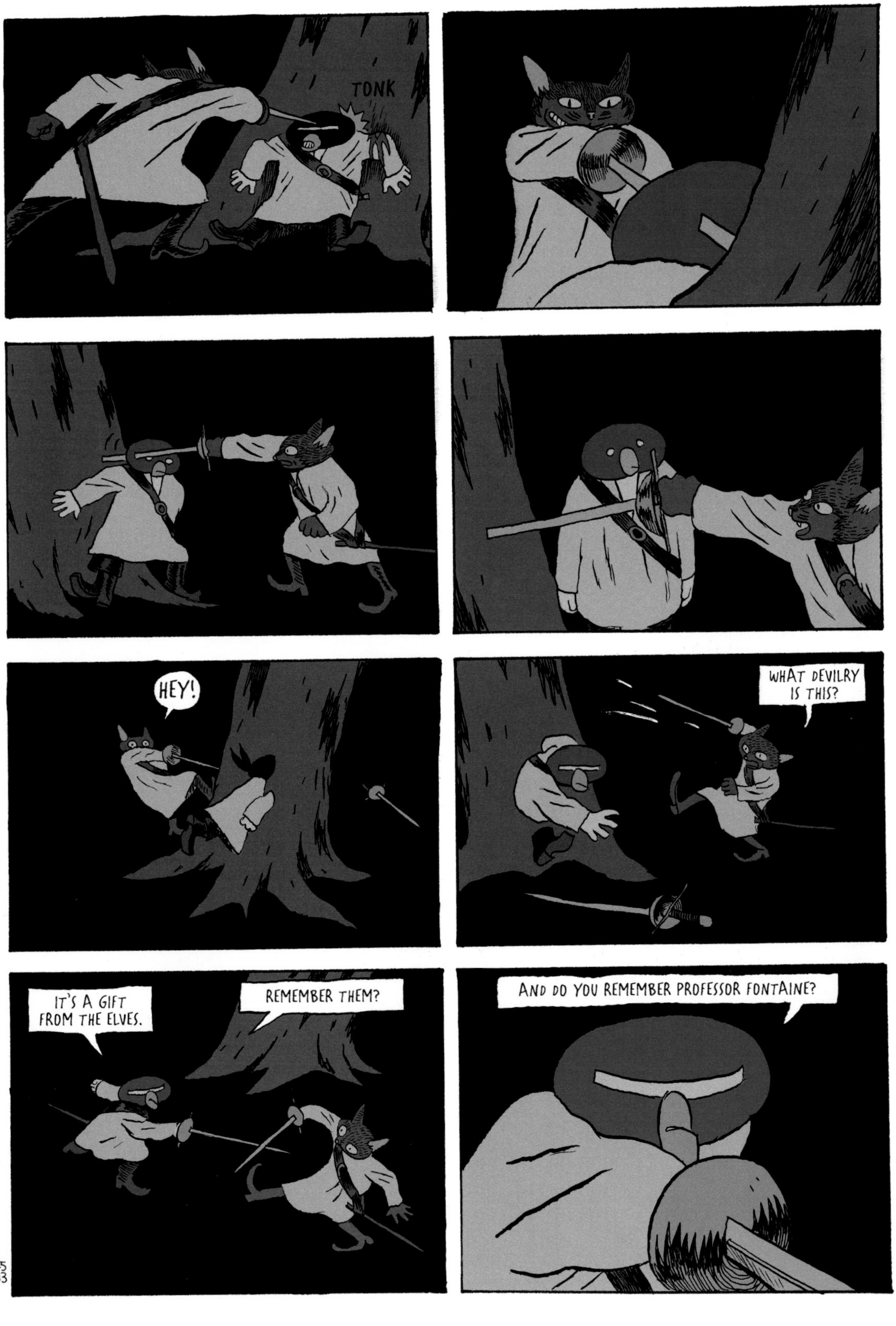
TONK
HEY!
WHAT DEVILRY IS THIS?
IT'S A GIFT FROM THE ELVES.
REMEMBER THEM?
AND DO YOU REMEMBER PROFESSOR FONTAINE?

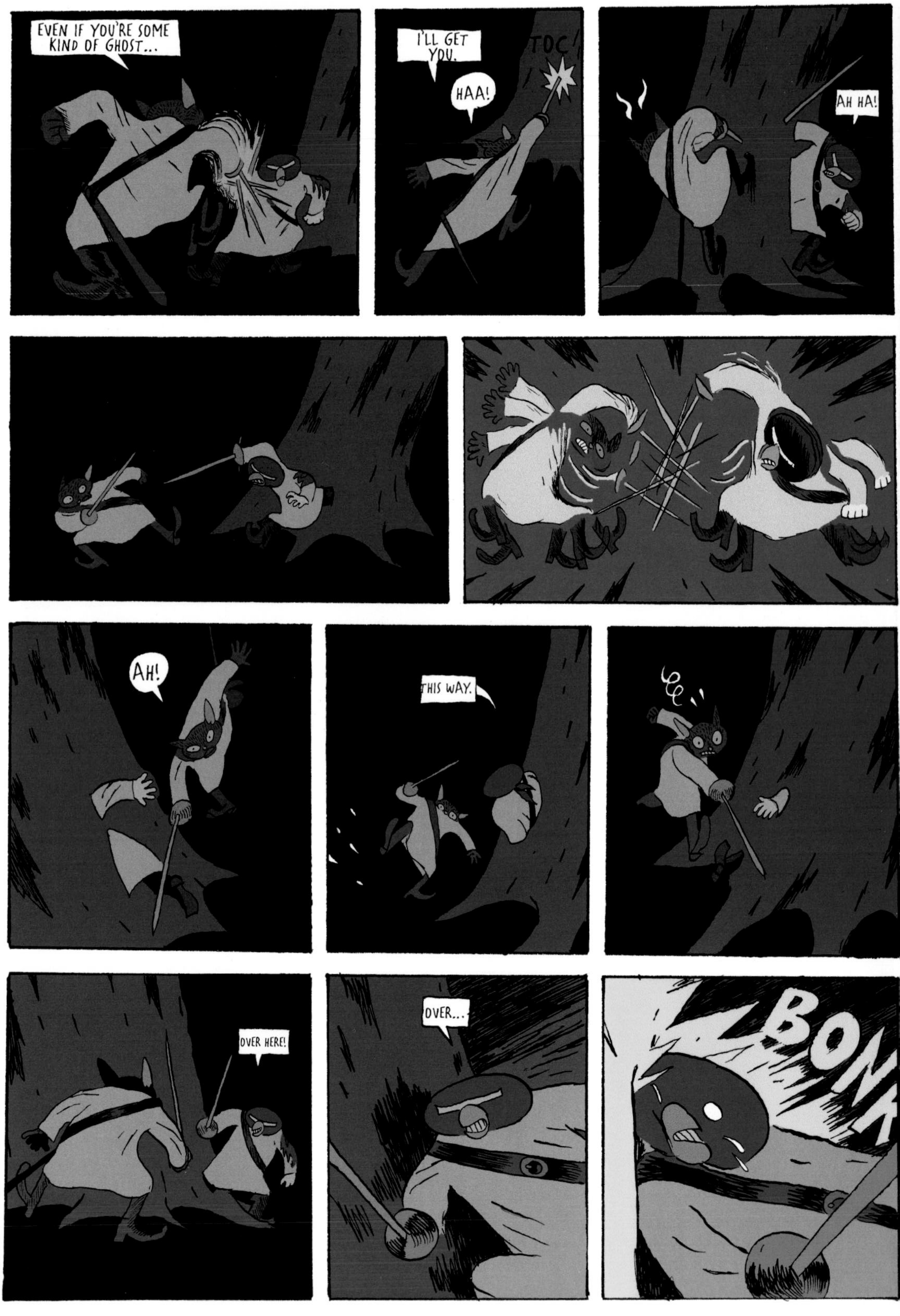
EVEN IF YOU'RE SOME KIND OF GHOST...
I'LL GET YOU.
HAA!
TOC
AH HA!
AH!
THIS WAY.
OVER HERE!
OVER...
BONK

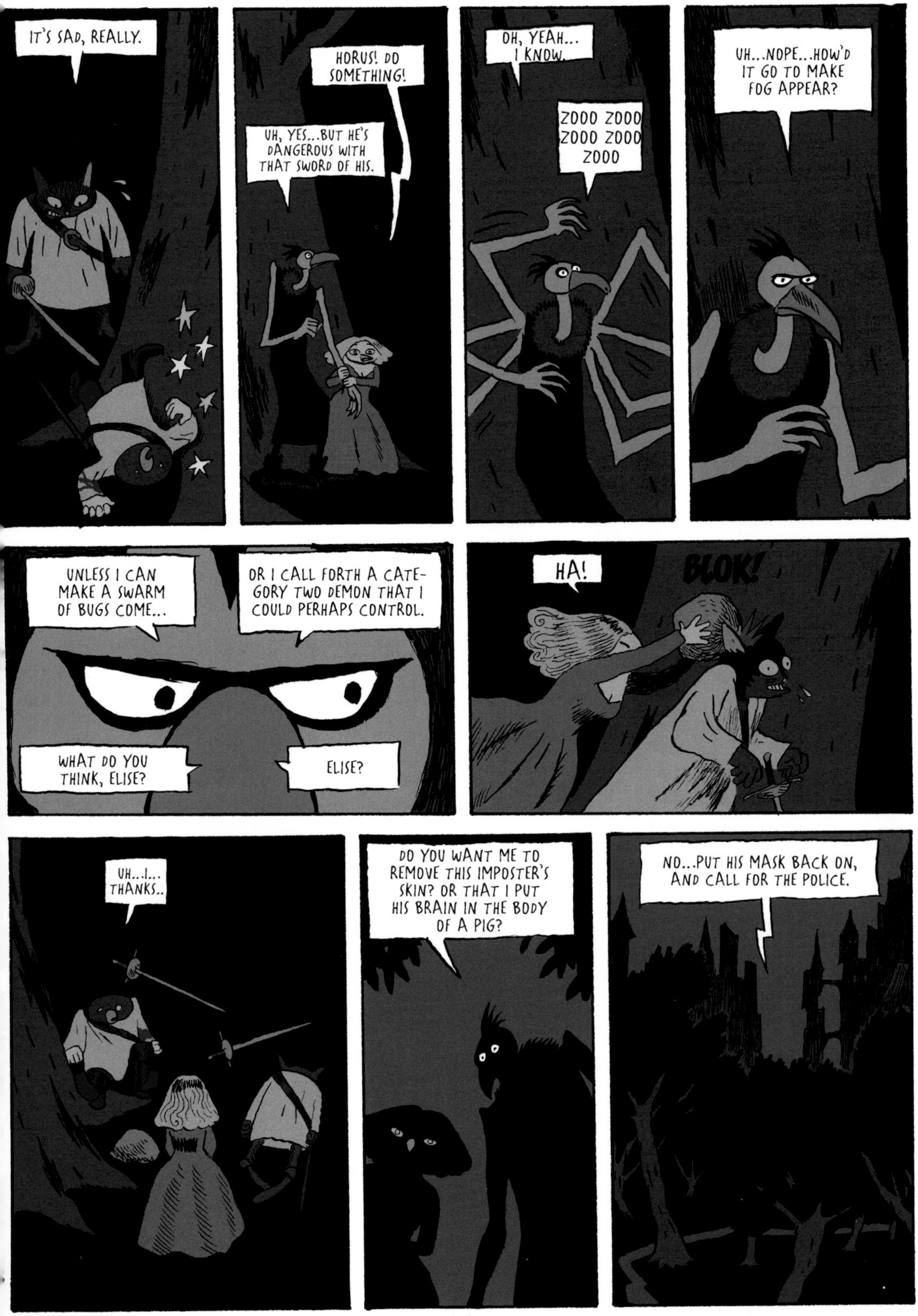
IT'S SAD, REALLY.
HORUS! DO SOMETHING!
UH, YES...BUT HE'S DANGEROUS WITH THAT SWORD OF HIS.
OH, YEAH... I KNOW.
ZOOO ZOOO ZOOO ZOOO ZOOO
UH...NOPE...HOW'D IT GO TO MAKE FOG APPEAR?
UNLESS I CAN MAKE A SWARM OF BUGS COME...
OR I CALL FORTH A CATEGORY TWO DEMON THAT I COULD PERHAPS CONTROL.
WHAT DO YOU THINK, ELISE?
ELISE?
HA!
BLOK!
UH...I... THANKS..
DO YOU WANT ME TO REMOVE THIS IMPOSTER'S SKIN? OR THAT I PUT HIS BRAIN IN THE BODY OF A PIG?
NO...PUT HIS MASK BACK ON, AND CALL FOR THE POLICE.

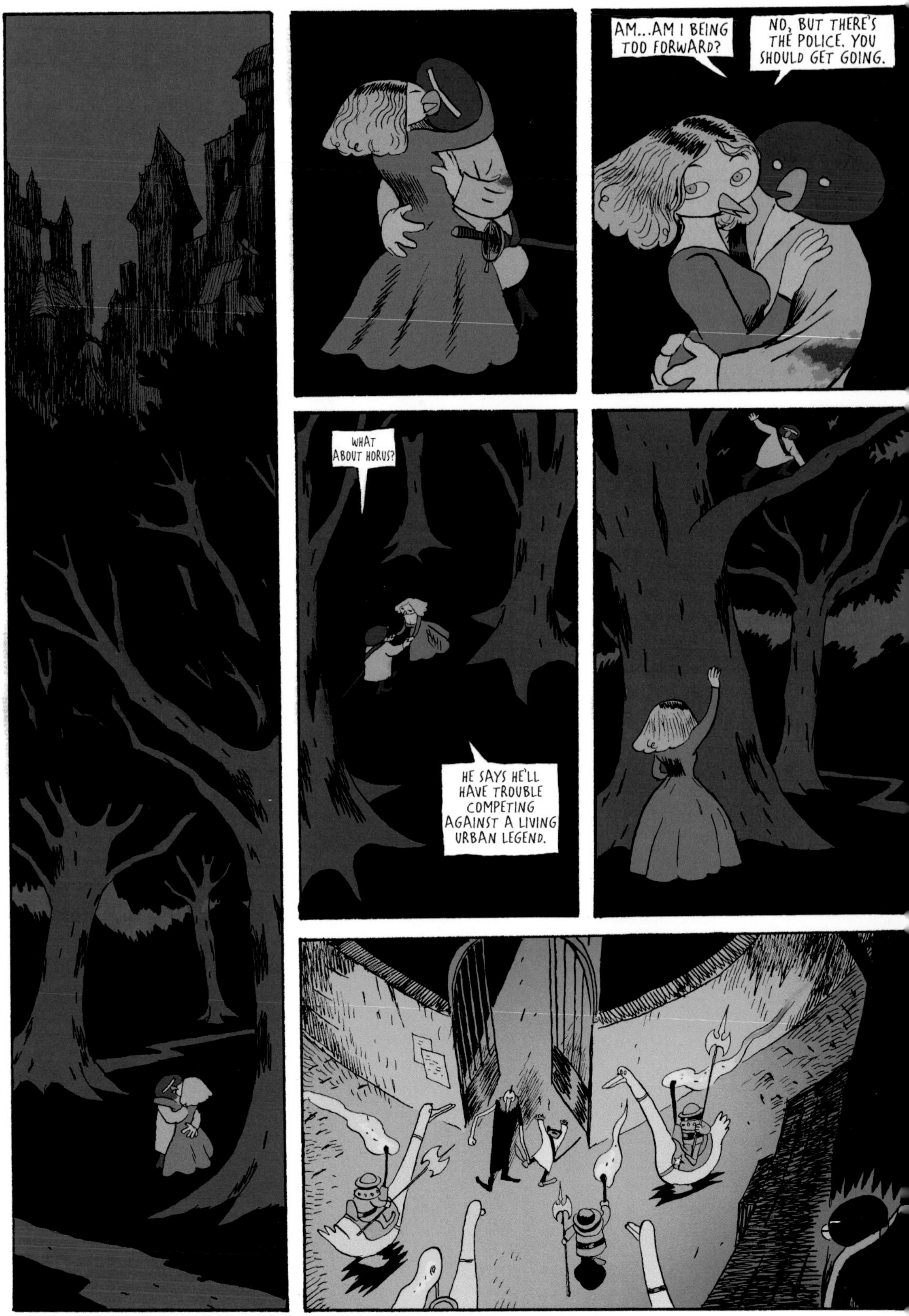
AM...AM I BEING TOO FORWARD?
NO, BUT THERE'S THE POLICE. YOU SHOULD GET GOING.
WHAT ABOUT HORUS?
HE SAYS HE'LL HAVE TROUBLE COMPETING AGAINST A LIVING URBAN LEGEND.

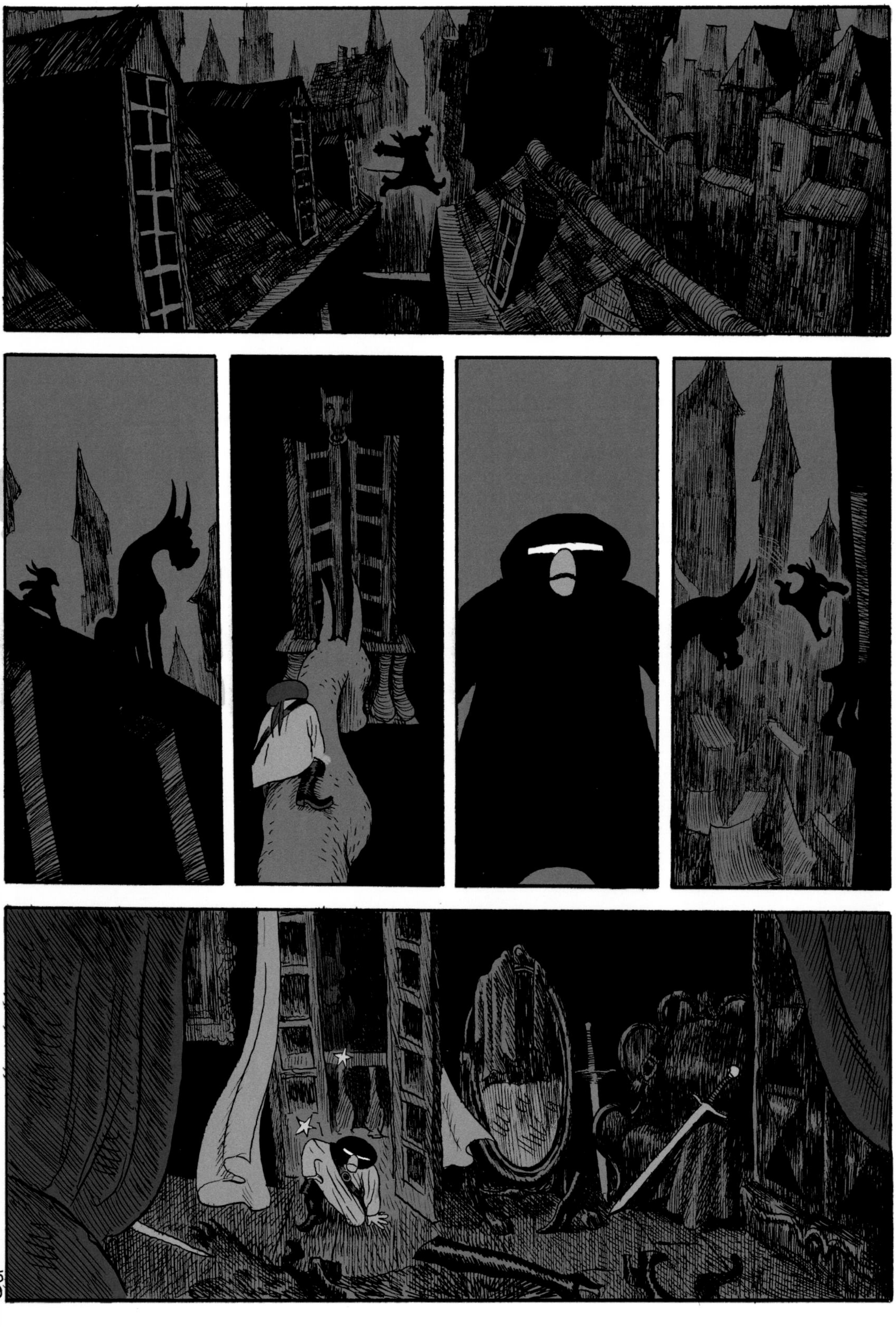

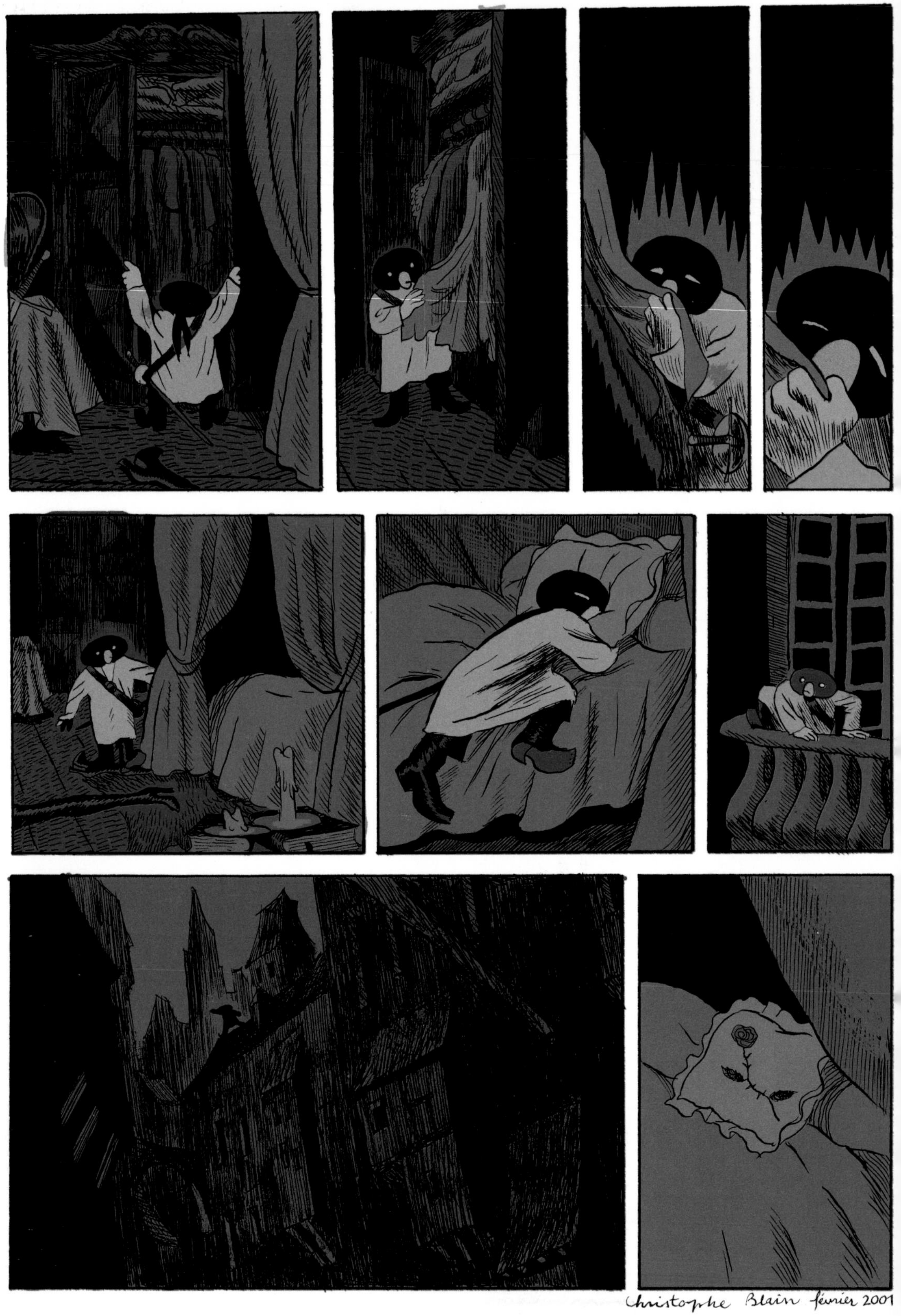

Christophe Blain février 2001